DISCOVERING MATTHEW

Discovering Biblical Texts

Content, Interpretation, Reception

Comprehensive, up-to-date and student-friendly introductions to the books of the Bible: their structure, content, theological concerns, key interpretative debates and historical reception.

PUBLISHED

Ian Boxall, *Discovering Matthew*

Ruth Edwards, *Discovering John*

DISCOVERING MATTHEW

Content, Interpretation, Reception

Ian Boxall

WILLIAM B. EERDMANS PUBLISHING COMPANY
GRAND RAPIDS, MICHIGAN / CAMBRIDGE, U.K.

© 2014 Ian Boxall

First published in the U.K. by
Society for Promoting Christian Knowledge
36 Causton Street
London SW1P 4ST

This edition published 2015
in the United States of America by
Wm. B. Eerdmans Publishing Co.
2140 Oak Industrial Drive N.E., Grand Rapids, Michigan 49505 /
P.O. Box 163, Cambridge CB3 9PU U.K.
www.eerdmans.com

Printed in the United States of America

21 20 19 18 17 16 15   7 6 5 4 3 2 1

Library of Congress Cataloging-in-Publication Data
Boxall, Ian.
Discovering Matthew: content, interpretation, reception / Ian Boxall.
        pages   cm
Includes bibliographical references and index.
ISBN 978-0-8028-7238-8 (pbk.: alk. paper)
1. Bible. Matthew — Criticism, interpretation, etc.   I. Title.

BS2575.52.B69   2015
226.2'06 — dc23
                                        2015010112

*With grateful thanks to the staff and students of
St Stephen's House, Oxford
1994–2013,
and in memory of Eric Franklin,
priest and scholar*

Contents

Acknowledgements

Many colleagues and friends have been instrumental in the writing of this book (most of them unwittingly). As always, Christopher Rowland has been a particular inspiration. Some years ago I was privileged to teach a lecture course on Matthew with Chris, who taught me so much about the marginal dimensions of this 'ecclesiastical' Gospel. I have also benefited from the companionship and wisdom of my New Testament colleagues in the Faculty of Theology and Religion in Oxford, especially those colleagues in OPTET (Oxford Partnership for Theological Education and Training) with whom I have had the privilege of teaching Matthew in more recent years: Justin Hardin, Helen-Ann Hartley, Michael Lakey and Peter Walker. Among friends and family who have encouraged me to bring this work to completion are William Whittaker, and my mother, Pam Boxall. I am especially grateful to Philip Law at SPCK for his generosity in entrusting me with this book, and his patience in waiting for the final manuscript.

Particular thanks are due to my colleagues and students over 19 years at St Stephen's House, Oxford. Most especially I am aware of my profound debt as a New Testament scholar to the late Eric Franklin, whose immense learning, persistent questioning and pastoral sense have continued to inspire me, along with countless generations of ordinands and undergraduates. Although Eric was no great fan of Matthew (he thought him rather too much of a 'Staggers man'), I trust that from the eternal perspective he will accept this dedication in the Lucan spirit in which it is intended.

Abbreviations

AUSS	*Andrews University Seminary Studies*
BETL	Bibliotheca Ephemeridum Theologicarum Lovaniensium
BNTC	Black's New Testament Commentaries
BZNW	Beihefte zur Zeitschrift für die neutestamentliche Wissenschaft
CBQ	*Catholic Biblical Quarterly*
HTKNT	Herders theologischer Kommentar zum Neuen Testament
HTR	*Harvard Theological Review*
HTS	*HTS Teologiese Studies/Theological Studies*
ICC	International Critical Commentary
JAAR	*Journal of the American Academy of Religion*
JBL	*Journal of Biblical Literature*
JETS	*Journal of the Evangelical Theological Society*
JSNT	*Journal for the Study of the New Testament*
JSNTSS	Journal for the Study of the New Testament Supplement Series
JTS	*Journal of Theological Studies*
LNTS	Library of New Testament Studies
NICNT	New International Commentary on the New Testament
NT	*Novum Testamentum*
NTOA	Novum Testamentum et Orbis Antiquus
NTS	*New Testament Studies*
SBL	Society of Biblical Literature
SJT	*Scottish Journal of Theology*
SNTSMS	Society for New Testament Studies Monograph Series
TS	*Theological Studies*
WUNT	Wissenschaftliche Untersuchungen zum Neuen Testament

1

Introduction

The First Gospel

The Gospel according to Matthew has had a profound impact on Christian history and on human culture more widely. In Christian worship, preference has been given to the Lord's Prayer in Matthew's version ('Our Father, who art in heaven', Matt. 6.9–13; cf. Luke 11.2–4: 'Father . . .'). The Matthean wording of Jesus' Beatitudes ('Blessed are the poor in spirit', 5.3) is far more familiar than Luke's equivalent ('Blessed are you poor', Luke 6.20). Through centuries of use, phrases from Matthew's Gospel have crept into common parlance: 'salt of the earth' (5.13); 'the left hand doesn't know what the right hand is doing' (6.3); 'wolves in sheep's clothing' (7.15). Even if modern scholarship now questions the traditional belief that Matthew was the first of the four canonical Gospels to be written, few will dispute its primacy of honour and usage. In its reception, if not its origins, it is the First Gospel.

A preference for Matthew over the other Gospels is manifest already in Christian literature of the late first and early second centuries (Massaux 1990–3). Early in the second century, Ignatius of Antioch quotes from or alludes to Matthew's Gospel on a number of occasions. He refers to the star of Matthew 2.2 heralding Christ's birth (Ignatius, *Eph.* 19.2). His description of Jesus' baptism as 'fulfilling all righteousness' (*Smyrn.* 1.1) echoes Matthew 3.15. His letter to Polycarp of Smyrna recalls Jesus' words to the Twelve about being 'wise as serpents and innocent as doves' (*Polycarp* 2.2 = Matt. 10.16; cf. *Smyrn.* 6.1 = Matt. 19.12; *Trall.* 11.1 = Matt. 15.13; *Eph.* 14.2 = Matt. 12.33). The *Didache* or 'Teaching of the Twelve Apostles' (possibly late first century) shares with Matthew the concern for the 'two ways' (*Did.* 1.1 = Matt. 7.13–14), and the rite of baptism 'in the name of the Father and of the Son and of the Holy Spirit' (*Did.* 7.1 = Matt. 28.19). It also cites Jesus' teaching about turning the right cheek (*Did.* 1.4–5 = Matt. 5.38–42) and avoiding the excesses of the 'hypocrites' when fasting (*Did.* 8.1 = Matt. 6.16–18). Indeed, the author of the *Didache* seems to know Matthew as the only Gospel: 'And do not pray as the hypocrites, but as the Lord commanded in his Gospel, pray thus: "Our Father, who art in Heaven, hallowed be thy Name . . ."' (*Did.* 8.2 = Matt. 6.7–13. Lake 1925: 1/321).

1

The evidence of surviving manuscripts of the Gospels in Greek and other languages points to a general preference for Matthew's version in the tendency among scribes to harmonize disagreements between the Gospels. In later centuries, scenes unique to Matthew, such as the magi worshipping the infant Jesus (2.1–12), the giving of the keys of the kingdom to Simon Peter (16.18–19) or the story of the soldiers guarding Jesus' tomb (27.62–66; 28.11–15), would inspire artists in their visual interpretations of the biblical text. Famous examples include *The Adoration of the Magi* by Botticelli (*c*.1475–6; Uffizi, Florence) and Rembrandt (1632; Hermitage, St Petersburg), Pietro Perugino's fresco *The Delivery of the Keys* (*c*.1481–2; Sistine Chapel, Rome) and *The Resurrection* by Piero della Francesca (*c*.1463–5; Museo Civico, Sansepolcro). Artists have also been inspired by the figure of the evangelist himself and his part in the story he recounts. The Church of San Luigi dei Francesi in Rome contains three canvases by Caravaggio, depicting *The Calling of St Matthew*, *The Inspiration of St Matthew* and *The Martyrdom of St Matthew*. Musically, the most famous interpretation of Matthew's account of Jesus' suffering and death is probably Johann Sebastian Bach's *St Matthew Passion*.

Reasons for Matthew's popularity, religiously and culturally, are at least threefold. First, the Gospel is superbly and memorably ordered, suggesting an author who is master of his material. This has led to specific proposals that the evangelist was a converted rabbi (von Dobschütz 1995: 31–2) or a scribe and 'provincial schoolmaster' (Goulder 1974: 5), as well as the more traditional identification of Matthew as a methodical tax-collector (9.9; 10.3). The Gospel's juxtaposition of narrative and discourse, story and sermon, often regarded as a key to its structure, has been frequently commented upon. Matthew uses frequent repetitions: for example, his rounding off each of the major teaching blocks with 'When Jesus had finished . . .' (7.28; 11.1; 13.53; 19.1; 26.1) or his liking for the colourful phrase 'weeping and gnashing of teeth' (8.12; 13.42, 50; 22.13; 24.51; 25.30). He is fond of 'triads' or groups of three: for example, Jesus' miracles are organized in groups of three in Matthew 8—9, and there are two triads of parables in Matthew 13 (for further examples, see Allison 2005: 202–5). He also uses doublets: examples of the latter are Matthew's inclusion of *two* stories of the healing of *two* blind men (9.27–31; 20.29–34) and his story of *two* Gadarene demoniacs (8.28–34), his counterpart to Mark's one Gerasene demoniac (Mark 5.1–20). Other numbers important to him include five (e.g. the five discourses or teaching blocks), seven (12.45; 15.34, 36, 37; 16.10; 18.22; 22.25, 26, 28; also seven 'woes' against the scribes and Pharisees, 23.13, 15, 16, 23, 25, 27, 29) and 14 (e.g. 1.17, repeated three times).

Matthew also makes use of chiastic (ABBA) and concentric (ABCBA) patterns (e.g. Matt. 5—7; 9.1b–8; 13.13–18; 18.10–14). He uses brackets, known by the technical term *inclusio*, to mark out significant sections of his book. One example is the repetition of the same summary statement at 4.23–25 and 9.35–38 (referring to Jesus' teaching, preaching and healing ministry in Galilee), which frames the Sermon on the Mount and the ensuing narrative of Matthew 8—9. Indeed, the book as a whole is located between a great *inclusio* (the statement at 1.23 that Jesus is Emmanuel, 'God is with us', is picked up at the very end by the risen Christ's statement 'I am with you always, to the end of the age', 28.20). Finally, there is a certain poetic rhythm to many of Jesus' sayings (e.g. 7.7–8; 12.25–26; 23.8–10; 25.35–39; Goulder 1974: 70–94).

Second, the widespread usage of Matthew in liturgy and catechesis has ensured the importance of this Gospel within the churches. It is the preferred Gospel in church lectionaries, a fact frequently noted across the centuries. 'Lastly, we may note the great honour in which his Gospel is held in the Church', declares a medieval lesson for the Feast of St Matthew (21 September), 'for it is read more often than the other Gospels, just as the Psalms of David and the Epistles of Saint Paul are recited more frequently than the other sacred writings' (Jacobus de Voragine 1941: 565). Matthew's catechetical value is due particularly to the prominence it gives to the teaching of Jesus. Indeed, for some scholars the careful ordering of the Gospel is evidence that it was originally written for the purpose of catechesis (teaching the faith). Paul Minear, for example, has offered a sustained reading of Matthew's Gospel as written by a teacher for other early Christian teachers, with the five Matthean sermons or discourses understood as teaching 'manuals' (Minear 1984). Minear is in fact picking up on a very ancient hunch about the Gospel. The Prologue to the influential fifth-century *Opus imperfectum* or 'Incomplete Work' on Matthew describes how the Christians of first-century Palestine, threatened with dispersion due to persecution, urged Matthew to compose his account of Christ's words and deeds, 'so that even if by chance they had to be without any teachers of the faith, they would still not lack their teaching' (Kellerman 2010: 1/1). It has very much the feel of a teacher's guide, to those in need of sound catechesis.

Others have seen a liturgical *Sitz im Leben* (or 'setting in life') for this Gospel. G. D. Kilpatrick proposed that it developed as a kind of running commentary and homiletic expansion of Mark's Gospel, and Matthew's other sources, as these were read in the context of community worship (Kilpatrick 1946: 59–71). Michael Goulder has developed this liturgical explanation into an intricate thesis according to which the evangelist reworks Mark in the light of the cycle of Old Testament readings in the Jewish festival lectionary (Goulder 1974). Whether or not this can account for the Gospel as a whole, Matthew's text certainly betrays some traits of early Christian worship. Matthew's version of the Lord's Prayer, with its communal 'Our Father' and its similarities to the formal prayer of the synagogue, the Eighteen Benedictions, may well reflect the liturgical practice of the Christian circles to which Matthew belonged. The triadic baptismal formula at 28.19 probably offers a window into how baptism was administered in those same circles (possibly in Syria, given a similar wording found in other Christian texts from that area: *Did.* 7.1; Ignatius, *Magn.* 13.2; *Odes of Solomon* 23.22).

A third reason for Matthew's popularity is the centuries-old belief that Matthew is the earliest of our four canonical Gospels, and one of only two (John being the other) attributed to an apostle and eyewitness of Jesus. The tradition linking this Gospel with someone called Matthew is reflected in the earliest Greek manuscripts, which include the title *Kata Matthaion* ('according to Matthew'). At an early stage, this Matthew was identified with Matthew the converted tax-collector and member of the Twelve (9.9–13; 10.3). 'I have learned by tradition', writes the third-century exegete Origen of Alexandria, 'that the first was written by Matthew, who was once a publican, but afterwards an apostle of Jesus Christ' (quoted in Eusebius, *H. E.* 6.25: Eusebius 1995: 273). This virtually unanimous tradition meant that Matthew's Gospel was viewed as closer to the source than Mark or Luke, both attributed to second-generation followers of apostles (Peter and Paul respectively). This seemed to be confirmed by its Jewish character, apparently unaffected by the reinterpretation of the Christian message as it moved out of its original Palestinian context into the wider Gentile world. Its greater length – covering almost all the content of Mark and much more besides – also made it a more complete and satisfying record than the other Synoptic Gospels.

The Breakdown of a Consensus

Since the nineteenth century, however, such a consensus has broken down, many scholars rejecting the age-old belief in authorship by an apostolic eyewitness. Rather, Matthew is now viewed as the *second* Gospel, composed by an anonymous author 50 to 60 years after Jesus' death, and dependent upon the work of another (the Gospel according to Mark). That is not to say, as we shall see, that questions of authorship, chronological sequence and dating have been definitively settled. A minority of eminent scholars have continued to hold to a variation of apostolic authorship, Matthean priority or early dating (e.g. Farmer 1964 on the priority of Matthew; Gundry 1994 and France 2007 on authorship and dating). Nonetheless, the scholarly consensus on these questions is sharply at odds with the testimony of the early centuries.

This shift away from the 'priority of Matthew' has sometimes led modern commentators to a more negative assessment of its merits. In his comparative study of Matthew's and Mark's passion narratives, Leslie Houlden regards Matthew as the 'villain of the piece, inferior and even reprehensible at almost every turn' in his capacity to 'spoil the purity of Mark's teaching' (Houlden 1987: 66). For Houlden, Matthew's almost obsessive tidiness, his desire to tie up loose ends in Mark and his other sources, makes his a less sympathetic Gospel. Yet Houlden also recognizes that there is a realism about Matthew, particularly when it comes to Mark's urgency about the imminence of the End. For good or for ill, he has had to come to terms with the longer term, which results in a toning down of Mark's urgency.

Others regard the realism of this Gospel as its greatest asset. Matthew is in a true sense 'the Gospel of the Church', laying down patterns for structured Christian existence in this world. One of the greatest Matthean scholars of recent times, the Swiss exegete Ulrich Luz, speaks of the 'transparency' of Matthew's Gospel (e.g. Luz 1995a). By this he means the way Matthew's story of Jesus and his disciples offers a window on to the post-Easter situation of the Church. Luz, like many other recent scholars, means specifically the local first-century congregations for whom Matthew wrote (though he is also interested in the ongoing 'transparency' in the life of the Christian Church: e.g. Luz 2005b: 115–42). However, this way of reading the Gospels as 'allegories' of specific Christian communities is by no means undisputed (see Bauckham [ed.] 1998). For other reasons too, readers of Matthew have found his a more compelling account than Mark's. The Italian film director Pier Paolo Pasolini, for instance, thought that Matthew captured the revolutionary spirit of Jesus' ministry more effectively than the rather crude Mark, the sentimental Luke or the overly mystical John. Thus it was the First Gospel that provided the inspiration for his classic 1964 film about Jesus, *Il Vangelo secondo Matteo* or *The Gospel according to St Matthew* (Clarke 2003: 113). Pasolini's response is worth pondering (and his film worth viewing), given the common scholarly tendency to denigrate Matthew as an inferior and institutionalized version of Mark's Gospel.

A 'Janus-like Book'

The ambivalence towards Matthew reflects tensions within the Gospel itself, leading John Riches to describe it as 'a Janus-like book' (Riches 2000: 228). Like the Roman god Janus, whose two faces enabled him to look both to the past and the future, Matthew's Gospel seems to look in two directions simultaneously. It contains a tension between a universal vision that embraces all the nations within the remit of the kingdom of heaven, and a 'particularist' concern for the 'lost sheep of the house of Israel', presenting Jesus' message as the only authentic Judaism. In many ways it seems to breathe the air of the Jewish world, negatively portraying 'Gentiles' or 'pagans' as outsiders. Although Gentile magi worship the infant Jesus, they come as outsider questers to the heart of the Jewish world, Jerusalem (2.1–4). Followers of Jesus are to behave differently from Gentiles (5.47). When they pray they are not to 'babble' as the Gentiles do (6.7). Christians expelled from the community are to be regarded as 'a Gentile and a tax-collector' (18.17).

Yet Matthew's Gospel can be equally vitriolic in its condemnation of certain Jews (especially the Pharisees, e.g. 9.11; 12.2, 14; 15.12; 19.3; 23.13; 27.62), and possibly even the whole Jewish people (27.25). It presents a Jesus who explicitly denies that he has come to abolish the Law and the prophets (5.17) and yet who appears to sit lightly to fundamental laws about Sabbath observance (12.1–8) or to challenge the Mosaic teaching about divorce (5.31–32; 19.3–9). The disciples are told at one point to beware of the teaching of the Pharisees (along with that of the Sadducees, 16.12); at another to do all that the scribes and Pharisees tell them, as authoritative teachers sitting on Moses' seat (23.2–3). The places where Moses' seat might be found are referred to derogatively as 'their synagogues' (4.23; 9.35; 10.17; 12.9; 13.54; cf. 23.34), where Jesus' followers can expect persecution (10.17, 23; cf. 5.10–12). This tension has led modern readers of Matthew to diametrically opposed assessments. On the one hand, George Nickelsburg can include Matthew's Gospel in his introduction to Jewish writings of the post-biblical period (Nickelsburg 1981). On the other, Dan Cohn-Sherbok draws a very different conclusion: 'In the Gospel of Matthew the belief that the Jews murdered the prophets evoked hatred and vituperation against official Judaism' (Cohn-Sherbok 1992: 19). It is a paradoxical text, often described as simultaneously 'Jewish' and 'anti-Jewish'. F. C. Grant arguably provides a more accurate definition: 'it is at once the most conservatively Jewish of the gospels and the most violently anti-Pharisaic' (Grant 1957: 137).

Precisely why the Pharisees come in for particular criticism will be explored later in this book.

This Janus-like tension extends to the portrayal of the Gospel's main protagonist, Jesus of Nazareth. Its portrayal of Jesus emphasizes his merciful character (on this see Byrne 2004). On several occasions we are told that Jesus looks on the crowds with compassion (9.36; 14.14; 15.32); he is moved with compassion by the two blind men at Jericho (20.34); he utters a blessing on the merciful (5.7), twice cites a passage from the prophet Hosea that prioritizes mercy over sacrifice (Hos. 6.6, quoted at 9.13 and 12.7), and castigates the scribes and Pharisees for their lack of mercy (23.23). On four separate occasions those in need of healing recognize Christ's merciful character by calling on him to 'have mercy' (9.27; 15.22; 17.15; 20.30–31). In Byrne's words:

> In Matthew I discovered a gospel that teaches us to look at humanity through the eyes of Jesus and see it as afflicted and weighed down with all manner of burdens. Far from adding to humanity's burdens, Jesus comes to bear and lift them.
> (Byrne 2004: vii)

Such a characterization is attractive to modern Western sensibilities. Yet Matthew's Jesus can also appear moralizing and judgemental, sharply dividing humanity into good and bad, wise and foolish, sheep and goats (e.g. 7.24–27; 13.24–30, 47–50; 25.1–13, 31–46). The apocalyptic (revelatory) and eschatological (end-time) interests of the Gospel present a hint of foreboding and cosmic collapse (e.g. 24—25; 27.51–54) that compound this sense of unease among certain contemporary audiences.

How can one reconcile these apparently contradictory elements? Possible answers – and what they reveal about the presuppositions of the interpreters who propose them – will be explored in more detail in the chapters that follow. One solution is to regard the evangelist Matthew as little more than a collator and transmitter of traditions, failing to integrate them into a coherent whole. Thus conservative Jewish-Christian sayings (e.g. 'Go nowhere among the Gentiles', 10.5) sit rather awkwardly alongside more radical traditions derived from Mark and non-Marcan traditions (e.g. the healing of the centurion's servant, in which a Gentile functions as a model of true faith for God's people Israel: 8.5–13). A more nuanced approach acknowledges the creative scribal activity reflected in Matthew's use of Old Testament quotations, but similarly shies away from treating the evangelist as a coherent author with a detectable 'theology'. This point of view is represented by two of the most prominent modern commentators on Matthew, W. D. Davies and Dale Allison: 'Matthew was more tradent than theologian, more exegete and commentator than innovator' (Davies and Allison 2004: xxv). Others emphasize the evangelist's creativity, viewing him as a rewriter of inherited traditions (e.g. Bornkamm, Barth and Held 1982; most especially Goulder 1974). The 'Janus-like' character of this Gospel means that both positions can claim supporting evidence.

Reading Matthew's Story

In order to lay the foundation for a more detailed exploration of Matthew in the remaining chapters, there now follows a brief outline of the Gospel's contents, to accompany a reading – or better reading aloud – of Matthew's Gospel from beginning to end. There is a growing scholarly acknowledgement that all the New Testament writings were intended to be heard, although scholars are divided as to whether a lengthy text like Matthew was designed to be read out in one sitting (in favour of the latter view, see e.g. Luz 2005b: 3–17). The following summary is intended simply as a preliminary guide for a first reading, which readers may wish to modify or reject as they reread Matthew's text (its complexity, use of keywords and repetitions suggests that the evangelist intended his audiences to experience repeated readings: Luz 2005b: 3–4). Precisely how the text is structured remains a matter of considerable debate. A fuller discussion of this and related issues will be offered in Chapter 3.

Origins of Jesus (Matt. 1.1—4.11)

Matthew's Gospel begins with a series of stories exploring Jesus' origins and setting the scene for his public ministry, together forming the Prologue to his book (Krentz 1964). The first two chapters are not found in Mark, but are paralleled – albeit with significant differences – in Luke 1—2. A brief title, identifying Jesus as Christ/Messiah (i.e. 'the anointed one'), 'son of David' and 'son of Abraham' (1.1), introduces a 'family tree' in which both Abraham and David feature. Those who know the Old Testament will detect echoes of Genesis (Gen. 2.4; 5.1) and the opening of 1 Chronicles (which contains a significant number of genealogies). Although readers may be tempted to skip over this long list of Christ's ancestors, close attention to the genealogy – notably its structure and the identity of the women mentioned – is worthwhile (see Chapter 6 below). The second half of Matthew's first chapter (1.18–25) contains a surprise: for the revelation that Jesus' mother Mary was a virgin means that Joseph's genealogy cannot straightforwardly belong to Jesus.

Matthew 2 describes events following Jesus' birth, and is rich in allusions to the Jewish Scriptures (as well as explicit Old Testament quotations). The journey taken by the child and his parents – from Bethlehem (the town of Israel's King David and appropriate birthplace of 'the son of David') to Egypt and back again to 'the land of Israel' – recalls earlier journeys of Jacob/Israel (Gen. 46—47) and Moses (Exod. 2—4; 12—14). Joseph's dreams evoke those of the Old Testament patriarch of the same name (e.g. Gen. 37.5–11), while the star recalls the messianic prophecy uttered by the pagan prophet Balaam (Num. 24.17). Finally, 'the prophets' are invoked in order to explain why the Messiah has come to be associated with the backwater town of Nazareth (2.23). The primary concern seems to be to clarify who Jesus is and what he has come for.

A further sequence of stories in Matt. 3.1—4.11 (paralleled to varying degrees in Mark and Luke) prepares the audience for the public ministry of Jesus: the appearance and preaching of John the Baptist as the 'voice' who prepares the Lord's way; Jesus' baptism by John in the river Jordan, in which he is revealed as God's Son; his 40-day temptation or 'testing' in the Judean wilderness, which recalls both Israel's 40-year wilderness wanderings (Num. 32.13) and the 40-day fast of both Moses (Exod. 34.28) and Elijah (1 Kings 19.8).

Jesus' Ministry in 'Galilee of the Gentiles' (Matt. 4.12—18.35)

Much of the first half of Matthew's Gospel describes Jesus' ministry of preaching, teaching and healing in the northern region of Galilee, which Matthew, following a prophecy from Isaiah, calls 'Galilee of the Gentiles' (4.15; cf. Isa. 9.1). It begins with the 'handing over' of John the Baptist (4.12; cf. 14.1–12), anticipating Jesus' own 'handing over' to crucifixion at the end of the Gospel. A comparison with Mark in this first part of the Gospel – at least until the end of Matthew 13 – reveals a significant divergence in the order of events, Matthew exhibiting a tendency to order stories thematically and to punctuate his narrative with carefully structured speeches or discourses containing Jesus' teaching. Thus after describing the call of the first four disciples (4.18–22), the narrative slows for the magisterial Sermon on the Mount (5.1—7.29). This, the first of five discourses ending with a similar concluding formula (7.28–29; 11.1; 13.53; 19.1; 26.1), sets out Jesus' radical teaching on discipleship. It also emphasizes the motif of continuity that is a feature of Matthew's Gospel: Jesus is adamant that he came not to 'abolish' the Law or the prophets but to 'fulfil' them (5.17–20).

The theme of healing and other deeds of power shapes the narrative as Jesus descends from the mountain at 8.1. Jesus, particularly in his role as

Isaiah's Servant and the Son of David (8.17; 9.27), is a healer. Interwoven with this collection of miracle stories in Matthew 8—9 are three stories revealing conflict between Jesus and other Jews ('some of the scribes'; the Pharisees; the disciples of John: 9.3, 11, 14). Thus it is no surprise to find, in Jesus' second discourse addressed to the 12 disciples who are to continue Jesus' mission to 'the lost sheep of the house of Israel' (Matt. 10), a warning that they will face hostility and persecution, particularly from synagogue authorities. The theme of division within God's people Israel, and hostility towards Jesus from religious leaders, grows in the narrative of Matthew 11—12. Even John the Baptist, now in prison, wonders whether Jesus is 'the one who is to come' (11.3). The present generation's inconsistent reaction to both John and Jesus (11.16–19) heralds further conflict, particularly over Sabbath observance and Jesus' authority to cast out demons (12.1–14, 22–32).

A collection of parables makes up Jesus' third discourse in Matthew 13. Matthew understands Jesus' parables to be difficult allegories (in which each detail corresponds to something or someone in the real world), and therefore requiring careful interpretation. Matthew's Jesus not only offers the key to the paradigmatic parable of the sower (13.18–23); he also provides interpretations of the weeds of the field (13.36–43) and the dragnet (13.49–50). Again, the motif of conflict and division emerges, accentuated by Matthew's preference for two-dimensional, dualistic terms (weeds and wheat; good seed and bad seed; good fish and rotten fish).

In the continuing narrative – where Matthew now follows an order of events much closer to that of Mark – the division within Israel over Jesus is juxtaposed with an anticipation of a wider mission to embrace all nations. The hostility of the Pharisees and scribes towards Jesus (15.1–20) is followed immediately by his encounter with a Canaanite woman (15.21–28), whose daughter Jesus heals despite an initial reluctance. This gradual inclusion of non-Jews is symbolized by the two feeding miracles in this section. The first (14.13–21) presents the feeding of the 'lost sheep of the house of Israel' (the five loaves and five thousand people recall the five books of Moses, while the 12 baskets reflect the 12 tribes). The second (15.32–39) symbolizes the feeding of the Gentile 'dogs', not with scraps from the master's table (see the words of the Canaanite woman in verse 27) but with the children's bread (the seven loaves and baskets recall the perfect number seven, e.g. Gen. 7.2, and the '70 nations' of biblical tradition: e.g. Gen. 10).

Along with this anticipation of a wider mission comes a more positive portrayal of the disciples than that found in Mark. Peter, like the other disciples, has 'little faith' rather than lacking faith completely (14.31; cf. 8.26; Mark 4.40). Peter's confession at Caesarea Philippi results in a blessing of Peter and the promise that Jesus will build his Church on him (16.13–20). This more favourable portrayal contrasts with the hostility of the Pharisees and Sadducees, the would-be leaders of God's people (16.1, 6, 11). Thus the fourth discourse (Matt. 18) contains disparate teachings for the life of this Church, as if reflecting a time when the followers of Jesus will be distinguished from the synagogues, with Jesus' disciples as the new shepherds of God's flock.

The Journey to and Ministry in Jerusalem (Matt. 19.1—25.46)

Many commentators will see the crucial turning point in the narrative back in Matthew 16, in the immediate aftermath of Peter's confession (notably 16.21: 'From that time on', e.g. Combrink 1983; Kingsbury 1986). Yet although the narrative has already turned the audience's attention towards Jerusalem, with a series of passion predictions spoken by Jesus (16.21; 17.22–23), it is only at 19.1 that Jesus 'left Galilee and went to the region of Judea beyond the Jordan'. The journey south to Jerusalem for the pilgrimage festival of Passover provides an opportunity for questioning and teaching, both from those hostile to Jesus (e.g. the Pharisees seeking to 'test' him over divorce, 19.3–9) and from his disciples and individuals sympathetic towards him (e.g. the rich young man, 19.16–22).

Jesus' approach to the holy city is understood by Matthew as the entrance of the royal Son of David into his capital. He is explicit that this fulfils prophecy (here Zech. 9.9, interpreted literally such that Jesus sits rather comically on two animals, 'on a donkey, and on a colt, the foal of a donkey', 21.5). The note struck by the prophet Zechariah, that the king coming to the daughter of Zion is 'humble' and rides on lowly animals, sets the scene for what is to follow.

Matthew's description of Jesus' activity in Jerusalem highlights both hostility and receptivity. A series of controversy stories (involving the chief priests and the elders, the Pharisees and Herodians, the Sadducees, a Pharisaic lawyer and finally the Pharisees once again: 21.23–27; 22.15–46) heightens the tension in the narrative, while Jesus' parables (the two sons, the tenants in the vineyard, the marriage feast: 21.28—22.14) hint at a dramatic rupture within the people, and even the destruction of the holy city (22.7). Unique to Matthew is a lengthy tirade against the hypocrisy of the 'scribes and Pharisees' (23.1–39), which many think reflects the fierce intra-Jewish debates against which the Gospel was composed.

By contrast there are characters more receptive to Jesus. The crowds are responsive (e.g. 21.9–11, 46; 23.1), even if they will ultimately be persuaded by the religious leaders to call for Jesus' crucifixion. Children acclaim him as 'son of David' in the Temple (21.15). Jesus himself recounts how tax-collectors and prostitutes are gaining priority entry into the kingdom (21.31).

This section of the narrative concludes with the fifth and final major discourse (Matt. 24—25), spoken by Jesus as he sits on the Mount of Olives overlooking Jerusalem and the Temple. From the perspective of the story, Jesus looks into the future to prepare his followers for the 'time of the Church' between his impending death and what Matthew calls the 'end of the age'. Original readers of the Gospel may well have detected within the stock 'end-time' language of this discourse allusions to events that by their time had come to pass (e.g. 24.15–20). Closely paralleled in Mark 13, the sermon also includes distinctly Matthean parables that explore different dimensions of the final judgement (the faithful and wicked slave, the wise and foolish bridesmaids, the talents, and the separation of the sheep and the goats: 24.45—25.46).

The Passion and Resurrection of Jesus (Matt. 26.1—28.20)

All four evangelists devote a significant percentage of their Gospels to the days and hours leading up to the crucifixion of Jesus. Matthew is no exception, recounting the story in terms almost identical to Mark. In a manner similar to the five discourses, narrative time slows at this point as the last two days of Jesus' earthly life unfold scene by scene. Of the twin themes of hostility and receptivity that have characterized this Gospel, it is the former that now dominates. Jesus, abandoned by his disciples in the Garden of Gethsemane following a final Passover meal (26.56), faces arrest, accusation, mocking and finally death.

Matthew's stress on the fulfilment of Scripture in the events of Jesus' life shapes his passion story, as it had the story of his infancy and ministry (though puzzlingly there are fewer explicit quotations from the Old Testament: 26.31, 64; 27.9, 46). Another theme, whose effects in history have been more sinister, is the heightening of the role of the Jewish leadership in the death of Jesus. Probably reflecting the evangelist's own experience of persecution by synagogue authorities, it nonetheless skews the historical record. As caricatures of their true selves, the chief priests and elders also function as foils to the figure of Jesus, who is depicted in a reverential way (contrast e.g. 26.59 with 26.63). Jesus dies, as he has lived, as the obedient Son of God determined to do his Father's will.

Jesus' death is not the end of the story, however. Matthew agrees with his fellow evangelists in recounting the discovery of the empty tomb early on the following Sunday. Unique details of his account include heavenly involvement (an earthquake and the presence of an 'angel of the Lord': 28.2–3), and an appearance of the risen Jesus to the women (28.9, though see the appearance to Mary Magdalene at John 20.11–18; cf. Mark 16.9). A final appearance to 'the eleven disciples' (the Twelve minus Judas Iscariot: 28.16–20) on a mountain in Galilee draws various threads together, and prepares for the mission of the Church no longer confined to the 'lost sheep of the house of Israel'. The Gospel ends, not with Jesus' ascension into heaven (cf. Mark 16.19; Luke 24.51; John 20.17), but with the promise of his abiding presence: 'I am with you always, to the end of the age' (28.20).

Setting the Scene

This opening chapter has set the scene for what follows by considering the historical prominence of the Gospel according to Matthew and sketching out some of its inherent ambiguities. An initial read-through has been offered in order to help readers get their bearings at the start of their exploration of Matthew's book. In the following chapters, different ways readers across the centuries have interpreted Matthew will be explored in support of the proposal that a multipronged approach – combining literary, historical and theological interests and attending to text, authorial context and communities of readers – is required for a rounded understanding of the Gospel. Further chapters will examine specific sections of Matthew and specific Matthean themes in more detail, with the purpose of opening up questions and fresh avenues for exploration. No claim is made to exhaustive coverage of scholarship on the First Gospel. Given the explosion of scholarly writing on Matthew, that would be an impossible task. Those wishing for a fuller treatment are directed to the many excellent surveys on Matthean scholarship available: for example, Stanton 1985; Anderson 1995; Senior 1996; Hare 1998; Clarke 2003; van Aarde and Dreyer 2010.

2

Interpreting Matthew: Strategies for Reading

Different Ways of Reading

When Thomas Aquinas (1225–74) was shown the magnificent buildings of medieval Paris, he reportedly claimed that he would rather possess a complete copy of the *Opus imperfectum* on Matthew's Gospel than be mayor of that beautiful city (Kellerman 2010: 1/xvii). The *Opus imperfectum* – as its Latin title, meaning 'Incomplete Work', suggests – is a now-incomplete commentary on Matthew, probably written in the fifth century and for centuries wrongly attributed to John Chrysostom. Although in places it betrays the Arian theological views of its author, it was highly prized by mainstream Latin Christians in the Middle Ages, as Thomas' approving words testify.

The interpretation of Matthew found in the *Opus imperfectum* is very different from that found in most modern critical commentaries. Its preference is often for a non-literal reading of the Gospel, in which the 'letter' of the text (the literal meaning), though important in and of itself, acts as a springboard for other, deeper meanings. The commentary on 4.18–22 (the call of the first four disciples), for example, sees the nets, boat and father left behind by the various characters as symbolizing 'everything that everyone who comes to Christ ought to leave behind: carnal deeds, worldly wealth and fleshly parents' (Kellerman 2010: 1/79). Here the figurative interpretation has a moral impetus: how the readers are to respond to Matthew's message in their everyday lives. Elsewhere, it tends to prioritize the theological meaning of the passage. In this the *Opus imperfectum* has much in common with other patristic and medieval commentaries, although these differ among themselves as to the degree of non-literal, especially allegorical, interpretation they employ. Their common presumption is that the text of Matthew is rich in meaning and potential for meaning for those who study it carefully and prayerfully.

Critical scholarship, by contrast (at least from the eighteenth century until recent decades), has sought a univocal meaning for Matthew in its quest for the historical circumstances that produced the Gospel. A cluster of 'historical' approaches have been employed to explore the sources, written and oral, used by the evangelist (*source criticism*: e.g. Streeter 1927; Farrer

1955; Farmer 1964; Goulder 1985); the history of those traditions prior to their use by Matthew (*form criticism*: notably Bultmann 1963); and the ways he has creatively edited or redacted the material at his disposal, whether through detailed examination of pericopae with parallels in other Gospels (*redaction criticism*: e.g. Bornkamm, Barth and Held 1982) or a more broad-sweep analysis of his overall message (*composition criticism*: e.g. Thompson 1970).

In other words, priority has tended to be given to the human author and to interpreting the text in the same way as other, more secular literature. The meaning of the text, moreover, has generally been equated with what that human author intended to convey to the first-century audience or audiences for whom he or she – in the case of Matthew, almost certainly 'he' – originally wrote. Such an approach is often referred to as the 'historical-critical method' because it is asking primarily historical questions – about the historical evangelist, his sources, method of composition and intended message, or the community for whom he wrote and their particular needs, or the 'pre-history' of his sources before he composed his Gospel.

Another set of recent critical methods has given priority to the text of the Gospel, in the final form we now possess. Perhaps most famous among these 'literary' approaches is *narrative criticism* (e.g. Kingsbury 1986; Powell 1992), which borrows from literary theory in other disciplines to identify the meaning embedded in the text (as opposed to a hypothetical reconstruction of the 'world behind the text'). Narrative critics pay attention to literary dimensions such as plot, characterization and point of view. Their approach tends to be holistic, as opposed to the more fragmentary treatment of the text by some historical-critical methods (narrative criticism is anticipated in the more historically focused composition criticism). Matthew is treated as a story to be entered into, or to which to respond, rather than an 'archaeological site' to be excavated. Other literary approaches include *rhetorical criticism*, which reads biblical texts in the light of ancient rhetorical techniques of persuasion (e.g. Kennedy 1984), and *structuralism* (e.g. Patte 1987), interested in the deep structures of the text.

Both historical-critical and many – though not all – literary approaches have in common a univocal quest for meaning. They generally agree that a given passage of Matthew has a single meaning, although differ over where that meaning is to be found – in the reconstructed 'intention' of the original author or in the text itself. Another cluster of approaches is more concerned with the interested reader, who interprets Matthew's Gospel from his or her particular perspective and ideological commitments and seeks to expose the extent to which all interpretations reflect the commitments of those who espouse them. Examples of ideological criticism, sometimes called *advocacy criticism*, include liberationist, feminist, and postcolonial readings (e.g. Anderson 1983; Levine [ed.] 2001; Wainwright 2009; Carter 2001; Riches and Sim [eds] 2005). As Warren Carter notes in his *Matthew and the Margins*, all readings are 'perspectival, partial, and shaped by the questions, experiences, and location of various communities of readers' (Carter 2000: xvii). Awareness of the various reading communities to which we belong, of our own political or religious stance and the questions we are predisposed to ask – and the answers we are predisposed to give – as a consequence of our own tradition of interpretation, is now very much on the agenda of biblical scholarship. Moreover there is a greater appreciation that biblical texts, like musical symphonies, are texts to be 'performed'. Even the same reader will not read Matthew in exactly the same way twice but will be engaged in a unique performance on each occasion.

One important strand of the turn to reader-orientated interpretation is the renewed interest in the 'reception' (or 'effective') history (a translation of the German term *Wirkungsgeschichte*) of biblical texts across the centuries and in a range of media, including music and art. The greatest exponent of *Wirkungsgeschichte* in relation to Matthew's Gospel has been the Swiss New Testament scholar Ulrich Luz, in his commentary for the ecumenical Evangelisch-Katholischer Kommentar (EKK) series (Luz 1989, 2001 and 2005a) and a flood of other publications (e.g. Luz 1994 and 2005b). Reception history has the merit of reminding interpreters of where they have come from, revealing the extent to which even their reconstructions of the 'original context' of Matthew are framed by the tradition of interpretation in which they stand. It also exposes interpreters to unfamiliar or forgotten ways of reading Matthew's Gospel, reflecting 'popular' as well as 'professional' readings.

Figurative and Allegorical Exegesis

Let us begin our survey with the *Opus imperfectum* and other early commentaries on Matthew's Gospel also available in English translation. These include the commentary on Matthew by Origen, surviving copies of which cover Matt. 13.36—22.33 (Origen 1994), and a short commentary by the fourth-century Latin biblical scholar Jerome, written in the space of just two weeks for his friend Eusebius of Cremona (Jerome 2008), together with two volumes of excerpts in the Ancient Christian Commentary on Scripture series, edited by Manlio Simonetti (Simonetti [ed.] 2001). There are also translations of John Chrysostom's homilies on Matthew (John Chrysostom 1991), and Augustine's homilies on the Sermon on the Mount (Augustine 1996).

Given the tendency of modern scholarship to dismiss patristic exegesis as unbridled allegorization, it is important to note the diversity between different interpreters. Jerome's, for example, tends to prefer a literal reading of the text and is not oblivious to 'critical issues', such as discrepancies between the Gospel accounts or Matthew's tendency to quote inexactly from Old Testament texts. The quotation from Zechariah at 26.31 is a case in point (the Old Testament passage has the imperative 'strike the shepherd', whereas Matthew has 'I will strike the shepherd'). For Jerome, Psalm 69.25 provides the key to explain the indicative verb in Matthew's quotation: 'Because they have persecuted him whom you have struck' (Jerome 2008: 299). Origen's commentary places more weight on the 'spiritual sense' of the Gospel text, while the fact that both Chrysostom and Augustine offer their interpretation of Matthew in sermons leads them to emphasize the meaning of the text for their hearers. Hence Chrysostom treats Jesus' withdrawal from Nazareth to Capernaum (4.13) as an example for Christians 'not to seek out temptation but to withdraw ourselves from its sphere of influence' (Simonetti [ed.] 2001: 66). A moral or 'tropological' interpretation – from the Greek *tropos* meaning 'way' or 'manner of life' – is also found in Jerome's commentary. Commenting on Jesus' command to the Twelve to go 'nowhere among the Gentiles' (10.5), Jerome first considers the literal sense and the tension it sets up with the command to 'make disciples of all the Gentiles/nations' at 28.19. Like many critical commentators, he offers a salvation-historical explanation: the Gospel was intended for the Jews first and only then for the Gentiles. But he also draws out a 'tropology': that Christians should 'not go into the way of the Gentiles and the error of the heretics' (Jerome 2008: 116).

Nonetheless there are common strategies employed by patristic commentators on Matthew. Manlio Simonetti identifies four (Simonetti [ed.] 2001: xlii). First, the Fathers employ etymological symbolism to explore the significance of a biblical name or other word. Hence Cyril of Alexandria, when commenting on Matthew's quotation from Isaiah 9 at 4.15, interprets 'Zebulun' as 'a sweet smell and blessing' (the latter interpretation perhaps from the Hebrew *zebed* meaning 'gift'), while 'Napthali' is 'a sprouted stump' (Simonetti [ed.] 2001: 74). Some of the etymological explanations, it must be admitted, are rather obscure.

Second is their interest in arithmetical symbolism. The Fathers are close enough to the world of the New Testament authors to appreciate that numbers have symbolic meaning for the classical world generally (e.g. five, seven, ten, twelve), and the Judaeo-Christian world in particular (thus the number 40 has associations with Israel's 40-year wanderings in the wilderness). This might be relevant for interpreting the text as a whole: Jerome, for example, finds significance in the fact that Matthew's Gospel contains 15 miraculous signs, although not specifying the precise significance of this number (Jerome 2008: 43). His reasoning might be that 15 is the sum of a number associated with the Old Testament (seven, as in the Sabbath) and one associated with the New (eight, on the understanding that the resurrection happened on the eighth day). But Jerome also explores arithmetical symbolism in specific passages. He proposes that the five loaves and two fish produced at the feeding of the five thousand (14.13–21) symbolize Moses (the five books of the Pentateuch) and the two Testaments (Jerome 2008: 171), and notes that the number of the loaves at the feeding of the four thousand is the perfect number seven (Jerome 2008: 186).

Third, patristic exegetes are attentive to incongruities in the text or what they sometimes call *defectus litterae* ('defect of the letter/literal sense'). Certain passages may contain improbable statements that cannot be literally true, alerting the reader to move beyond the letter to uncover a more satisfying spiritual meaning. Finally, the Fathers, borrowing a technique from the rabbis, will often 'interpret Scripture with Scripture'. This involves juxtaposing the biblical text with a passage from elsewhere in the Bible that shares a common word or idea. Thus for Augustine the symbolic role of the centurion as prefiguring the conversion of the Gentiles is explained by appeal to Psalm 18.43: 'A people whom I have not known has served me' (Simonetti [ed.] 2001: 162). This stands in sharp contrast to modern historical-critical commentators, and even narrative critics, who want to allow Matthew's narrative to speak on its own terms. But it has its own inner logic: the theological conviction of the overarching unity of Scripture, one divine Author working in and through the diverse voices of the human authors. Moreover one finds already in Matthew's Gospel the rabbinic tendency to combine and conflate two or more Old Testament passages (e.g. Mic. 5.2 and 2 Sam. 5.2 at 2.6; Jer. 18–19 and Zech. 11.12–13 at 27.9–10; Isa. 62.11 and Zech. 9.9 at 21.5).

Reassessing Pre-critical Readings

The tendency of many modern scholars has been to dismiss patristic and medieval exegesis out of hand as unbridled allegorizing owing more to the interpreter's imagination than the text of Matthew or the meaning intended by the evangelist in writing. But it would be premature to do so (see e.g. Johnson and Kurz 2002; Daley 2003). Certainly there are aspects of patristic interpretation of Matthew that seem naïve to modern sensibilities and gloss over some of the critical difficulties raised by different Gospel accounts of the same event. Yet there are also similarities between so-called 'pre-critical' exegesis and the postmodern conviction of a plethora of meanings contained in, or capable of being produced by, Matthew's text. Authorial intention, in so far as that is recoverable, cannot be the sole arbiter of the Gospel's meaning. But even authorial intention is not necessarily univocal. As one prominent Matthean scholar puts it, Matthew's sentences are 'intertextually, intratextually, and theologically dense' (Allison 2005: 125).

Equally important, as Simonetti has shown, is the recognition that 'pre-critical' exegesis was as disciplined as any modern critical method. Moreover there are specific parallels between how they read Matthew and certain strands in recent New Testament scholarship. The appeal to etymology, for example, is not inappropriate for understanding Matthew's Gospel in its ancient context. When the angel of the Lord tells Joseph to name the child 'Jesus, for he will save his people from their sins' (1.21), the evangelist is offering an etymological explanation of the name *Yeshua/* Joshua, meaning 'YHWH helps' or 'YHWH is salvation' (a point noted by many critical commentators: e.g. Davies and Allison 1988–97: 1/209).

Nor are allegorical readings of Matthew in the Fathers qualitatively different from the evangelist's own interpretative strategy. Matthew famously interprets Jesus' parables as complex allegories (in which there is a point-by-point, character-by-character correspondence between the story world and the real world), accompanied by detailed interpretations (e.g. 13.18–23, 37–43, 49–50). Other stories in Matthew are also regularly given symbolic significance by modern critical scholars, even if these are rooted in the literal sense. Günther Bornkamm's famous article on the stilling of the storm in Matthew (Bornkamm 1982) interprets the story as an allegory of discipleship in the post-Easter Church. The story of Peter sinking as he steps out of the boat at 14.28–33 is another example, in which the character of Peter serves as a reassuring model for the wavering faith of other Christians. It is not far from this to the kind of figurative reading one finds in Jerome's commentary. His interpretation of Matthew 13.1, where Jesus leaves the house and sits beside the Sea of Galilee to teach in parables, reads as follows: 'Therefore, the compassionate the merciful Lord goes out from his own house and sits near the sea of this world' (Jerome

2008: 152). Again, this reading is rooted in the literal sense but brings the contemporary life of Christians, called to live out their vocation as disciples in the world, firmly into the world of the story.

Another example is 26.30, where Jesus and the disciples leave the room of the Last Supper and go out to the Mount of Olives. Jerome does not deny that this is describing an actual journey across the Kidron Valley outside Jerusalem. But he emphasizes the sequence of events – akin to modern narrative criticism – linking the Last Supper with the Mount of Olives, combined with the symbolic significance often given to mountains in the ancient world, to connect this story with the Christian reader's reception of the Eucharist:

> According to this citation, the one who has been filled with the Saviour's bread and made merry with his cup can praise the Lord and ascend the Mount of Olives, where there is refreshment from labors and solace from grief and there is knowledge of the true light. (Jerome 2008: 298)

The reference here to 'the true light' encountered on 'the Mount of Olives' exploits the fact that olive oil was used in lamps.

Finally, patristic interpreters are concerned primarily with the theological subject matter of Matthew's Gospel, and what it teaches about the protagonist Jesus, rather than historical questions such as the mind of the author. This theological concern sometimes manifests itself in 'reading back' developed doctrinal beliefs into the biblical text, in a manner many critical scholars would regard as 'unhistorical'. Thus, for example, Jerome finds a fully developed doctrine of the Trinity in the triadic baptismal formula at 28.19 (Jerome 2008: 327). On the other hand, ecclesial and other commitments are rather more explicit in the Fathers than they are in many modern critical scholars.

Historical Criticism

Perhaps the dominant approach in scholarly study of Matthew since the nineteenth century has been the historical, often known as the 'historical critical' method. In contrast to patristic and medieval commentators, the main focus of historical critics has been to understand the Gospels, Matthew included, within the original historical environment of their authors. *Historical criticism* is often used as an umbrella term encompassing a variety of methods (source, form, redaction and composition criticism). Somewhat confusingly, early practitioners of these approaches sometimes referred to them as 'literary criticism', given that they are interested in literary texts such as

Matthew's Gospel, the literary sources they employ and the literary techniques used in their composition. In more recent scholarship, 'literary criticism' describes narrative criticism and similar approaches, which often sidestep issues of history and sources and concentrate on holistic readings of the text in its final form.

Source criticism seeks to uncover the sources, both written and oral, used by the human author (for a fuller discussion, see Chapter 3). The traditional view, that Matthew's Gospel is the work of an eyewitness and the first of the four canonical Gospels to be written, has no obvious need to seek for underlying sources. However, what has become the scholarly consensus view, popularized in the English-speaking world by B. H. Streeter (Streeter 1927), is the Two Source Theory. This theory maintains that Mark was the first Gospel to be written, and was used by both Matthew and Luke, who also drew – independently of each other – on another written source, mainly made up of sayings of Jesus, referred to as Q (from the German *Quelle* = 'source'). Matthew also contains material paralleled neither in Mark nor in Luke (e.g. the story of the magi; the command of Jesus not to go in the way of Gentiles; the parable of the wise and foolish virgins: 2.1–12; 10.5–6; 25.1–13), which is often referred to for convenience as M (= Matthew's Special Material). Other scholars have proposed alternative solutions, including the Griesbach or Two Gospel Hypothesis (Mark is the third Gospel, combining Matthew and Luke), the Farrer-Goulder theory (holding to the priority of Mark but dispensing with Q through positing that Luke used Matthew as well as Mark), and more complex solutions that place more weight on shared oral traditions (Sanders and Davies 1989: 84–119).

Form criticism (from the German *Formgeschichte*) seeks to identify different units or pericopae that make up a text like Matthew, categorize them according to literary type or form (e.g. parables, miracle stories, conflict or controversy stories where Jesus or his disciples are engaged in debate with other Jewish groups) and trace how those units of tradition were reshaped in the period between Jesus and the writing of the Gospels (e.g. the Lord's Prayer as a piece of early Christian liturgy; the story of the centurion's servant being used in early Church discussions about the status of Gentiles; or the story of plucking grain on the Sabbath as reflecting ongoing debates between followers of Jesus and the Synagogue: 6.9–13; 8.5–13; 12.1–8). Form critics have often been rather sceptical about the historicity of many of these traditional stories, seeing them as composed of layers of tradition and interpretation by an anonymous 'community'. More recent scholarship has invited a rethink, whether through reflection upon oral tradition with its combination of fixity and fluidity (e.g. Dunn 2011: 35–44), or giving a greater role to named eyewitnesses in passing on the Jesus tradition (e.g. Bauckham 2006).

Redaction criticism built on form criticism but emphasized the creative role of the evangelist in collating these units of tradition in a narrative framework, and reworking available source material. Pioneering work on Matthew was done by Günther Bornkamm and his colleagues (Bornkamm, Barth and Held 1982). However, the shift brought by redaction criticism in the middle of the twentieth century can be overstated. Already in his 1907 International Critical Commentary, for example, Willoughby Allen acknowledged the 'individuality of the respective Evangelists' that treated them as writers who 'selected, arranged, compiled, redacted, with the intention of trying to set before their readers the conception of the Christ as they themselves conceived Him' (Allen 1907: iii).

Redaction criticism has significantly illuminated the study of Matthew, highlighting many of the Gospel's distinctive features discussed in Chapter 1 above (a fine example of a redactional-critical approach is R. H. Gundry's commentary: Gundry 1994). However, it is not without its critics. Does it not, for example, presuppose a theological consistency within the Gospel that requires more careful demonstration? In other words, it treats the evangelist as a creative individual with a coherent theology rather than a conservative collator of tradition and preserver of his sources. But how can one be sure that features regarded as 'Matthean' spring from the pen of the evangelist rather than his sources? Moreover – at least as practised by European scholars – redaction criticism has often focused on minute changes made by Matthew to those sources (generally believed to be Mark and Q). This underestimates the extent to which Matthew may have been in agreement with his sources and therefore preserved them virtually unchanged (see Goodacre 2006). Partly as a reaction, William Thompson championed *composition criticism*, which pays greater attention to the whole Gospel and the characteristic motifs that emerge as a result (Thompson 1970 and 1971).

Social Sciences

Hand in hand with redaction criticism has gone the application of the social sciences to the study of Matthew and the other Gospels. Whereas history tends to focus on the individual or unusual, the social sciences seek to explore what is typical and social. As will be seen in Chapter 5, one area in which social-scientific approaches have illuminated Matthew's

Gospel is the discussion of the evangelist's social context. Overman and Saldarini have utilized the social model of the sect, and 'deviance' theory respectively, to illuminate the Gospel's social dynamics and specifically its polemical language against the Pharisees and other Jewish leadership groups (Overman 1990; Saldarini 1994). Such an approach reads the Gospel's 'name-calling' (e.g. the series of woes against the 'scribes and Pharisees, hypocrites': 23.13–36) as the result of a minority Jewish group defining itself over against a parent or sibling group dominated by the Pharisaic party in late first-century Judaism. The sociology of knowledge – derived from Berger and Luckmann – has been employed by Philip Esler to explore the social function of Matthew's strong emphasis on 'righteousness' (*dikaiosunē*). For Esler, the 'righteousness' language does not only make ethical demands; it also serves to differentiate the followers of Jesus from rival Jewish groups (Esler 1994: 8).

Insights from cultural anthropology (e.g. Malina 1981; Malina and Rohrbaugh 2003) have also been used effectively to shed light on aspects of Matthew. Malina discusses several features of ancient Mediterranean culture that may be obscure to modern readers of the Gospels. Honour was especially prized in ancient Mediterranean society, in sharp contrast to shame. This ancient concentration on honour and shame illuminates specific features of Matthew's book. Against such a background Matthew's genealogy (1.2–17), which links Jesus (via Joseph) to the great King David and the patriarch Abraham, may have the function of ascribing honour and nobility to Jesus, as might also the fact that his birth was heralded by a special star. The declarations of Jesus as 'innocent' in the passion narrative (27.4, 19, 24) accord honour to one who died an apparently shameful death.

The concept of a dyadic personality – from the Greek *duo* meaning 'two' – describes the ancient tendency to define someone's personality according to the group to which he or she belonged, as opposed to the individualism typical of contemporary Western society. Dyadic personality may shed additional light on the negative portrayal of the Pharisees, and other groupings, in Matthew's story, which looks to the modern mind like stereotyping and caricature. Ancient ideas of kinship and marriage are also relevant to interpreting Matthew's Gospel. The world was divided into 'kin' and 'non-kin', relationships to non-kin being marked by competitiveness. Marriage, in contrast to the modern understanding, was generally arranged, the female being 'embedded' in the dominant male, and the interests of the two families rather than the husband and wife being the primary consideration. Jesus' saying about his alternative family ('For whoever does the will of my Father in heaven is my brother and sister and mother': 12.50) has particular significance against this background. So too does his teaching about divorce (5.31–32; 19.3–9): in ancient terms this would be seen less as the breakdown of a relationship between two individuals than as a feud between two families (Malina and Rohrbaugh 2003: 96–7).

Finally, issues of purity, the distinction between 'clean' and 'unclean' (people, animals, places and time) that preserved order in society, also emerge in the pages of Matthew. Purity was particularly significant in Jewish society; yet Jesus regularly comes into physical contact with people considered unclean (a leper, 8.1–4; two demoniacs who lived among the tombs and therefore would have contracted ritual impurity through their close proximity to corpses: 8.28–34).

Holistic Readings

If historical criticism and social-scientific criticism are interested in the 'referential function' of the Gospels (what they reveal about 'the world behind the text'), a variety of literary approaches focus their attention on the 'world within the text' (see Powell 2009). Such readings tend to be more holistic than source-, form- and even redaction-critical approaches, which risk chopping the text into its constitutive parts. Particularly prominent among literary approaches is narrative criticism, which could be seen as a development of the more holistic composition criticism advocated, for example, by William Thompson. The narrative or story world explored by narrative critics is not the real world, nor a window on to the real world of early Christian communities, although entering into it has an effect on readers such that they return to their real world changed or with a different perspective. An increasing number of scholars have applied the tools of narrative criticism to Matthew's Gospel (e.g. Edwards 1985; Kingsbury 1986; Matera 1987; Powell 1992; Stock 1994).

As a literary rather than historical approach, narrative criticism is less interested in the real author (the historical evangelist traditionally called Matthew, about whom we know little for certain) than in the 'implied author' (the version of the real author implied by the text itself) and the 'narrator' (the voice telling the story, and just occasionally speaking explicitly: e.g. 1.22; 28.15). Whereas in other texts there may be a clear distinction between the implied author and the narrator, in Matthew's text this is less pronounced.

Similarly, narrative critics speak of the 'implied reader' or 'ideal reader': 'an imaginary person who is to be envisaged, in perusing Matthew's story, as responding to the text at every point with whatever emotion, understanding, or knowledge the text ideally calls for' (Kingsbury 1986: 36). Thus the implied readers of Matthew are followers of Jesus familiar enough with the Jewish tradition that they need no explanation of distinctive Jewish traditions (e.g. 15.1–2; cf. Mark 7.1–5), who recognize Jesus' 'point of view' as the truly authentic one, and who feel antipathy towards such characters as the Pharisees. Some narrative critics further define the implied reader as a first-time reader of Matthew (e.g. Edwards 1985). This may be too restrictive, however, given evidence that the Gospel was designed for repeated reading and careful study (see Luz 2005b: 3–4).

In their analysis of Matthew's narrative, narrative critics are interested in features such as plot, 'discourse time', 'point of view', narrative setting and structural markers that help the reader identify transitions in the narrative, as well as the characterization of the key players in the story. 'Plot' describes the sequence of incidents or 'events' that make the whole meaningful (Kingsbury 1986), or what Matera calls their 'narrative logic' (Matera 1987). An important dimension of the plot is 'discourse time' (focusing on the order, duration and frequency of events recounted, and those events that are omitted or only alluded to), which is to be distinguished from 'story time' (the natural order and duration of events). The amount of space devoted to Jesus' Last Supper, arrest, passion and death, for example (26.20—27.61), is disproportionate to its actual length (less than 24 hours) in the totality of Jesus' ministry (Powell 1992: 192–4). This accentuates the solemnity of the death and resurrection, which have been prepared for by a succession of predictions earlier in the story (e.g. 16.21; 17.9, 22–23; 20.18–19). By contrast, the time between the return of the child Jesus from Egypt to the appearance of John the Baptist (a period of some years) is glossed over in an instant (3.1). John's own death is mentioned out of chronological sequence (14.1–12), as a 'flashback' to an event that has occurred previously (although Matthew forgets he is recounting a flashback: see Goodacre 1998; Donaldson 1999).

'Point of view' refers to those literary indicators through which the implied author's viewpoint is made clear. This is particularly in evidence when the voice of the 'narrator' is heard. Matthew's so-called 'formula citations' are a good example. These are Old Testament quotations, introduced by a stereotypical formula ('This happened in order that what was spoken by the Lord through the prophet might be fulfilled'), which stand outside the narrative, passing a running commentary on the action (e.g.

1.22–23; 2.15, 23; 12.17–21). Other examples of Matthean 'point of view' include the depiction of scribes and Pharisees as 'hypocrites' (e.g. 23.13) and of the chief priests as bribers and plotters (28.12–13). Readers of Matthew's Gospel may not necessarily share its point of view (e.g. that Pharisees as historical figures are hypocrites, or that angels appear to human beings in dreams). In a narrative-critical approach, however, they are invited to suspend their presuppositions temporarily and enter into the world the text describes, with its time, space and value system.

Narrative critics pay attention to additional narrative features such as the 'setting' within which particular events occur. The setting might be a geographical location (e.g. Bethlehem, Capernaum, the desert or the Temple), a particular time (e.g. 'the consummation of the age') or particular social circumstances (e.g. a time of persecution: Kingsbury 1986: 27–9). Structural markers are also important for reading the Gospel holistically, though narrative critics debate the relative importance of particular markers. For example, is the repetition of 'From that time' (4.17; 16.21) more significant structurally than the conclusion to the five main discourses: 'Now when Jesus had finished' (7.28; 11.1; 13.53; 19.1; 26.1)?

Finally, narrative critics of Matthew's Gospel are interested in the way characters are portrayed, the way they develop (or fail to) throughout the narrative and the response they evoke from the implied reader. Specific characters or character groups might evoke sympathy (Jesus, given his rejection by members of his own people), empathy (the disciples, in whose 'little faith' the implied readers might recognize themselves) or antagonism (the leadership who are hostile to Jesus). Some characters are not straight-forward: how, for example, is the implied reader to respond to the Canaanite woman (15.21–28)? She belongs to the hated Canaanites, and even Jesus is initially reluctant to help her ('I was sent only to the lost sheep of the house of Israel', 15.24); yet her persistence leads to her faith being praised (15.28).

Turn towards the Reader

If in simplistic terms historical critics are interested in the human author and the 'world behind the text', and narrative critics prioritize the text itself in its final form, a cluster of recent approaches focus attention on the readers or audience and their active role in creating meaning through their engagement with the gaps in and ambiguities of the biblical text. An important dimension of these approaches is acknowledgement of the 'interested reader': the extent to which all interpretations are shaped by the interests and commitments of the interpreter. Reader-focused inter-preters are not only upfront about their own commitments but seek to expose the – sometimes unacknowledged – commitments of others, especially those who claim 'objectivity' for their interpretations.

A significant example that has impacted the interpretation of Matthew is *feminist criticism* (e.g. Anderson 1983; Levine [ed.] 2001; Wain-wright 2009). This does not so much represent a specific methodology as a perspective or hermeneutical stance from which any methodology – whether redaction-critical, narrative-critical or social-scientific – might be employed. Feminist criticism may involve the rehabilitation of the for-gotten history of women in the ministry of Jesus or the life of the early Church (e.g. Schüssler Fiorenza 1983), by a process of historical recon-struction employing a 'hermeneutic of suspicion'. Some feminist critics seek to unmask the androcentric character of a text like Matthew, and its encoding of patriarchal structures, while also noting its ambiguities and instability. The presence of a small number of women in Matthew's genealogy is one example of the latter (Anderson 1987). Another is Matthew's story of the Canaanite woman (15.21–28): Gail O'Day has made an interest-ing case for the woman, rather than Jesus, being the protagonist in the story (O'Day 2001). Other feminist critics are more concerned to identify the androcentric assumptions of previous Matthean scholars.

Postcolonial interpretation has also left its mark on the interpretation of Matthew (e.g. Carter 2001; Riches and Sim [eds] 2005). This is an umbrella term for readings, initially emerging from the non-Western world, that critique the influence of colonialism, both as embedded in the biblical text and as found in critical biblical scholarship, attempt to retrieve silenced voices in the text, and foreground the political dimension (Segovia 2009). But postcolonial critics differ considerably in their assessment of Matthew. For Musa Dube, it is a thoroughly imperializing text, presenting Rome in a positive fashion (Dube 2000). For Warren Carter, by contrast (Carter 2001), Matthew's Gospel offers a subversive counter-narrative to the imperial ideology of the Roman Empire. In other work too, Carter has attempted to read Matthew 'from the margins', offering a perspective on the Gospel very different from that of most privileged Western academics. He believes that this is justifiable on historical, literary and contemporary ecclesial grounds. Historically, Matthew is a text produced by a marginal group in an urban setting (for Carter, Antioch in Syria). In literary terms it presents its protagonist as in opposition to the religious elite, and finally killed as the result of an alliance between the political and religious elites. Meanwhile, the alternative vision – of the 'kingdom of the heavens' – that he teaches his disciples heightens the marginality of his community. Carter's reading 'from the margins' also connects with the increasingly marginal status of the Christian Church, including in the USA where Carter writes.

A final example of reader-focused interpretation is the recent interest in reception history, often referred to by the German term *Wirkungsgeschichte* (borrowed from the philosopher Hans-Georg Gadamer, and variously translated 'history of effects', 'history of influence' and 'effective history'). If there is a technical distinction between the two terms, reception history focuses on the reader/interpreter and his or her engagement with the biblical text, while *Wirkungsgeschichte* emphasizes the text as active agent. Although Ulrich Luz has been the most famous pioneer of *Wirkungsgeschichte* in relation to Matthew's text, other scholars have explored particular dimensions of the Gospel's reception, embracing history, literature, music and art as well as more traditional biblical studies. Martin O'Kane has written on the visual impact of Matthew's Gospel, especially in artistic interpretations of the adoration of the magi (e.g. O'Kane 2005). Rachel Nicholls has examined the reception of Matthew's story of the walking on the water (Nicholls 2008). From outside the guild of biblical scholars, the classical scholar Howard Clarke has authored a wide-ranging exploration of historical receptions of the First Gospel (Clarke 2003).

Coming Full Circle

The reference to *Wirkungsgeschichte* and reception history brings us full circle, for a reception-historical approach is receptive to rather than dismissive of so-called 'pre-critical' exegesis of Matthew such as we find in the Fathers. Indeed, the postmodern emphasis on multivalency of meaning has meant the rediscovery of patristic and medieval exegesis as a complement, and sometimes a check, to more historically focused methods of interpretation. Moreover although this chapter has attempted to differentiate between historical, social-scientific and literary approaches, such distinctions have their limits. Thus, for example, historical-critical methods have literary as well as historical dimensions, such that they were in earlier decades referred to by the umbrella term 'literary criticism' (nowadays generally reserved for holistic readings such as narrative criticism). Hence source criticism of Matthew has traditionally focused on uncovering the evangelist's *literary* sources, and redaction criticism on the shape of the text created by the evangelist's editing. Moreover anticipations of discrete approaches may be detected in the work of earlier interpreters: as noted above, an Edwardian commentary on Matthew

(Allen 1907) can use language similar to that of redaction critics of the 1960s and 1970s.

Similarly, literary approaches cannot totally insulate themselves from historical questions. A narrative-critical reading of Matthew will be sadly deficient if it fails to ask about the origins and beliefs of the Pharisees (minimal information is provided by the text), the location of Galilee vis-à-vis Judea or when Herod the Great ruled as 'king of the Jews'. Further, Matthew's book (unlike Mark's) is not straightforwardly narrative, for it is punctuated with substantial teaching discourses that limit the usefulness of interpreting Matthew as story.

Hence a rounded interpretation of Matthew invites an interweaving of historical, literary and theological questions, together with an honest recognition of the perspective from which I read the text and an openness to the different readings of other ages, cultures, theological traditions and interest groups. Such has already been suggested by this book so far, especially in its appeal to earlier receptions of Matthew, and will continue to be the unashamedly eclectic approach in the discussion that follows.

3

The Text of Matthew:
Puzzles and Possibilities

Different Textual Questions

For all the diversity of the interpretations explored in the last chapter, which can be positioned on a spectrum from author through text to reader, they arguably have one thing in common. They all agree, to greater or lesser degrees, that *textual* questions are central. Some prioritize the creation or production of Matthew's text: what can be gleaned about its author and how did that author construct the text? For others, known as textual critics, the important task is to reconstruct the original words of the Gospel from the multiplicity of variant readings found in the ancient Greek manuscripts and in early translations (though see Parker 1997). With the recent interest in reception, textual criticism has become increasingly attentive to what can be learned from those later scribal corrections and errors about how Matthew's Gospel was being read in different contexts. Still others, with more holistic interests in the narrative, are concerned with the shape of the narrative, attempting to undercover structural patterns in this complex literary work, at both the macro- and the micro-level. Finally, some readers prioritize the interplay between reader and text, exploring the text's ambiguities and gaps – which may be highlighted by different English translations – and the variety of responses to those in differing reading contexts. These different textual questions will be the subject of this chapter, although particular attention will be paid to the interests of textual critics proper: reconstructing the original Greek text and account-ing for the various readings in the manuscripts.

The Writer of the Text

For many centuries the evangelist called 'Matthew' was believed to be Matthew the apostle, one of Jesus' chosen Twelve (9.9; 10.3; Mark 3.18; Luke 6.15; Acts 1.13) and a former tax-collector or customs officer (9.9; the parallel in Mark 2.14 and Luke 5.27, 29 describes the call of a disciple named Levi, not listed among the Twelve). This gave Matthew's Gospel, along with John's, particular priority, given that it was the work of one of Jesus' closest associates and an eyewitness of many of the events described. According to early patristic testimony, Matthew the apostle wrote his Gospel for the Jews in their own language (e.g. Irenaeus, *Adv. Haer.* 3.1.1; Origen in Eusebius, *H. E.* 6.25.4; Jerome, *De Vir. Illustr.* 3). Much of the patristic testimony is probably dependent on the statement of the second-century bishop Papias of Hierapolis, citing 'the Elder'. According to Papias, Matthew the Lord's disciple compiled the 'oracles of the Lord' (variously interpreted as Jesus' sayings, Old Testament prophecies about the Messiah or the Gospel as a whole) 'in the Hebrew language/dialect' (possibly Aramaic), or 'in a Hebrew manner' (Eusebius, *H. E.* 3.39.16). Whatever the meaning of Papias' words, there seems to have been no rival contender for the authorship of this Gospel in the early Church. This tradition of Matthean authorship is reflected in the earliest Greek manuscripts, which include the title *Kata Matthaion* ('according to Matthew').

Since the nineteenth century, however, this tradition of apostolic authorship has been increasingly rejected by scholars. As one early twentieth-century commentator expressed it: 'He was certainly not Matthew the apostle' (McNeile 1928: xxviii). A major reason is the widespread acceptance of Marcan priority, coupled with evidence for a close literary relationship between Matthew and Mark (strong similarities in content, order and wording between the two Gospels). It seems implausible to many scholars that a firsthand witness like Matthew would need to resort to the work of one who was neither an apostle nor an eyewitness (Mark) in composing his Gospel. Others (e.g. Farmer 1964) resolve the difficulty by appeal to the priority of Matthew, with Mark as the later redactor. Still others (e.g. France 1989: 73; Hagner 1993: lxxvi; Gundry 1994: 609–22), while holding to Marcan priority, have questioned whether this argument is quite so compelling, particularly if Mark's Gospel derived from the authoritative testimony of Peter (as Papias also claimed). They raise the legitimate question as to whether this denial of apostolic authorship is too dependent on modern ideas about authorial originality and fear of plagiarism. However, defence of authorship by Matthew the tax-collector remains a minority scholarly position.

A second argument is particularly directed against the Papias tradition (at least if that is understood to be claiming that Matthew originally wrote in Hebrew or Aramaic). Although our Greek Matthew contains some Semitic phrases (e.g. 'And it happened'; 'Behold!' etc.: Moule 1966: 215–19), it does not look to many scholars like a translation from a Semitic language, particularly if it is dependent upon Mark, a text composed in Greek (Kilpatrick 1946: 3). Further, its Old Testament quotations represent a mixed collection of textual traditions, including the Septuagint (LXX). If our Matthew were the result of translation from Aramaic or Hebrew, one might expect its translator to be more consistent in using an existing Greek biblical translation. However, some caution should be expressed here, given that educated Greek speakers as eminent as Irenaeus, Clement of Alexandria and Origen believed our canonical Greek Matthew to be a translation from a Semitic version (Davies and Allison 1988–97: 1/12).

One further issue regarding authorship of Matthew is sometimes raised: should we be looking for a single author at all, whether the inspired apostle of Christ, a rather cautious editor of inherited traditions or a particularly creative second-generation Christian (for the latter view, see for example Farrer 1966)? Or does this reflect a modern understanding of authorship? Krister Stendahl famously interpreted the Gospel as the product of a school, akin to the *tannaim* or early rabbinic sages of Judaism (Stendahl 1954), rather than of an independent individual. Stendahl, influenced particularly by the form-critical focus on the community dimension of the oral tradition, saw striking parallels between the biblical interpretation in the Qumran *pesharim* or interpretative commentaries (notably its *pesher* on Habakkuk) and the Old Testament interpretation presupposed by Matthew's formula citations.

In a similar vein, Benedict Viviano notes not only the expense of producing a manuscript, which would have involved commissioning and financial support, but also signs that the evangelist had significant sacred texts available: 'His gospel was not the product of a solitary genius, but of a qualified representative of a community with its own point(s) of view' (Viviano 2007: 4). Nonetheless, Viviano also believes that the coherence of the whole points to a 'single controlling mind' responsible for the Gospel's final form. This is in sharp contrast to the interpretation of Ernest Abel (Abel 1971), who is more impressed by Matthew's *lack* of coherence (the tension between its universalist dimensions and its emphasis on Jewish continuity). Thus he claims that Matthew was the work of two editors. The first, Jewish-Christian, editor was responsible for traditions that emphasize Jewish continuity and for specifically anti-Pharisaic sentiments. Abel attributes elements of 'universalism' (e.g. 2.1–12; 4.14–16; 12.21; 28.19; contrast e.g. 10.5), along with 27.25 (which condemns not just the Pharisees but 'all the people'), to a second editor, a Gentile Christian.

The Writer of the Text in Reception History

Even if – as seems likely – Marcan priority is to be preferred and author-ship by the apostle Matthew rejected, that does not necessarily require a wholesale rejection of earlier traditions about the evangelist and his book. In the first place, what modern narrative critics call the 'implied author' of Matthew's Gospel – the author proposed by the text – emerges as a figure utterly at home in the world of Judaism. This is confirmed by the extensive quotations from the Old Testament, some of them reflecting rabbinic patterns of exegesis (e.g. 2.6; 27.9–10), the Gospel's interest in 'righteousness' (Greek *dikaiosunē*, translating the Hebrew *tsedek*, e.g. 3.15; 5.6, 10, 20; 6.1, 33; 21.32), and the lack of explanation of distinctly Jewish practices (e.g. 15.1–2; cf. Mark 7.1–4; 23.5). The evangelist may not be one of the original apostles, but he breathes the same air and inhabits a similar cultural heritage.

Second, there are indications that so-called 'pre-critical scholars' were interested in the figure of Matthew for his symbolic potential as well as his literal association with Jesus. One such symbolic aspect was Matthew's role as a model of conversion. The author of the *Opus imperfectum* writes how Matthew was in a special way the evangelist of sinners, 'since he proclaimed the gospel to sinners not only by his words but by the emendation of his life' (Kellerman 2010: 1/1). His transformation from a tax-collector to Gospel writer was a consequence of his repentance and experience of divine mercy. This is well exemplified in *The Calling of St Matthew* (1599–1600) by Caravaggio, where the figure of Matthew – art historians are divided as to whether he is the old man looking up or the young man with head downcast – reacts to the finger of Jesus pointing directly at him.

Another aspect of patristic and especially medieval interpretation was interest in the symbolic significance of the evangelist's name. Jacobus de Voragine's *Golden Legend*, a popular medieval collection of saints' lives, offers an etymology of Matthew's name ('a gift hastily given', referring to his 'speedy conversion') possibly derived from Hebrew ('gift of God'). Voragine follows this up with a rather less convincing combination of the Latin *magnus*, 'great' (or *manus*, 'hand'), and the Greek *theos*, 'God'. Matthew then means 'great unto God' or 'the hand of God'. This etymological solution shifts emphasis away from apostolic authorship per se to the quality of his Christian discipleship, and to the Gospel text that bears his name: 'For Matthew was . . . great unto God by the perfection of his life, and the hand of God by his writing of the Gospel' (Jacobus de Voragine 1941: 561).

Voragine's ingenious etymological solutions will fail to convince modern readers of Matthew. Yet they are not qualitatively different from the way modern critical scholars occasionally exploit the similarity between the name Matthew or *Matthaios* and the Greek word for 'disciple', *mathētēs* (literally meaning 'one who learns'). Kiley has highlighted the wordplay at work in Matthew's account of the call of Matthew (9.9–13), in which Matthew's name, two references to 'disciples' (*mathētai*), and Jesus' command to 'go and learn (*mathete*)', are closely juxtaposed (Kiley 1984).

Composing the Text

The traditional association of Matthew's Gospel with Matthew the apostle was often combined with the view that the normal canonical order – Matthew, Mark, Luke – reflected the order of composition. For Augustine, Mark was an epitome or abbreviation of the much fuller and earlier Matthew. Although few would now hold to this Augustinian position, the twentieth century saw some robust defences of it (e.g. Butler 1951).

As noted above, the dominant scholarly position on Matthew's sources reverses Augustine's order. Matthew is regarded as the second Gospel, using the more primitive Mark as its main source, together with a collection of other Jesus traditions (mainly sayings, though including two miracle stories, the centurion's servant and the dumb demoniac: 8.5–13; 9.32–34; cf. 12.22–24) known as *Quelle* (German = 'source'), generally shortened to Q. Q explains that material common to Matthew and Luke but absent from Mark, used by both of them independently along with Mark (this is known as the Two Source Theory). A development of this is the Four Source Theory, which seeks to explain the fact that both Matthew and Luke have traditions unique to themselves (Matthew's Special Material or M, and Luke's Special Material or L), as well as Mark and Q.

Though still the dominant view among critical scholars, the Two Source/ Four Source Hypothesis has its detractors. Some have revised the theory of the eighteenth-century scholar Johann Jakob Griesbach, which maintains that Matthew was the first Gospel, Luke the second and Mark a conflation of the two (e.g. Farmer 1964; for a critique, see Tuckett 1983). An alternative, which is gaining popularity, remains convinced of Marcan priority but dispenses with the need for Q by claiming that Luke also knew Matthew (e.g. Farrer 1955; Goulder 1985; Goodacre 2002). This attempts to account for the minor and major agreements between Matthew and Luke against Mark, as well as the differences that the Two Source Hypothesis emphasizes.

Finally there are more complex theories, which account for similarities and differences between the Gospels through a combination of oral and written sources (see Sanders and Davies 1989: 84–119).

Leaving aside the question of Q, many scholars are convinced that Marcan priority makes best sense of the substantial amount of material found in Matthew (and Luke) that is not found in Mark, together with the fact that Mark's version of many stories also found in Matthew is often considerably longer (which does not look like the work of a later abbreviator: compare e.g. 8.28–34 with Mark 5.1–20). Yet there are also several Marcan passages that are not found in Matthew's Gospel. Although sometimes used in support of Matthean priority, most of these are readily explicable on the theory that Matthew is editing Mark.

For example, having revised Mark's order substantially in order to give a typical selection of Jesus' miracles (Matt. 8—9), Matthew may well have regarded the healing of the demoniac in the Capernaum synagogue (Mark 1.23–28) as superfluous. Two healings (of the deaf man, and the blind man at Bethsaida, Mark 7.32–37; 8.22–26) have their own ambiguities (magical elements and a two-stage healing), which might have given Matthew cause for concern. Similarly, he might have chosen to omit the story of the independent exorcist (Mark 9.38–40) because of its maverick implications, legitimating healing activities outside the boundaries of the Church. The apparent absence of the parable of the seed growing secretly (Mark 4.26–29) is resolved if we allow that Matthew has reworked it into his allegorical parable of the wheat and the tares (13.24–30: Drury 1985: 87). Finally, sheer puzzlement might account for his omitting the strange story of the naked young man in the garden (14.51–52). This leaves unexplained only the story of the widow's mite (12.41–44).

But if Matthew was using Mark as his major source, can any conclusions be drawn about his purposes? Was Matthew intending to supplement Mark with additional material and make explicit what was implicit in his source? Or was Matthew's Gospel intended as a replacement for Mark, such that the latter could be abandoned? David Sim holds to the latter view: 'What role could Mark have possibly played in the Matthean community once Matthew had published his own corrected, revised, enlarged, improved and updated edition of Mark?' (Sim 2011: 182). There are strengths to Sim's view. For example, it is unlikely that Matthew would have wanted his intended audiences to read those sections of Mark he chose not to include. There are also detailed redactional changes Matthew makes (e.g. the omission of Mark's editorial comment that Jesus 'declared all foods clean', Mark 7.19) that reveal criticism of Mark.

Yet Sim surely goes too far here. By contrast, Mark Goodacre has offered a positive portrayal of Matthew as the first, and relatively successful, commentator on Mark (e.g. largely sharing Mark's ambiguous portrayal of Simon Peter, and both accepting and making more explicit Mark's novel presentation of John the Baptist as the returned Elijah: Goodacre 2006 and 2008). Goodacre has warned against the tendency of redaction critics to prioritize difference in comparing Gospels, while neglecting the shared material that the later evangelist was content to take over substantially unedited (in Matthew's case, approximately 90 per cent of Mark). The very fact that Matthew has used Mark at all (in Luz's words a 'new edition of Mark': Luz 1995b: 8) points to its authoritative status within Matthew's circles. Indeed, this is heightened if Matthew's reworking of Mark is understood liturgically, as a homiletic expansion similar to the exposition of Scripture in the Synagogue (e.g. Kilpatrick 1946: 59–71; Goulder 1974). The early emergence of a Four Gospel Canon shows that Mark continued to hold an authoritative place within the early Church rather than being eclipsed by its longer and more detailed successor.

Dating the Text

The presumption of patristic and medieval writers is that Matthew's Gospel was written relatively early. Admittedly not all early commentators explicitly consider the relative order of the canonical Gospels. Nevertheless, the identification of the evangelist with Matthew the apostle pointed to a date of composition earlier rather than later in the first century. According to Irenaeus, Matthew's Gospel was composed while Peter and Paul were still preaching in Rome (i.e. prior to c.64: Irenaeus, *Adv. Haer.* 3.1.1).

By contrast, modern critical scholarship has moved to a relatively late dating for this Gospel (c.80–90). The *terminus ad quem* is provided by the knowledge of Matthew by Ignatius of Antioch, Papias, Polycarp, the author of the *Epistle of Barnabas*, and Justin Martyr (and probably also the author of the *Didache*). This means that the Gospel must have been written prior to c.100. There are two basic arguments in favour of a date late in the first century. The first is source-critical: belief in Marcan priority necessitates a later date for Matthew (Mark is generally dated to the late 60s or early 70s CE).

The second argument relies on identifying allusions within the text to dateable events. The strange statement that the king 'burned their city' in the parable of the wedding banquet (22.7; cf. Luke 14.15–17; *Gos. Thom.* 64) is widely interpreted as a reference to the destruction of Jerusalem.

According to the first-century Jewish historian Josephus, the Romans under Titus set fire to the Temple in the last stages of the siege of Jerusalem (Josephus, *War* 6.249–53). Other claimed references to Jerusalem's destruction are 21.41 ('He will put those wretches to a miserable death, and lease the vineyard to other tenants who will give him the produce at the harvest time'), 23.38 ('see, your house is left to you, desolate') and 24.15 ('so when you see the desolating sacrilege standing in the holy place, as was spoken of by the prophet Daniel').

While the scholarly consensus view of a post-70 dating is probably correct (and will be presupposed in the discussion of the Gospel's historical setting in Chapter 5), it lacks certainty. The precariousness of dating Matthew in relation to Mark is flagged up by recent arguments in favour of redating the latter to the late 30s or early 40s (Crossley 2004). As for the internal evidence, the reference to the burning of the city at 22.7 is probably the strongest. Not all scholars are persuaded even by this (e.g. France 2007: 18, 825; Evans 2012: 4–5), on the grounds that it would have been possible for either Jesus or Matthew to predict the destruction of Jerusalem, particularly in the light of Old Testament prophecies about the burning of Jerusalem (e.g. Jer. 21.10; 32.29; 34.2). Yet the odd location of the reference – in the middle of a parable and in response to the bizarre reaction of those invited to the king's banquet – points to its allusion to an actual event rather than reflection on what might be in the light of the prophets.

Ordering the Text

Almost from the beginning, readers of Matthew have commented on the Gospel's neat structure. Patristic and medieval commentators regularly detected an arrangement in the text that was thematic no less than chronological. The author of the *Opus imperfectum* identified seven stages – seven signifying completeness – in Matthew's narrative of Christ:

> first, his birth; then his baptism; third, his temptation; fourth, his doctrine; fifth, his miracles; sixth, his passion; seventh, his resurrection and ascension. Through these sections he intended not only to set forth the history of Christ's life but also to teach the disposition of an evangelical life.
>
> (Kellerman 2010: 1/1)

Modern critical commentators also acknowledge Matthew's tendency to organize material thematically, particularly in the first half of his Gospel (as comparison with the order of Mark and Luke reveals).

However, despite this universal recognition of Matthew's concern for order and patterning, no real consensus has emerged over the structure of the Gospel as a whole (leading Robert Gundry to conclude that Matthew is 'structurally mixed': Gundry 1994: 11). One influential pattern is reflected in the chapter divisions in modern Bibles, worked out by Stephen Langton, a twelfth-century Archbishop of Canterbury, while he was lecturing at the University of Paris. Some of Langton's divisions work well: the Sermon on the Mount, for example, manifestly begins at 5.1 and comes to a natural conclusion at the end of chapter 7. Other chapter divisions seem rather more arbitrary: Jesus' parables discourse finishes several verses before the close of Langton's chapter 13, at 13.53. The story of the Transfiguration (17.1–8) is intimately connected with the preceding chapter, especially 16.28. Some commentators would view the 'ecclesiastical discourse' as beginning not at 18.1 but with the Temple tax discussion in 17.24–27 (e.g. Thompson 1970).

At least in its present form, the *Opus imperfectum* makes a crucial break in the middle of chapter 3 between the preaching of John and the coming of Jesus for baptism (3.13). It also presents the beginning of Jesus' public ministry as 4.12 ('Now when Jesus heard that John had been arrested, he withdrew to Galilee'), rather than 4.17 ('From that time') preferred by many modern commentators. Indeed, this focus on new sections beginning with references to specific locations is a recurring feature: for example, the wilderness (4.1), the sea (4.18), the mountain (5.1 and 8.1), Capernaum (8.5), the boat (8.23), Judea beyond the Jordan (19.1), Jericho (20.29), Jerusalem (21.1, 10), the Temple (24.1). On other occasions a temporal clause ('At that time', *in illo tempore*) functions as a structural division (e.g. 8.23; 10.16, 26, 34; 11.2; 12.38).

In modern scholarship three main solutions have been proposed. The first, a 'Pentateuchal' structure, emphasizes the five major discourses that punctuate the narrative, each concluded by a similar phrase (7.28; 11.1; 13.53; 19.1; 26.1). Its most famous proponent was the American scholar Benjamin Bacon, building on the work of nineteenth-century predecessors (Bacon 1918 and 1930). For Bacon, the Gospel comprised five books, each with a combination of narrative and discourse: Matt. 3—7; 8—10; 11—13; 14—18; 19—25. The infancy narrative (Matt. 1—2) and passion and resurrection narratives (Matt. 26—28) were described as Preamble and Epilogue respectively.

Bacon's theory has been justly criticized, despite its recognition of Matthew's interest in the figure of Moses. Some feel that the precise divisions drive too great a wedge between the discourses and the narratives that follow (although Bacon himself saw the concluding formula of the discourses to be 'not so much a rounding-off' as a link to the following narrative: Bacon 1918: 65). Nor is the juxtaposition of narrative to discourse in Matthew quite so closely patterned on the Mosaic Pentateuch, where the two are interwoven in a much more haphazard fashion (Genesis, for example, has little 'discourse', whereas Leviticus is severely lacking in narrative!). The neglect of the infancy, and the passion and resurrection narratives, is certainly a serious objection to the thesis as an overall explanation, for both sections are integral to the whole. Finally, Bacon's hypothesis has been criticized for its failure to take seriously the story character of Matthew.

Kingsbury's alternative structures the narrative around what he regards as the transitional phrase *apo tote* ('From that time on', 4.17; 16.21: Kingsbury 1976). This basically follows Mark's narrative pattern: a prologue (expanded by Matthew through the addition of 'infancy narratives': 1.1—4.16), a ministry in Galilee (4.17—16.20) and a movement towards Jerusalem and the cross (16.21—28.20). This narrative explanation has much to commend it, not least its appreciation of Matthew's narrative flow and his adoption of Mark's overall structure. But it needs some refining, especially in its concentration on the *apo tote* phrase. First, 4.17 cannot be so easily divorced from 4.12–16; similarly, 16.21–23 continues the conversation with Peter begun in 16.13–20. Instead, the wider passages, rather than the *apo tote* phrase itself, should be seen as the narrative turning points. However, there is a further difficulty with focus on *apo tote*: it occurs again at 26.16 ('And from that moment he [Judas Iscariot] began to look for an opportunity to betray him'), without introducing a significant transition in the narrative.

A variation on Kingsbury's narrative structural pattern is offered by Frank Matera (Matera 1987). Matera pays attention to 'kernels' – major events or cruxes in the narrative on which other events depend as 'satellites' – as significant indicators of turning points in Matthew's story, alongside the linguistic indicators identified by both Bacon and Kingsbury (e.g. 'And when Jesus had finished'; 'From that time Jesus began'). He identifies the following kernels: the birth of Jesus; the beginning of Jesus' ministry; the question of John the Baptist; Jesus' conversation at Caesarea Philippi; the cleansing of the Temple; the Great Commission. As a result Matera structures the Gospel into five narrative blocks: 1.1—4.11 (the coming of the Messiah); 4.12—11.1 (the Messiah's ministry to Israel of preaching, teaching, healing); 11.2—16.12 (the crisis in the Messiah's ministry); 16.13—20.34 (the Messiah's journey to

Jerusalem); 21.1—28.15 (the Messiah's death and resurrection); 28.16–20 (the Great Commission).

The third type of explanation finds a chiastic pattern in the Gospel as a whole, or more accurately a concentric pattern (structured around a central passage: e.g. Fenton 1959; Ellis 1974). Again, this theory has something to commend it. The first and fifth discourses, for example, could be paralleled to each other (they are the two longest discourses), and this parallel is increased if Matthew 23 is treated as part of the final discourse (the first then begins with blessings and the last with woes: 5.3–12; 23.13–36). Yet significant differences between chiastic interpretations of Matthew leave one wondering how far structure is in the eye of the beholder. For some such as Ellis, Matthew 13 is structurally at the centre, with a theme of rejection and division in surrounding chapters (typified especially by the role of the Pharisees in chapters 11—12). Others, however (e.g. Green 1968), locate the chiastic centre in Matthew 11.

The lack of a consensus over structure may be indicative of the evangelist's brilliant writing skills. The intricacy of Matthew's text, reflected in a variety of overlapping patterns, allows different interpreters to identify different possibilities for ordering the text, not all of which are mutually exclusive. Moreover the detection of patterns may depend on whether one is looking for literary structure or prioritizing the aural experience of hearing Matthew's Gospel read. Search for structure is further compounded by Matthew's complex editorial pattern. Presuming Marcan priority, he is much more radical in the treatment of his sources in the first half of his Gospel. There his policy seems to be thematically determined. He groups miracle stories and conflict stories into blocks, revising the Marcan order in the process. He shifts some of Jesus' teaching about the End (Mark 13) from Jesus' final sermon on the Mount of Olives to his much earlier discourse to the Twelve as he prepares to send them out as missionaries (Matt. 10). By contrast, from chapter 13 onwards he fairly slavishly follows the chronological sequence of Mark.

Establishing the Text

Despite Papias' claim that Matthew wrote 'in the Hebrew language' (or style), our Matthew is a Greek document, and shows no evidence of being translation Greek. Yet the ancient Greek manuscripts of this Gospel contain a large number of variants in wording. Assessing these differences, explaining how they came about and identifying 'families' of manuscripts with similar wording is the task of the New Testament textual critic (see Parker 2012).

Older textual critics saw their primary task as uncovering the 'original text' as it left the pen of the evangelist or his scribe (although with greater awareness of oral performance and the fluidity of textual traditions, the very concept of an 'original text' of the New Testament has recently been challenged: e.g. Parker 1997; Epp 1999). More recent interest in reception has shifted the focus somewhat to the secondary variant readings and what they reveal about how Matthew's Gospel was read and the assumptions of the scribes who copied the manuscripts (in Latin and other translations as well as the original Greek).

In some cases the reasons for variant readings in the surviving Greek manuscripts of Matthew are fairly clear. Scribes appear to be clarifying an ambiguity in the text or correcting what they think are errors in the version they have inherited. The conclusion to Matthew's genealogy of Jesus is a case in point. Very well attested is the reading 'Jacob the father of Joseph the husband of Mary, of whom Jesus was born, who is called the Messiah/Christ' (1.16). Although this reading does not contradict what is later said about Mary's virginal conception while still betrothed to Joseph (1.18–25), the reference to 'husband' might be understood to imply physical descent from Joseph (the point, indeed, of the genealogy). Thus it is logical to regard an alternative reading as a secondary scribal emendation clarifying ambiguity: 'being betrothed to whom (i.e. Joseph) the virgin Mary gave birth to Jesus the one called Christ'. One Syriac translation has Joseph begetting Jesus and Mary giving birth to a son by Joseph, while still acknowledging the virginal conception later in the chapter. This apparent contradiction is resolved when read against the ancient Semitic conviction that *legal* paternity was *real* paternity (Stock 1994: 29).

An example of scribal correction for christological purposes may be found in some manuscripts at 24.36. This verse is potentially problematic given that it posits ignorance on the part of Christ about the timing of the End: 'But about that day and hour no one knows, neither the angels of heaven, nor the Son, but only the Father.' Some manuscripts omit the phrase 'nor the Son', and this is probably due to scribal activity. On the other hand, given that this reading is also found at Mark 13.32, it may have been Matthew himself who omits the phrase for christological reasons (just as he modifies Mark's account of Jesus' visit to Nazareth: 13.53–58; cf. Mark 6.1–6). The presence of 'nor the Son' would then be the result of harmonization of manuscripts of Matthew to Mark (although harmonization between these two Gospels normally works in the other direction). On balance, the first explanation is more probable.

Another passage that has been christologically important is 11.19. The variant reading preferred affects whether or not Matthew's Jesus is to be identified with divine Wisdom. In this passage, paralleled in Luke, Jesus is comparing the reaction of his generation to himself and John the Baptist to a fickle group of children, constantly changing the rules of the game. The NRSV opts for the reading 'Yet wisdom is vindicated by her deeds' (not the best attested, though found in some early codices such as the fourth-century Codex Sinaiticus), supporting the identification of Jesus and Wisdom. The Lucan parallel, by contrast, treats both John and Jesus as Wisdom's 'children' (Luke 7.35). However, a significant number of manuscripts of Matthew have a reading either very close ('by her children') or identical to Luke ('by all her children'). Is this the result of scribal harmonization to Luke or does it reflect an earlier version?

Scribes may correct the received text for other reasons besides the theological. Matthew 14.3 follows Mark 6.17 in describing Herodias, the would-be bride of Herod Antipas, as 'the wife of his brother Philip'. Yet according to Josephus, Herodias was the wife of another brother (confusingly also called Herod), while Philip was married to Herodias' daughter Salome (Josephus, *Ant*. 18.136–7). Thus a scribe who was better informed historically could have chosen to omit the reference to Philip (see also Luke 3.19). Other examples relate to the correction or modification of errant or puzzling geographical references. After the feeding of the 4,000, for example, Matthew recounts how Jesus crossed the sea to another region (15.39). While many manuscripts read Magadan (or occasionally Magedan), some may have chosen a more recognizable location, hence the variants Magdalan or Magdala, the town from which Mary Magdalene came.

A variation of scribal correction is the common tendency for copyists to harmonize the different Gospel texts to one another, thus overcoming or resolving discrepancies between them. This is almost certainly motivated by theological concerns: that Scripture speaks with one voice and that therefore discrepancies need to be resolved. Often Matthew, as the pre-eminent Gospel, is the text to which Mark and Luke are harmonized (e.g. some manuscripts of Mark 1.8 add to the description of Jesus' coming baptism 'in the holy Spirit' the words 'and fire', conforming it to Matthew 3.11). Another example, this time harmonizing Matthew to Luke, is 1.25. The original version probably read 'and he (i.e. Joseph) did not know her until she had borne a son'. Some manuscripts expand this reference to 'a son, her firstborn', linking the text of Matthew to the parallel account in Luke 2.7. Harmonization to the text of Luke can also be found in some witnesses to 5.44 (which add 'and pray for those who abuse you and persecute you', cf. Luke 6.27–28). Finally 17.21 ('But this kind does not come out except by prayer and fasting'), a verse totally absent from several manuscripts, represents a harmonization of the text of Matthew to Mark 9.29.

A less straightforward example of the scribal tendency to harmonize is the parable of the lost sheep, located within the fourth Matthean discourse, on life in the Church (18.10–14). Some manuscripts insert verse 11 ('For the Son of Man came to save [*or* 'to seek out and save'] the lost'), which is found in Luke's Gospel (not, however, in the Lucan parallel to this parable, Luke 15.3–7, but rather Luke 19.10).

In other cases the variation may be explained by the transcription of words that look or sound similar (the latter is a particular issue when several scribes were simultaneously copying a text being read aloud by another). Many English translations render 1.18 as explaining the 'birth' of Jesus Christ. This presupposes the reading *gennēsis* in the Greek, a word meaning 'birth' (from the same root as the verb translated 'begat' or 'was the father of', which is used throughout Matthew's genealogy). In context, however, that is odd, for the subject of the passage is how Joseph's genealogy – that of the royal line of David – could be Jesus' family tree despite Joseph not being his natural father. A solution may be found in the fact that the Greek manuscripts opt for one of two similar-sounding nouns at this point. Many have the alternative reading *genesis*. While this word can be translated 'birth', it has wider associations of 'origin', 'generation' and even 'genealogy' (see 1.1). Another obvious example of a scribal mistake is found at 11.2, where misreading or mishearing one word could lead to a different meaning. Did John send a message to Jesus 'by/through his disciples' (*dia tōn mathētōn*)? Or did he send 'two of his disciples' (*duo tōn mathētōn*) to interrogate Jesus?

Reception and Fresh Rereadings

As already noted, the tendency of earlier textual critics, concerned to undercover the 'original version' of Matthew's Greek text, was to dismiss secondary readings. However, the greater interest in the reception of biblical texts among current scholars encourages closer attention to what these tell us about how the Gospel was subsequently read. There is an interesting variant in some Latin versions of Matthew's baptism account. Inserted between verses 15 and 16 are the following words: 'And when Jesus was being baptized a great light flashed from the water, so that all who had gathered there were afraid' (see Metzger 1971: 10). Clearly this reference is not original, although the light in the Jordan also seems to have been mentioned in Tatian's *Diatessaron* (a second-century Syriac harmony of the four Gospels), and was known to Justin (*Dial.* 88.1) and the *Gospel of the Ebionites* (Epiphanius, *Haer.* 30.13.7–8).

A second example illustrates how particular passages were used in the ongoing life of the early Church. Many English-speaking Christians are familiar with the following appendage to the Lord's Prayer: 'For thine is the kingdom, the power, and the glory, forever and ever. Amen.' This is almost certainly secondary, given that it is missing from a number of early manuscripts representing different 'families' of manuscripts. It nonetheless sheds interesting light on how the Lord's Prayer was subsequently adapted for use in Christian worship. The doxology is found in various forms (including at *Did.* 8), probably reflecting different liturgical practices. Orthodox Christians will be most familiar with the Trinitarian form found in some late manuscripts: 'for thine is the kingdom and the power and the glory of the Father and of the Son and of the Holy Spirit for ever. Amen' (Metzger 1971: 16–17).

Two final examples illustrate how a scribal addition can show the scribe concerned to be a good and sensitive reader of Matthew. In the first the scribal emendation links one passage to another place in Matthew's Gospel, where the connection might only be implicit. In Matthew's account of the temptation, Jesus' parting shot to the devil is 'Depart, Satan!' (in Greek, *hupage Satana*: 4.10). But what lies at the heart of the testing of Jesus? Matthew seems to understand this as the temptation to reject the Father's will. Central to Jesus' role as 'son of God', by contrast, is his total obedience to the Father, which will bring him to the cross. Thus it should not surprise us to find a scribe accommodating 4.10 to the story of Peter's 'temptation' of Jesus at 16.23. In this latter passage Peter resists Jesus' prediction that he must suffer and die, thus casting himself in the role of the Satan in the wilderness and provoking Jesus' rebuke: 'Get behind me, Satan' (Greek *hupage opisō mou Satana*). Exactly the same phrase occurs in some versions of 4.10.

The second example concerns an additional formula citation in some versions of 27.35: 'in order that what had been spoken through the prophet might be fulfilled, "They divided my clothing among themselves, and for my clothing they cast lots"' (quoting from Psalm 22.18). Psalm 22 has provided the mood music for Matthew's crucifixion scene, as it has also for Mark's. In both, the opening words of the psalm are placed on the lips of the dying Jesus. This scribal edition is in line with the general tenor of the evangelist, making explicit the ways Scripture both anticipates and conforms to the life and death of Jesus. It is possible that this was originally inserted by a scribe as a marginal note, finding further scriptural warrant for the details in the passion narrative. It would then have been copied into the main text of Matthew at a secondary stage.

Hearing the Text

This chapter has discussed the different ways diverse interpreters of Matthew are nonetheless united by their concern for the text (whether its origins, its sources, its structure or the details of its wording). There is one sense in which speaking of Matthew's Gospel as text is misleading, however. Matthew's Gospel, like many other ancient writings, was intended to be performed and heard as well as pored over in study. The occasional reference to 'the reader' in the singular (e.g. 24.15) refers to the one who reads the text aloud to the assembled community. The Gospel itself is replete with verbs of speech, hearing and seeing that become more central when the text is heard (see Knowles 2004): 'You have heard that it was said . . . But I say to you . . .' (e.g. 5.21–22, 27–28); 'Beware . . .' (e.g. 6.1; 7.15); 'Therefore I tell you . . .' (e.g. 6.25); 'Everyone then who hears these words of mine' (e.g. 7.24); 'Listen!' (e.g. 13.3); 'Hear then . . .' (e.g. 13.18); 'Let anyone with ears listen!' (e.g. 13.9, 43); 'Listen and understand!' (e.g. 15.10). The command to 'See!' or 'Behold!' is very frequent (e.g. 1.23; 2.9, 13; 3.16; 10.16; 11.10; 12.18; 19.16; 28.2), in reference both to Jesus' words and to the fulfilment of Scripture. Some words are even more expressive in the Greek original, as in the piercing shriek of the word for 'Woe!' (*ouai*, an onomatopoeic word: e.g. 11.21; 23.13–29). Rhythmic patterns may also be more prominent when the Gospel is read. The rhythmic pattern of the genealogy (X begat Y) is particularly striking in oral performance, thus accentuating any additional phrases that break the rhythmic pattern (e.g. 'and his brothers'; 'by Tamar'; 'and his brothers, at the time of the deportation to Babylon'). Appreciation of the aural experience is also relevant to discussions of Matthew's structure: some structural features become more prominent when heard orally (arguably the phrase 'From then on' is less noticeable that the repeated and rhythmic 'When Jesus had finished all these sayings' or even 'They will be cast into the outer darkness, where there will be weeping and gnashing of teeth').

4

Characters and Places in Matthew's Story

The Importance of Character and Place

Reading or hearing Matthew as story, especially as a story that is in some sense also the story of the reader, invites attention to the characters within the Gospel. These characters include the huge cast of minor characters – many of them unnamed – who interact with Jesus in different ways. Ancient commentators often saw their exemplary role, and this way of reading the Gospels is amply attested in the medieval mystery plays and the various passion plays that survive to this day, such as at Oberammergau in Bavaria. Modern narrative critics, meanwhile, have wanted to explore the effect of particular characters on the implied or ideal reader. Which characters invite sympathy, empathy or antipathy? Or is the characterization more complex than this, with the same character evoking differing responses in specific situations (Peter may be a case in point)?

Reading Matthew as narrative also highlights the significance of 'place' or narrative 'setting' in which Jesus and the various other characters interact with each other. Places may be geographical locations (such as Capernaum, Egypt or Jerusalem) or specific buildings or other 'settings' (a synagogue, a house, the seaside). Particular places contain a complex web of association and memory, linked to what has occurred there or people who have been there in the past, which may be triggered by the mere mention of their name. In the case of Matthew's Gospel this is especially so if they have been significant places in the Hebrew Bible or wider Jewish tradition. Other unspecified topographical 'settings' may also have particular associations: for example, a mountain might evoke associations of sacred mountains in the ancient world or of specific biblical mountains such as Mount Sinai, Mount Nebo or the Temple Mount in Jerusalem.

This chapter explores both characters and places, engaging with contemporary narrative criticism as well as older elements in Matthew's reception history. Certain characters will be considered in more detail at the appropriate point later in this book: for example, Joseph and Mary in Chapter 6; Judas Iscariot and Pilate and his wife in Chapter 11. A key narrative critic who has engaged with characterization in Matthew in a number of publications is Jack Dean Kingsbury (e.g. Kingsbury 1984,

1986, 1988 and 1995). Kingsbury utilizes E. M. Forster's distinction between 'round' and 'flat' characters in his analysis of Matthew's characters (Kingsbury 1986: 9–10). 'Round' characters possess a variety of character traits. Examples include Jesus and 'the disciples' (as a character group), whose traits sometimes conflict with his, inviting the readers to react to them differently at different stages in the story. 'Flat' characters behave in predictable ways due to their possessing few traits – such as 'the crowd[s]' and the Jewish leaders. Kingsbury also identifies 'stock' characters: minor characters who may only appear once in the story and possess only one trait, such as the woman with haemorrhages at 9.20–22 whose sole distinguishing feature is 'faith'. While open to some criticism, such as the undifferentiated treatment of 'the leaders' as a single character group, Kingsbury's analysis offers insight into the key players in Matthew's story.

God

Although often standing 'behind' the narrative and only occasionally breaking into it, God is the main actor in Matthew's story – indeed, in the whole of salvation history that Matthew presupposes (Kingsbury 1984: 6). His presence is even more pervasive than the occurrences of the Greek word for 'God' might suggest – *theos* occurs 51 times in the Gospel, compared to 48 occurrences in the much shorter Mark and 122 in Luke. The frequent phrase 'the kingdom of the heavens' functions as a circumlocution for God, as do the 'divine passives' (e.g. 'they will be comforted', 5.4; 'they will receive mercy', 5.7; 'You have heard that it was said', 5.21; 'Do not judge, so that you may not be judged', 7.1; 'Ask, and it will be given you', 7.7: see Viviano 2010).

Matthew presupposes the standard beliefs of Judaism: there is one God, the God of Abraham, Isaac and Jacob (22.32), who is uniquely good (19.17) and who has revealed himself to Israel (e.g. 15.31), although he has power to raise up children for Abraham from stones (3.9). God is the only object of true worship (4.10; 6.24), whose face is seen by the angels of the 'little ones' in heaven (18.10) and who will be seen by the pure in heart (5.8). He is omniscient, being the only one to know the day or the hour of the End (24.36). As 'the Lord', God speaks to his people, and to the reader of the Gospel, in different ways: through angelic mediators, especially in dreams (e.g. 1.20; 2.13, 19); through scriptural quotations from the prophets (e.g. 1.23; 2.15; 13.35) and the Law (e.g. 15.3–4; 22.32); and other means of revelation (e.g. 16.17). Occasionally God speaks directly from heaven (e.g. 3.17; 17.5).

Yet although transcendent and the object of worship, God is not remote or disinterested. He feeds the birds of the air and clothes the grass of the field (6.26, 30) and has particular care for the 'little ones' (18.14). Jesus reveals him as 'Father', 'my Father' or 'your heavenly Father' (e.g. 6.1, 4, 6, 8, 9, 14–15, 18), thus initiating his followers into a relationship of intimacy with him. Mowery locates this title in the context of a progressive 'revelation' in the first seven chapters of Matthew, from Lord to God to Father (Mowery 1997). God has come near to humanity pre-eminently in Jesus, who is 'God-with-us' (1.23). At times God can appear absent (e.g. at 27.46 when Jesus cries 'My God, my God, why have you forsaken me?'). But ultimately he sends his angel to announce his vindication of Jesus (28.2–7).

Jesus

Jesus is the main protagonist of Matthew's narrative, towards whom the implied reader feels sympathy. A narrative-critical approach to the character of Jesus can complement the older scholarly focus on 'christological titles', which often obscured how those titles were being used, or where important biblical figures or narratives were being evoked when no specific title was present (see Keck 1986).

That is not to say that titles are irrelevant in exploring the character of Jesus (Kingsbury 1984: 4). In the opening verse of the Gospel he is introduced as 'son of David' (highlighting his royal messianic credentials, through his adoption by Joseph, 1.21, 24) and 'son of Abraham' (linking him not only to the wider Jewish people but also anticipating the Gentile mission; see Gen. 17.4; 22.17). The 'son of David' remains an important title, particularly in relation to Jesus' healings (e.g. 9.27). He is also described as 'Christ' (e.g. 1.1, 16; 11.2; 16.16), Teacher (e.g. 10.25) and the heavenly Son of Man who comes in judgement (e.g. 24.30, 37; 25.31). Given that 'the Lord' refers elsewhere to God speaking through his prophets, it is striking that those who seek healing and Jesus' own disciples regularly address him as 'Lord' (e.g. 8.2, 6, 8, 21, 25; 14.30; 15.22, 25).

If God is 'Father' then Jesus (God-with-us) is pre-eminently God's Son. Indeed, Kingsbury has argued that Son of God is the most important christological title in Matthew (Kingsbury 1976: 40–127), occurring at all the key moments in his story (2.15; 3.17; 4.3, 6; 8.29; 14.33; 16.16; 17.5; 26.63; 27.40, 54; 28.19). This title combines several overlapping motifs: Jesus as king and royal Messiah (e.g. 3.17; 17.5; cf. 2 Sam. 7.14; Ps. 2.7); his filial obedience to his Father (e.g. 4.3, 6; 27.40); his role as the perfect personification of God's 'son' Israel (e.g. 2.15; 4.1–11; cf. Hos. 11.1); the conviction that he was born without a human father, by the creative act of God's Spirit (1.18–19).

However, the character of Jesus is glimpsed by more than titles. His personal name has significance. Jesus (Greek *Iēsous*, Aramaic *Yeshua*) is linked etymologically to his role of saving 'his people from their sins' (1.21). Typologically he is connected to the great figure of Moses, filling a variety of Mosaic roles: 'leader and king, savior and deliverer, teacher and revealer, and intercessor and suffering prophet all at once' (Allison 1993: 91). There are also connections between Jesus and Wisdom (e.g. 11.19, 25–30: see Suggs 1970; Deutsch 1990; though see also Johnson 1974), including the extraordinary statement, reminiscent of John's Gospel, that the Son has had all things handed over to him by the Father (11.27).

But it is Jesus' engagement with other characters in the story that tends to be the focus of narrative-critical studies. Kingsbury's narrative reading of Matthew sees conflict as the key to the Gospel's plot (e.g. Kingsbury 1986 and 1987). Hence Jesus' character is revealed in his conflict with his opponents, whether Satan and the demons (reflecting the cosmic nature of the conflict: see Powell 1992) or the political and especially Jewish religious leaders, as well as his engagement with his disciples.

Angels and Demons

Though Powell considers the non-human actors whose activity betrays the cosmic conflict underlying the terrestrial conflict between Jesus and his human opponents, they are surprisingly absent from several narrative-critical discussions of Matthew's characters (even Kingsbury, who notes the supernatural dimension to the conflict, devotes little space to them: Kingsbury 1988: 3–4, 55–7). Yet given the prominence of the supernatural world for Matthew, reflecting the apocalyptic dualism so characteristic of Matthew's text (see Sim 1996), they ought to be accorded a more central role.

Angels are key players in Matthew's story, particularly in their role as divine messengers mediating between heaven and earth. Both Jesus' birth and his resurrection are heralded by 'an angel of the Lord' (1.20–24; 2.13, 19; 28.2–7), assuring the readers of the authority of the message to Joseph on the one hand, and to the women at the tomb on the other. Jesus' life is as transparent to the angelic world as it is to his heavenly Father. Angels minister to him in the wilderness (4.11) and he knows that he could rely on their protection (26.53; see also the devil's words at 4.6, quoting Ps.

91.11). Matthew's Jesus reminds his disciples that the children have their own guardian angels in heaven, who have the privilege of looking upon God's face (18.10; cf. e.g. Ps. 34.7; Tobit 5.4, 22; *Jub.* 35.17; *T. Levi* 5.3), and that at the resurrection married people will be 'like angels in heaven' (22.30). When Jesus comes in judgement as the vindicated Son of Man he will be accompanied by angelic armies (13.41–42, 49; 16.27; 24.31; cf. *1 Enoch* 1.9; 54.6). Matthew specifies that these angels are 'his angels'; that is, Christ's (contrast Mark 8.38; 13.27).

On the other side of the cosmic battle are the devil and his angels (25.41; cf. Rev. 12.7–9). The devil or 'slanderer' (4.1, 5, 8, 11; 13.39) is also known as Satan (from the Hebrew meaning 'accuser', 4.10; 12.26; 16.23), the 'tempter' (4.3), Beelzebul/Beelzebub or the 'lord of the flies' (10.25; 12.24, 27), and the 'prince of demons' (9.34; 12.24). The Lord's Prayer, setting out the pattern of prayer for followers of Jesus, concludes with a petition to be delivered or rescued 'from the Evil One' (6.13; cf. 5.37; 13.19, 38). Satan tempts or tests Jesus. While in the background could be the non-malevolent figure of the Satan as God's accuser as in the book of Job (Job 1—2), his connection with the devil and the 'Evil One' gives him a sinister profile in Matthew. His kingdom (12.26) is a rival to the kingdom of the heavens. Satan's grip on human beings is evident from time to time throughout Matthew's story, as when the religious leaders 'test' Jesus (e.g. 16.1; 19.3; 22.18) or when Jesus rebukes Peter with the words 'Get behind me, Satan!' (16.23).

Also in league with the devil are the demons (e.g. 9.33) and unclean spirits (e.g. 12.43), by whom certain human beings are possessed. Central to Jesus' battle with Satan's kingdom is his authority to cast out demons (4.24; 8.16, 28, 33; 9.32; 12.22; 15.22; 17.18), an authority he shares with his disciples (7.22; 10.1, 8). On occasion Jesus is accused of casting out demons by 'the ruler of the demons' (9.34) or Beelzebul (12.24, 27), although the implied reader knows that he does so by the Spirit of God (12.28). This greater authority ensures that, however much Satan seems to have the upper hand in Jesus' suffering and death, his kingdom will ultimately be defeated – having refused Satan's offer of all the kingdoms of this world at 4.8–9, the risen Jesus receives 'all authority in heaven and on earth', 28.18.

Political and Religious Leaders

The conflict in the supernatural realm is mirrored in the hostility towards Jesus, 'God-with-us', from human characters in Matthew's story. Particular hostility comes from the politico-religious leadership. Narrative critics tend to focus their discussion on the Jewish religious leaders as the chief opponents of Jesus. Kingsbury, for example, traces the growing conflict between Jesus and the religious leaders almost from the start (with the appearance of the Pharisees and Sadducees at John's baptism: 3.7), albeit sporadic and tentative (and in Matthew 9 still rather indirect) but becoming increasingly intense and confrontational as the story unfolds (Kingsbury 1986: 3–5).

Although they represent different Jewish roles (e.g. scribes, elders, priests, the high priest Caiaphas) and interest groups (e.g. Pharisees, Sadducees, Herodians), and are mentioned in different permutations (e.g. 'the Pharisees and Sadducees', 16.1; 'the elders and chief priests and scribes', 16.21; the scribes and Pharisees, 23.2), the Jewish leaders are generally interpreted by narrative critics as a 'monolithic front' against Jesus (e.g. Kingsbury 1995: 180, although Kingsbury acknowledges minor distinctions between them). To use Forster's terminology, they are a single 'flat character' group because they do not develop nor have traits unrelated to their root trait of 'evilness'. This is underscored by the fact that several of these religious leaders – the Pharisees and Sadducees (16.1); the Pharisees alone (19.3); the disciples of the Pharisees together with the Herodians (22.16); a 'lawyer' (22.35) – 'test' Jesus, thus aligning themselves with 'the tempter', Satan (4.3).

While it is undoubtedly the case that the Jewish religious leaders are the main opponents of Jesus in Matthew, and that Matthew can combine unlikely groupings in an 'unholy alliance' (e.g. the Pharisees and Sadducees at 3.7 and 16.1), the analysis of narrative critics is arguably too 'monolithic' and simplistic. For example, Matthew's treatment of the scribes is rather more nuanced than Mark's wholly negative view. On occasion, Matthean redaction seems to avoid negative references to 'scribes' (e.g. compare 21.23 with Mark 11.27; 22.34 with Mark 12.28; 22.41 with Mark 12.35). Moreover he knows of scribes 'trained for the kingdom of heaven' (13.52). Second, a monolithic approach risks underestimating the dominant role of the Pharisees (e.g. 3.7; 5.20; 9.11; 12.2; 23.1–36) as antagonists in Matthew's story.

An alternative criticism is that the definition of Jesus' opponents in Matthew is too narrow. The distinction between 'religious' and 'political' leaders in the ancient world was much less clear than for the contemporary Western world. Other 'political' leaders – perhaps better described as 'religio-political' leaders – also exercise a malevolent role in Matthew's story of Jesus. Herod the Great orchestrates the slaughter of the innocents out of fear of the rival 'king of the Jews' (2.1–12). His son, Herod Antipas, is responsible for the execution of the forerunner John the Baptist (14.3–12). Other Herodian rulers play a more marginal role (Archelaus is mentioned as an 'offstage' threat to the infant Jesus, 2.22; Herod Philip, brother of Antipas, receives only a passing reference, 14.3), suggesting a relativizing of their significance compared with the 'kingdom of the heavens'. These share with the Pharisees, Sadducees, chief priests and scribes the fact that they are Jewish rulers – though ambiguously so in the case of Herod the Great, who was half-Idumean. On the other hand, Roman political and military characters have a less negative portrayal. Of the two Roman centurions mentioned, the first is held up as a model for faith (8.5–13) while the second correctly acknowledges Jesus as 'God's Son' (27.54). Pontius Pilate, Roman prefect of Judea and Samaria, publicly acknowledges Jesus' innocence (27.24), even though he cannot be completely exonerated given that he ultimately hands Jesus over to be crucified (27.26).

John the Baptist

Firmly on the divine side of the conflict is John the Baptist (see Meier 1980). This fiery prophet of the coming judgement appears suddenly on the scene accompanied by the sonorous words 'In those days' (3.1–17). The close match between his message and that of Jesus is revealed in the fact that they both speak the same words: 'Repent, for the kingdom of heaven has come near' (3.2; 4.17; contrast Mark 1.4). But he is clearly inferior to Jesus, as his attempt to dissuade Jesus from accepting baptism (3.14) reveals; indeed, even 'the least in the kingdom of heaven' is greater than John (11.11). John's role as the forerunner for Jesus is confirmed by two quotations from the prophets (3.3; 11.10). The first is from Isaiah (3.3, citing Isa. 40.3), quoted in the Greek LXX version, which identifies John as the voice in the wilderness who prepares the Lord's way (the Hebrew text reads 'A voice cries: "Prepare in the wilderness"'). A second biblical citation from Malachi confirms that he is the Lord's messenger or 'angel' (11.10; Mal. 3.1). In the reception history, the statement that John is an *angelos* has sometimes been interpreted as evidence for John's heavenly origin (hence in many Orthodox icons John the Baptist has angel's wings).

But Matthew's story is even more specific about John, evoking Jewish speculation about the last days. Given that the prophet Elijah had been taken up to heaven in a whirlwind (2 Kings 2.11), it was believed that he would return from heaven before the Lord. Indeed, the 'messenger' or 'angel' in Malachi is the returning Elijah. Three points make clear that John is the returned Elijah. The aforementioned quotation from Malachi is the first, which is clarified by Jesus' words: 'and if you are willing to accept it, he is Elijah who is to come' (11.14). Second, in the scene when he introduces John to his audience, Matthew mentions John's clothing first (3.4–6; cf. Mark 1.4–6). His 'camel's hair with a leather belt around his waist' recalls Elijah's clothing at 2 Kings 1.8 ('A hairy man, with a leather belt around his waist'). Third, Matthew again makes the connection explicit, as Jesus and his disciples discuss Elijah's return during their descent from the Mount of Transfiguration: 'Then the disciples understood that he was speaking to them about John the Baptist' (17.13, a narratorial comment unique to Matthew). Here he shows himself to be a sympathetic reader of Mark, who has also made the connection between John and Elijah (Goodacre 2008). Some interpreters over the centuries have wanted to nuance this bold identification (e.g. Jerome, who is concerned about interpretations that suggest a form of reincarnation: Jerome 2008: 132–3), particularly given that Elijah appears in his own right at Jesus' Transfiguration (17.3). Indeed, Luke may be an early example: for example, the more nuanced description of John as coming with 'the spirit and power of Elijah' (Luke 1.17); his lack of reference to John's clothing (Luke 3.1–6); his omission of the post-Transfiguration conversation about Elijah's return (Luke 9.36).

Finally, John is the forerunner in a very concrete sense. He dies at the hands of a local political ruler (Herod Antipas, tetrarch of Galilee and Peraea). The story of John's beheading uses verbs that will occur again in the story of Jesus' passion, such as 'arrested', 'bound', 'put to death', 'buried'. Jerome is one early commentator who sees a link between the death of John the Baptist ('His disciples came and took the body') and that of Jesus. He proposes that 14.12 can be understood 'as referring to disciples both of John himself and of the Savior' (Jerome 2008: 169).

The Disciples

Closely related to Jesus are that character group called 'the disciples' (Greek *mathētai*, meaning 'those who learn'). The disciples of Jesus are part of the action in almost every chapter of the Gospel, from the call of Simon Peter, Andrew, James and John at 4.18–22 through to their desertion and Peter's threefold denial in the passion narrative (26.56, 69–75). Kingsbury notes the contrast between the disciples and the Jewish leaders, despite the fact that both groups are in conflict with Jesus: 'Jesus has conflict with the disciples because although they aspire to appropriate his evaluative point of view, they falter at times and fail' (Kingsbury 1986: 129).

Although the disciples abandon Jesus before his passion, their portrayal in Matthew is rather more nuanced than in Mark (as redaction criticism makes clear). They are not completely devoid of faith (with the notable exception of Judas Iscariot: 10.4; 26.14–16, 25, 47–50; 27.3–10), but 'people of little faith' (*oligopistoi*, 6.30; 8.26; 14.31; 16.8; cf. Mark 4.40; 6.50–51; 8.17). Peter's confession is a more positive recognition of Jesus' Messiahship than the Marcan parallel ('For flesh and blood has not revealed this to you, but my Father in heaven': 16.17; cf. Mark 8.30). Matthew replaces James and John with their mother, leaving her to ask the offending question about seats at right and left in the kingdom (20.20–21; cf. Mark 10.35). Moreover the Twelve (or the Eleven, minus Judas Iscariot) are explicitly rehabilitated after the resurrection (28.16–20).

The precise relationship between 'the disciples' and 'the Twelve' – symbolizing the 12 tribes of Israel – in Matthew is somewhat unclear. With the change of Levi to Matthew at 9.9, all five named disciples up to that point (also Simon Peter, Andrew, James and John) are members of the Twelve (who are all listed at 10.2–4). Moreover Matthew can speak in places of 'the/his twelve disciples' (10.1; 11.1; 20.17) or 'the twelve apostles' (10.2, so-called because they have been 'sent out' by Jesus), suggesting an identification between the two groups, rather than viewing the Twelve as a core group chosen from among the wider group of disciples (as in Mark: 3.13–15). Most of the time, however, Matthew speaks simply of 'the [or 'his'] disciples' (e.g. 9.10–11; 12.1–2; 13.10; 15.2; 17.16; 23.1) and occasionally of 'the twelve' (26.20).

This ambiguous evidence is read in different ways. For some (e.g. Strecker 1963: 191; Collins 2003: 104–8), Matthew is looking back to an unrepeatable golden age of the 'twelve disciples'. However, against straightforward identification of the disciples with 'the twelve', as well as the inconsistency already mentioned, is the fact that the Twelve are not mentioned at all in Matthew's story until 10.1. Luz, by contrast, sees the disciples functioning as models for contemporary readers of the Gospel in their own call to discipleship (Luz 2005b: 115–42).

However they function for the reader, the disciples fulfil various roles within the narrative. They listen to and learn from Jesus, as their title suggests. They are more receptive than the crowds; indeed, they have been given *to know* the secrets of the kingdom of heaven (13.11; cf. Mark 4.11). They are commissioned to continue the preaching of Jesus, just as Jesus continued that of John the Baptist – the same message, 'The kingdom of heaven is at hand', is proclaimed by all of them (3.2; 4.17; 10.7). They also share in Jesus' authority to cast out unclean spirits (10.1). They often act as a foil for Jesus, asking him questions that provoke teaching from him (e.g. 18.1 (the disciples); 18.21 (Peter)). Their questioning, however, unlike that of religious leaders such as the Pharisees (e.g. 19.3), is not hostile, even if they do not always understand. Moreover at various points in his story Matthew describes how Jesus privileges particular individuals from within the Twelve: for example, Peter, James and John witness the Transfiguration of Jesus and are called apart with him in Gethsemane (17.1; 26.37–46). Chief among these is Simon Peter, whose shaky faith is contrasted with his naming as the Rock (14.28–33; 16.16–19). Given the importance of Matthew's Petrine traditions for the life of the Church, particularly in the Roman Catholic tradition, Peter will be considered in more detail in Chapter 10 below. The problematic character of Judas Iscariot will be treated in Chapter 11.

The Crowds and Minor Characters

Much of the action in Matthew's story revolves around the action of 'crowds' (Greek *ochloi*: e.g. 4.25; 5.1; 7.28; 8.1; 9.8; 12.15; 14.13) or occasionally the singular 'crowd' (e.g. 9.23; 14.14; 15.10). Their presence can be obscured in certain English translations: Paul Minear has criticized the RSV for its inconsistent policy in translating the term *ochlos/ochloi* variously as 'crowd', 'multitude', 'throng' and 'people' (Minear 1974). In narrative-critical studies the crowd/crowds, like the leaders, are treated as a mono-lithic character group. Kingsbury regards them, like the leaders, as 'flat' characters with few character traits, who do not change until they come with Judas to arrest Jesus (26.47, 55: Kingsbury 1986: 23–4). Just as there is differentiation between the different groups of Jewish leaders, however, it is debatable whether all the various references to 'the crowds', 'the crowd' or 'a large crowd' should be treated as descriptions of the one character group. Is it legitimate to identify the crowd that comes with Judas to arrest Jesus (26.47, 55), for example, with the crowds who flock to listen to Jesus' teaching or to be fed by him (e.g. 5.1; 14.13)?

Leaving aside this last ambiguous example, however, the bulk of the references to the crowds/crowd point to characters with similar traits. Generally speaking the crowds are positive towards Jesus (Minear 1974), praising God for his healings (e.g. 9.8; 15.31), and even on occasion acclaiming him as 'son of David' (21.9; though see 12.23). Jesus has compassion on them because they are 'like sheep without a shepherd' (e.g. 9.36). This identifies them as the 'lost sheep of the house of Israel' to whom Jesus and the disciples are sent (e.g. 10.6; 15.24), their own 'shepherds' having failed them (i.e. the Jewish religio-political leaders: see Ezek. 34). At times they 'follow' Jesus; that is, they behave as disciples should (e.g. 4.25; 8.1; 12.15; 14.13; 19.2). But they lack consistent faith in Jesus (Kingsbury 1986: 23–4) or regard him simply as a prophet (e.g. 16.13–14; 21.11, 46) – not an untrue assessment but an inadequate one. So they are contrasted both with the disciples (unfavourably) and with their leaders (favourably).

Interwoven with the crowds are individual 'minor characters' who make sometimes fleeting appearances in Matthew's story. Any discussion of minor characters inevitably requires selectivity, which will reveal something of the interests and prejudices of the interpreter. Kingsbury restricts the term 'minor characters' to 'the persons who dot the pages of Matthew's story and, except for one like "Joseph" (1.18—2.23), appear briefly in a scene and then vanish' (Kingsbury 1986: 25). Many of them are unnamed and some are incidental to the story being told, such as the flute-players in the raising of the ruler's daughter (9.23) or the blind and lame in the Temple (21.14). They tend to serve as foils for other characters: for Israel (e.g. the centurion of 8.5–13, whose faith is praised); for Pilate (e.g. Pilate's wife, who confesses Jesus' innocence as the result of a dream, 27.19); for Jesus (e.g. Barabbas, whose release is achieved through Jesus' death, 27.15–20). Many of them serve as foils for the disciples, contrasting with their 'little faith', such as the friends of the paralysed man (9.2) or the woman with haemorrhages (9.22).

Of the many different characters and character groups, some comment should be made of the female characters. With the notable exception of Jesus' mother Mary (1.16, 18, 20; 2.11; 13.55), and the mothers listed in the genealogy, the women in Matthew's story remain unnamed almost until the end. The fact that the female recipients of Jesus' healing touch (e.g. Peter's mother-in-law; the woman with an issue of blood; the daughter of the 'ruler'; the Canaanite woman and her daughter) are not named is not significant, given that the same applies to the men Jesus heals (even Mark's Bartimaeus has become two unnamed blind men: 20.30). But other examples are surprising. The brothers of Jesus are named (James, Joseph, Simon and Judas: 13.55) but not his sisters (13.56). We are told the name of the owner of the house visited by Jesus in Bethany ('Simon the leper') but not of the woman who anointed Jesus' head with ointment, despite his promise that what she had done would be told 'in memory of her' (26.6–13). We are dependent upon an imaginative reception history to give a name (Procula or Claudia) and a biography to Pilate's wife (27.19). Only at the climax to the story, with Jesus' male disciples having deserted him, do the faithful women come out of the shadows: Mary Magdalene (27.56, 61; 28.1, 5, 8–10); Mary the mother of James and Joseph or 'the other Mary' (27.56, 61; 28.1, 5, 8–10), as well as the still unnamed 'mother of the sons of Zebedee' (27.56). Feminist critics would find in the lack of names evidence for the essentially androcentric perspective of the evangelist, or of the inherited tradition (e.g. both Mark and Matthew name Simon Peter but not his wife or his mother-in-law).

The Significance of Geographical Place

One further point at which ancient commentators on Matthew and modern redaction, composition, and narrative critics converge, despite their different methodologies, is in attaching significance to geographical locations. We noted in Chapter 3, for example, how the author of the *Opus imperfectum* identified particular places as having an important structural function (e.g. 4.1, 18; 5.1; 8.23; 21.1, 10). An interest in topography, and its symbolic function, is also regularly found in modern critical scholars. For some, places are 'transparent' to the situation of the evangelist and his audience(s): the hostility towards Jesus and his disciples encountered in 'their synagogues' is a case in point (see Chapter 5 below). For others, the significance is not tied to any particular historical period but has a more universal appeal. What is shared is the conviction that the broad geography of the Gospel, and other 'locations' such as houses, synagogues and mountains, convey more than a literal reading might imply.

This is not a phenomenon unique to Matthew: in the Bible generally, significance is attached to particular places as a result of memories preserved in them, or similarities with other places that have been significant in Israel's history. In the Jewish apocalypses, with whose world view Matthew seems especially familiar, there is a very definite blurring of the boundary between terrestrial and mythic geography (see e.g. the journey of Enoch in *1 Enoch* 24—25: Himmelfarb 1991). Indeed, although the action in Matthew's narrative takes place on the earth (unlike many of the apocalypses), heaven is never far in the background. Heaven is the place where God dwells ('your Father in the heavens', e.g. 5.16, 45; 6.1, 9), where God's will is done (6.10) and where angels behold his face (18.10). As the 'place' of ultimate significance it is where lasting treasures are to be stored (6.20; 19.21) and where great rewards are kept (5.12), at least until heaven and earth 'pass away' (5.18; 24.35). Matthew's preferred designation for the kingdom of God proclaimed by Jesus is 'the kingdom of the heavens' (3.2; 4.17; 5.3, 10, 19–20; 7.21; 8.11; 10.7; 11.11–12; 13.11, 24, 31, 33, 44, 45, 47, 52; 18.1, 3, 4, 23; 19.12, 14, 23, 24; 20.1; 22.2; 25.1). In an important apocalyptic moment when Jesus is baptized by John, 'the heavens' are opened to allow the Spirit to descend and a heavenly voice to be heard (3.16–17).

The role of terrestrial sacred geography is evident almost from the beginning of Matthew's Gospel. As noted above, the infancy narrative (Matt. 1—2) emphasizes the significance of place in the events surrounding the birth and infancy of Jesus. All of these recall particular figures or events in Israel's history. Jerusalem is the holy city, the 'city of the great King' (5.35) and the location of God's Temple. Bethlehem, a town in Judea near Jerusalem, is the birthplace of King David (1 Sam. 17.12) and therefore appropriately the birthplace of Jesus, the Son of David (2.1, 5–6, 8, 16; cf. Mic. 5.2). The story of the flight into Egypt, interwoven with the motif of threat to a newborn child by a troubled ruler, recalls a cluster of stories in the books of Genesis and Exodus: the journey of Jacob/Israel to Egypt under Joseph, the story of Moses' infancy and the exodus of the people of Israel from Egypt.

As Matthew's story unfolds, geographical references continue to recall the events of Israel's history. Jesus' baptism by John (3.13–17) takes place at the River Jordan, which the Israelites crossed when they entered the promised land, the miraculous drying up of the water recalling Israel's crossing of the sea at the exodus (Josh. 3.14–17; cf. Exod. 14.21–25). Jesus' 40-day temptation or testing in the 'wilderness' (4.1–11), though located literally in the Judean desert north of the Dead Sea, recalls the 40-year testing of the Israelites in the wilderness of Sinai.

Jesus' ministry proper begins in Galilee, the territory that contained both his childhood home of Nazareth (2.23; 4.13; 21.11) and his adopted city of Capernaum (4.13; 8.5; 11.23; 17.24). Linking the latter location with a prophecy from Isaiah (4.15–16, quoting Isa. 9.1–2), Matthew identifies Galilee as 'Galilee of the Gentiles', suggesting a symbolic significance beyond its literal sense. It is from Galilee that Jesus occasionally goes forth to encounter non-Jews (e.g., at least by implication, the two demoniacs in the country of the Gadarenes, 8.28; the Canaanite woman in the district of Tyre and Sidon, although in Matthew's account Jesus avoids entering her house: 15.21–22; cf. Mark 7.24). Moreover Gentiles encounter Jesus in Galilee itself (e.g. crowds who come to Jesus from the Decapolis and beyond the Jordan, as well as Galilee, Jerusalem and Judea, 4.25; the centurion in Capernaum, 8.5). William Thompson noted a major *inclusio* marking out the Galilean section of Jesus' public ministry, denoted by the repeated use of Galilee and Capernaum (Thompson 1970). This is where Jesus' ministry begins (4.12–16). Galilee is mentioned again together with Capernaum towards the end of that Galilean phase at 17.22, 24, before the transition to the journey to Jerusalem at 19.1.

Jerusalem (2.1, 3; 3.5; 4.25; 16.21; 20.17–18; 21.1, 10; 23.37) or Zion (21.5; sometimes referred to simply as 'the holy city': 4.5; 27.53) is also a place with strong resonances, whether as David's capital city, the site of God's Temple or the tragic city devastated by the Babylonians in the sixth century BCE – a memory evoked by the fourfold reference to 'the deportation to Babylon' in Matthew's genealogy (1.11, 12, 17). As the place of Jesus' rejection and crucifixion its tragic associations are to the fore (e.g. 23.37–39; though it is also the location of the eschatological resurrection of the dead: 27.52–53; 28.1–10).

Other Settings

However, 'place' in Matthew is not only confined to geographical place names. The settings for particular events also have symbolic significance. The Gospel's references to 'the sea' (only occasionally identified explicitly as the Sea of Galilee: 4.18; 15.29) evokes the Bible's association of the sea with danger and chaos (e.g. Gen. 1.2, 9; Job 38.8–11; Ps. 74.13–15; 104.6–9; 107.23–30). It is the location of two of Jesus' miracles that display his authority over nature (8.23–27; 14.22–33). It is into the sea that the demon-possessed pigs are sent at 8.32. However, the shore of the sea is a place of receptivity, where Jesus teaches in parables (13.1–2).

By contrast the synagogues – or at least those synagogues dominated by Jesus' opponents – are presented as places of hostility and separation: 'their synagogues' or 'your synagogues'. Jesus teaches 'in their synagogues' (4.23; 9.35; cf. 13.54) and occasionally heals in a synagogue (12.9–14); but these visits result in people taking offence (13.57) or even conspiring to destroy him (12.14). He teaches the Twelve that they can expect to be flogged in 'their synagogues' (10.17; cf. 23.34).

Finally, mountains play a prominent topographical role in Matthew's narrative. Some are borrowed from Mark: the mountain on which Jesus prays before walking on the water (14.23); the 'high' mountain of the Transfiguration (17.1), traditionally identified as Mount Tabor in Galilee; the Mount of Olives to the east of Jerusalem (21.1; 24.3; 26.30). But Matthew has several more. In his lengthy account of the temptation of

Jesus, Matthew has the devil show him the kingdoms of the world from 'a very high mountain' (4.8; in Luke, the devil simply 'led him up', Luke 4.5). Matthew's Jesus delivers his first sermon from a mountain in Galilee (5.1; 8.1), paralleling his last sermon, delivered on the Mount of Olives. At 15.29 Jesus heals many while seated on 'the mountain' overlooking the Sea of Galilee, perhaps the mountain of the earlier sermon (cf. Mark 7.31–32). These healings provoke the second feeding miracle, of four thousand people (15.32–39). Finally the risen Jesus meets his disciples on a mountain in Galilee, having received 'all authority in heaven and on earth' (28.16; the contrast with the temptation by the devil on the 'very high mountain' is surely deliberate).

Again, the topography may be more symbolic than literal (see e.g. Donaldson 1985). This is accentuated by the fact that there is no 'exceedingly high mountain' in Judea (4.8). Thus the mountain where Satan tempts Jesus is either a visionary mountain, or so described as to recall another 'exceedingly high mountain' in Israel's story. Mount Pisgah, from where Moses is shown the promised land, is one good candidate (Deut. 34.1: Clarke 2003: 41). More generally mountains are places of revelation and encounter with the divine. Jewish readers of Matthew would recall Mount Sinai, where Moses received the Law and the covenant was established (e.g. Exod. 19.16–25; 34.1–28); Sinai's alter ego Mount Horeb where the prophet Elijah encountered God (1 Kings 19.8–13); Mount Zion (e.g. Ps. 125.1; Isa. 40.9), which like other sacred mountains became a point of entry into the heavenly realm; or the association of the Mount of Olives with eschatological events (building on Zech. 14.4–5). There are also possible prophetic promises. The juxtaposition of healing and feeding, for example, in Matthew 15 may recall the promise of Ezekiel that the Lord will bind up the injured sheep, and feed his flock 'on the mountains of Israel' (Ezek. 34.13–16; cf. 34.4).

5

Matthew's World: Locating the Text Historically and Socially

The Gospel for Jewish Converts

In the Preface to his brief commentary on the Gospel according to Matthew, St Jerome writes that Matthew:

> published a Gospel in Judea in the Hebrew language, chiefly for the sake of those from the Jews who had believed in Jesus and who were by no means observing the shadow of the Law, since the truth of the Gospel had succeeded it.   (Jerome 2008: 53)

Jerome's assessment of Matthew's authorship and intended audience is a typical one in the early Christian centuries. Origen – on whom Jerome may be partly dependent – had similarly begun his commentary with the claim that the apostle Matthew composed his Gospel 'in the Hebrew tongue and published it for the converts from Judaism' (Eusebius, *H. E.* 4.25.3–6; Origen 1994: 412). Even earlier, Irenaeus had claimed that Matthew wrote for his own people in Hebrew (*or* Aramaic) at an early stage, while Peter and Paul were preaching in Rome (cited in Eusebius, *H. E.* 5.8).

What these early commentators have in common is the conviction that Matthew wrote with a very specific audience in mind, and that this audience comprised followers of Jesus from a Jewish background, albeit those who no longer belonged to the Synagogue – at least viewed from the perspective of these later commentators. For Origen, Matthew's intended readership were 'converts from Judaism'; for Jerome, alluding to Colossians 2.17, they were Jewish believers who had exchanged the 'shadow of the Law' for the truth of the gospel. Moreover, at least some were of the opinion that Matthew's Gospel was composed close to where the original events took place, in Judea itself (so Jerome, who lived in Judean Bethlehem). It may be that some of these conclusions were deduced from Papias' tradition about Matthew collating the *logia* of the Lord 'in the Hebrew [*or* Aramaic] dialect [*or* style]' (Eusebius, *H. E.* 3.39.15–16), though believing it to apply to our Greek Matthew. Whatever their source, patristic and later medieval discussions of the circumstances that provoked the evangelist to write bear some striking similarities to a common view found among twentieth- and twenty-first-century Matthean scholars.

Matthew's Jewish World

Although few modern scholars would argue for the apostolic authorship of Matthew, or an early dating, many agree that the evangelist writes for Christians of Jewish descent. They are struck by how far the Jesus of Matthew's Gospel inhabits the world of first-century Judaism even more thoroughly than the Jesus of Mark. This indeed is one of the arguments occasionally put forward by proponents of Matthean priority. For those who regard Mark as the first Gospel, Matthew represents a 'rejudaizing' portrait of Jesus of Nazareth, reclothing him with the prayer shawl of his Jewish heritage (O'Leary 2006). For Matthew, Jesus is a pious, observant Jew who nonetheless claims to provide the definitive interpretation of the Torah. His debates about legal interpretation (e.g. over divorce, Sabbath observance or ritual purification: 5.31–32; 12.1–14; 15.1–20; 19.3–9) echo those of his Pharisaic contemporaries. Matthew seems keen to downplay any suggestion that Jesus came to 'abolish' rather than 'fulfil' the Law and the prophets (5.17).

Matthew's Jesus also assumes that his followers will understand and observe Jewish practices. In his teaching he presumes that they will wear phylacteries or *tefillin* and prayer shawls with tassels (23.5; cf. Deut. 6.4–9; Num. 15.38–40). He expects them to comprehend the Jewish practice of whitewashing tombs to prevent pious Jews from walking over them inadvertently, at the risk of becoming ritually unclean through contact with corpses (23.27). He urges them to pray that, when they are forced to flee from Judea when 'the desolating sacrilege' appears in the Temple, it does not happen on a Sabbath (24.20). He expects that they, or at least the 'reader' who reads his Gospel out to them, will know what the prophet Daniel has to say about this 'desolating sacrilege' (24.15, referring to Dan. 7.27; 11.31; 12.11). Nor does the implied author, or narrator, see fit to explain to his audiences Pharisaic regulations about washing hands before meals (15.2; cf. Mark 7.3–4).

On the other hand, Matthew's text betrays sharp hostility towards some other Jews. As we have seen, Jewish leaders of different varieties are antagonistic towards Jesus, and there is a particularly negative presentation of the Pharisees (e.g. 9.34; 12.14, 24; 15.1–9; 16.6; 22.15) or a coalition of 'the scribes and Pharisees' (especially in Matt. 23). There is a distancing between Jesus' followers in Matthew and 'their synagogues' (which has become something of a mantra for Matthew: 4.23; 9.35; 10.17; 12.9; 13.54;

23.34). This hostility towards the synagogue and its leaders may well explain why Jairus, the 'ruler of the synagogue' whose daughter Jesus restores to life (Mark 5.22), has become simply a 'ruler' in Matthew's version (9.18, despite the misleading translation in the NRSV).

Matthew and Jamnia

At least since W. D. Davies' 1964 classic work *The Setting of the Sermon on the Mount*, a specific historical and social context has been proposed as explanation for Matthew's ambivalent presentation. Building on the work of scholars such as E. von Dobschütz, B. W. Bacon and G. D. Kilpatrick, Davies argued that early rabbinic Judaism provides the interpretative key for understanding Matthew's text. This is the world of the so-called Council of Jamnia and the radical process of redefining Judaism following the destruction of Jerusalem and its Temple in 70 CE. Jamnia, or Yavneh, is a town on the Palestinian coast near Ashdod to which the predecessors to the rabbis – a coalition of various parties, the Pharisees having a dominant role – retreated in order to salvage the Jewish tradition from the wreckage of the Jewish War against Rome. The response of 'Jamnian Judaism' was to transform the diverse but fragmented pre-70 Judaism – made up of such diverse groups as the Pharisees, Sadducees, Essenes, the Qumran Community (probably a particular branch of Essenism) and Jewish followers of Jesus and John the Baptist – into a uniform community that could survive the loss of the Temple and the Land. It gave a more central place to Torah and emphasized those 'cultic' acts that could be performed without a Temple or sacrificial altar. This is exemplified in a quotation from the prophet Hosea beloved of the leader of the Jamnian movement, Johanan ben Zakkai: 'I desire mercy and not sacrifice' (Hos. 6.6).

In Davies' thesis, Matthew's Gospel represents an alternative attempt to reclaim the Jewish tradition after the destruction, but one centred on the following of Jesus (see especially Davies 1989: 256–315). It betrays both similarities to Jamnia – evidence for Matthew's close proximity to this Pharisee-led movement – and hostility towards it. Matthew's Jesus also values Hosea 6.6 ('I desire mercy and not sacrifice', 9.13; 12.7). Matthew prioritizes interpretation of the Torah (e.g. 5.17–20) and shares with Jamnia those 'cultic' actions that could be performed without a Temple (almsgiving, prayer and fasting: e.g. 6.1–18). But the hostile language of 'their synagogues' can be explained by Matthew's rejection of Jamnian-led synagogues (a point already made by Kilpatrick 1946: 110–11) and their attempts to excommunicate via the so-called *Birkath ha-Minim* with its curse on the Nazarenes and other *minim* or heretics (Matthew's Jesus presents an alternative form of excommunication at 18.15–20). Jesus' warning at 23.8 that disciples are not to be called 'rabbi' is indicative of the post-70 shift from 'rabbi' (literally 'my lord') being a purely honorific title to a specific office within the Synagogue.

Since Davies' work, this way of reading Matthew's Gospel has been further refined by a succession of Matthean scholars (e.g. Stanton 1992; Hare 1993; Overman 1990; Saldarini 1994; Sim 1998; but see Gundry 1994: 599–609 for a pre-Jamnian dating). Some prefer Jacob Neusner's terminology of 'formative Judaism' to 'Jamnian Judaism', emphasizing that what the later rabbis presented in idealized form as a single event (the so-called 'Council' of Jamnia/Yavneh, and the related traditions about Johanan ben Zakkai) was more likely the beginning of a lengthy and complex process of transition that culminated in the emergence of rabbinic Judaism (Overman 1990: 38–43).

Many of these scholars go further than the historical claim that Matthew and his intended audience were living against the backdrop of formative Judaism. They often treat that intended audience as synonymous with Matthew's own church, quite narrowly conceived as living in one city – rather more specific than the claims of the patristic authors. Matthew's Gospel, in other words, is written for internal consumption by the congregation to which Matthew belonged, and should be read, in all its redactional details, as a kind of allegory of the life of that 'Matthean Community'. For example, when Matthew's Jesus refers to persecution and warns that 'they will flog you in their synagogues' (10.17), this statement reflects the current or recent experience of his specific audience. Stanton represents a modified version of this, for he prefers to speak of the 'communities of Matthew' as opposed to one congregation in the city where the evangelist himself dwells (Stanton 1992).

Against the Community Hypothesis

Such an 'allegorical' reading of Matthew as a window on to the 'Matthean Community' has been heavily criticized from some quarters in the past two decades. Stanton himself notes that the issue of genre is relevant to discussion of the evangelist's social history. For Stanton, Matthew's Gospel is an example of a Graeco-Roman *bios*, telling the story of Jesus rather than the encoded story of a group of Matthean Christians. The hypothesis of a 'Matthean Community' tends to treat the Gospel like a Pauline letter, composed in order to address very specific community situations. If we are to draw analogies between Matthew and a New Testament letter, 1 Peter might serve as a better comparison. This is a circular letter, addressed to 'a loose network of communities over a wide geographical area', without revealing detailed knowledge of any specific church (Stanton 1994: 11). Further criticism of the community hypothesis has come from a collection of essays edited by Richard Bauckham (Bauckham [ed.] 1998). Reiterating Stanton's statement about genre, Bauckham proposes that scholars who speak of 'the Matthean Community' or 'the Johannine Community' (the community behind John's Gospel) fail to distinguish carefully enough between an author's *background* and his or her intended *audience*. Moreover he claims that far from being composed with very specific audiences in mind (still less for internal consumption by the local congregation to which the evangelist belonged), the Gospels were intended for a general Christian readership. He argues for an early Christian movement as a network of communities in close communication with one another rather than living in splendid isolation.

These criticisms deserve to be taken seriously, and indeed scholars are now rather more precise when talking about Gospel communities. However, Bauckham has overstated his case. One must allow for specific circumstances to have left their imprint on Matthew's story (though see the cautious words of Carson 1982). Indeed Paul Foster points to several texts in Matthew that appear transparent to the evangelist's situation, and presuppose a fairly precise set of intended audiences. These include the references to the Temple tax (which Foster connects to the post-70 *fiscus iudaicus* or 'Jewish tax', 17.24–27) and the contemporary Jewish claim that the disciples stole Jesus' body (28.11–15), the repeated references to 'their/ your synagogues' and the interest in church order (e.g. 18.1–10: Foster 2004: 5–6; for other criticisms of Bauckham, see Esler 1998; Sim 2001). Moreover some of Bauckham's evidence for communication between churches reflects a second- rather than first-century situation. Nor is the writing of a religious text for internal consumption by the author's own community or close associates without precedent either in Judaism (e.g. the Qumran *Damascus Document*, which seems to be an allegory of the community's early history, including its foundation by the Teacher of Righteousness) or early Christianity (e.g. the Johannine Epistles).

Intra muros or *extra muros*?

Scholars who continue to hold to the view that Matthew's Gospel was written for a quite specific audience or set of audiences from a predominantly

Jewish background are nonetheless divided over their precise relationship to other Jews. What is the relationship of Matthew's original audience(s) to Israel or the Synagogue? Are those whom Matthew addresses best described as *Christian Jews* (Jews who follow Jesus as Messiah) or *Jewish Christians* (a particular subset of the Christian Church that continues to observe certain aspects of the Jewish Law)? In Stanton's words (Stanton 1992: 113–45), are they *intra muros*, still 'within the walls' of the Jewish community, or does Matthew's Gospel reflect a stage in which, due to a mixture of persecution and excommunication, they now find themselves *extra muros*, 'outside the walls'? Unsurprisingly, given the 'Janus-like' character of Matthew and its ambiguous evidence, strong cases can be made for both positions.

Overman is an example of a Matthean scholar who holds firmly to the *intra muros* view (Overman 1990). He demonstrates the benefits of combining a historical-critical, and specifically redaction-critical, approach with a broader social-scientific analysis. He employs the sociology of knowledge, in particular the concept of a 'sect', in order to illuminate Matthew's polemic against 'their synagogues' while maintaining that Matthew's group remains within the wider Jewish community. Following J. Blenkinsopp, Overman defines a sect as a minority group that considers itself to be in opposition to a dominant parent group. Matthew's community is one such sect, presenting one alternative option to the increasingly dominant parent of 'formative Judaism' (other options include the visionary outlook of Jewish apocalypses such as *4 Ezra*, *2 Baruch* and the *Apocalypse of Abraham*, and a revolutionary stream that would lead to the Bar Kochba revolt of 132–6 CE).

Overman could be criticized for working with too broad a definition of 'sect' to be useful. His parent–child model might also be less useful to the discussion of the parallel Jamnian and Matthean groups than the alternative model of rival siblings, both emerging from the parent community of pre-70 Judaism (indeed, occasionally Overman uses the alternative language of 'fraternal twin' to express the relationship). Nonetheless, his interpretation provides a plausible explanation for the 'heat' of the Gospel's polemical language. A similar view of Matthew's Gospel as an alternative re-envisioning of Judaism after the loss of the Temple is espoused by Anthony Saldarini, drawing upon the work of Bryan Wilson. For Saldarini, the Matthean group is a 'deviant' group, objectionable to the wider Jewish community but attempting to reform it from the inside (Saldarini 1994 and 1995). David Sim is another scholar who argues strongly for an *intra muros* setting for Matthew (Sim 1998).

Others (e.g. Luz 1989; Stanton 1992; Hagner 2003; Foster 2004) regard proponents of the *intra muros* position such as Overman, Saldarini and Sim as having overstated their case, downplaying the Gospel's emphasis on 'newness'. They claim that contrary evidence tips the balance in favour of Matthew representing a form of Jewish Christianity now divorced from the Synagogue and definitively *extra muros*. The repeated reference to 'their/your synagogues' strongly suggests that the Synagogue has become an alien institution. The Gospel presupposes a separate Church with its own entrance rite in baptism (28.19), and other sacred rites such as the Eucharist (Matthew's Last-Supper narrative has a more liturgical feel than Mark's: compare 26.26–28 with Mark 14.22–24). Indeed the Great Commission, with its extension of the mission to the Gentiles (whether in addition to or in place of Israel), points to a significant breach. This is also believed to be reflected in a number of passages (e.g. 8.5–13; 15.13; 21.41, 43) envisaging the transference of the kingdom to a new people that includes Gentiles. The statement, in relation to the Jewish charge that Jesus' disciples stole his body from the tomb, that 'this story is still told among the Jews to this day' (28.15) also implies a certain distancing. A nuanced version of this *extra muros* position is that of Donald Hagner: that 'Matthew's community *had* broken with the synagogue, but that it remained in proximity to the synagogue and inescapably in an ongoing situation of debate and controversy with it' (Hagner 2003: 198). For Hagner, the Matthean Community finds itself in a kind of 'no man's land', having displaced the central Jewish pillar of Torah by Jesus and his authoritative teaching.

However, the evidence is not as decisive as often claimed. To speak of 'their synagogues' need not imply that Matthean Christians avoid all synagogues but only those dominated by the 'scribes and Pharisees'. The claim that baptism has replaced circumcision as an entrance rite is essentially an argument from silence, given that circumcision is mentioned neither negatively nor positively in this Gospel. Nor is an initiation rite or ritual meal necessarily evidence for a definitive breach with Judaism per se (the Qumran Community had its own initiation rite and communal meal, while John the Baptist seems to have required penitent Jews to 're-enter the Covenant' through baptism in the Jordan). The pericopae interpreted in terms of 'transference' from the old Israel to a new people incorporating the Gentiles are also open to alternative explanations. For instance, Matthew's distinctive interpretation of the tenants in the vineyard – 'Therefore I tell you, the kingdom of God will be taken away from you and given to a people [Greek *ethnos*] that produces the fruits of the kingdom', 21.43 – may be referring not to a shift from Israel to the Church but to a change of leadership (this parable will be discussed in more detail in Chapter 10 below). Nor is it clear that the phrase 'among the Jews' at 28.15 is a hostile reference from an outsider. The phrase literally means 'among Jews' (the definite article is absent in the Greek), and could be read as a neutral observation about the circles within which such a story still circulates. This is not necessarily any more hostile than claiming that a story is told 'among the English' or 'among Welsh people'. The ongoing debate attests to the ambiguity of much of the internal evidence.

Moreover, the answer to the *intra/extra muros* debate depends very much on who is asking the question and how that question is phrased. Proponents of the *extra muros* position sometimes treat 'Israel' as synonymous with 'the Synagogue' or membership of 'their synagogues'. However, given the diversity of pre-70 Judaism – where different Jewish groups might disagree vehemently without removing themselves from the people of Israel – it might well be possible for post-70 Jewish followers of Jesus to regard themselves as still part of the wider community of Israel while not frequenting, or being prevented from frequenting, the Synagogue or at least specific synagogues. Moreover, the answer to the question 'Are Matthew and like-minded Christians still within the walls?' will depend on who is being asked. A useful analogy might be the status of early Methodists who began as essentially a reform movement within the Church of England. As the breach widened, Anglican authorities may well have treated them as beyond the boundaries while the Methodists may have regarded themselves as still 'inside the walls'. This complicates the question as to whether the First Gospel presents the followers of Jesus as 'the new Israel' or 'the true Israel' (or even Stanton's 'new people'). Indeed, Stanton modified his position somewhat as a result of studying Justin's *Dialogue with Trypho*, which attests to a complex relationship between Jewish and Christian communities as late as the second century (Stanton 1994: 13–14; see also France 1989: 100–1).

Matthew a Gentile Christian?

Despite the ancient tradition that Matthew wrote his Gospel for converts from Judaism, and the dominant view among modern scholars that the Gospel represents a Christian-Jewish (*intra muros*) or Jewish-Christian (*extra muros*) reaction to formative Judaism, there have been prominent modern dissenters. A minority argue, on the basis of the tensions inherent in Matthew's narrative, that the evangelist was in fact a Gentile. They point, for example, to the positive portrayal of particular Gentile characters. The faith of the Roman centurion in Capernaum is praised beyond that of Israel (8.10). The story of the Canaanite woman, whose stubborn faith moves Jesus to act to cure her daughter (15.21–28), is juxtaposed with the blindness of the Pharisees (15.12–14). Pilate's wife rightly acknowledges Jesus' innocence as a result of a dream (27.19), placing her in the same category as righteous Joseph and the Gentile magi, who also received divine revelation by dreams (1.20; 2.12, 13, 19). Moreover, one of the formula citations explicitly identifies Jesus as the Servant of the Lord in whose name 'the Gentiles will hope' (12.21, quoting Isa. 42). Combined with the fierce denunciations of the Pharisees or the cry of 'all the people' at 27.25 ('His blood be on us and on our children'), this evidence, it is claimed, points in favour of a Gentile rather than Jewish evangelist.

In an important article published in 1947, Kenneth W. Clark detected what he described as a 'Gentile bias' in Matthew's Gospel, which was not taken sufficiently into account by those who posited a Jewish provenance. This was reflected in the story of the virgin birth of Jesus (which Clark saw as influenced by pagan myths), the heightened place given to the miraculous and the omission of Aramaic phrases found in Mark (e.g. Mark 3.17; 5.41; 7.11; 10.46, 51; 14.36). He also included the polemic against both Pharisees and Sadducees, and the Great Commission of making disciples of 'all the Gentiles' (28.19). Like proponents of the *extra muros* position, Clark also found evidence for the definitive rejection of Israel (specifically 21.43, along with the reference to the expulsion of the 'sons of the kingdom' at 8.12). He found it impossible to believe that a Jewish Christian of the late first century would present such a damning picture (Clark 1947). His explanation of particularist Jewish dimensions of Matthew, including the concern for fulfilment of the Torah, was that they reflect the Gentile evangelist's use of earlier tradition.

Others have come to similar if more nuanced conclusions about the first evangelist. John P. Meier, while not absolutely excluding the possibility that Matthew was a Jewish Christian, believes that the balance of probability points in the direction of the evangelist being a learned Gentile scholar, even if he has learned his trade in the Jewish-Christian scribal tradition. He points to two sets of examples that in his view reveal a glaring error on the part of Matthew regarding Judaism (Meier 1991: 18–22). The first is his treatment of the Sadducees. Matthew 16.12 links together 'the teaching of the Pharisees and Sadducees' (with one definite article;

contrast Mark 8.14–21). A further example of this is the dispute over the resurrection (22.23; cf. Mark 12.18; Luke 20.27), where Matthew's change to his Marcan source – from Mark's 'who say there is no resurrection' to 'saying there is no resurrection' – seems to lack awareness that the denial of the resurrection doctrine was a defining feature of the Sadducean party. The second 'mistake' is Matthew's overliteral interpretation of Zechariah in his account of Jesus' entry into Jerusalem, which has Jesus sitting on *two* animals, a donkey and a colt (21.2, 7; cf. Zech. 9.9; Isa. 62.11). For Meier this reveals a failure to understand the Hebrew parallelism of the Zechariah passage, whereby the same idea is stated twice using different words – the 'colt' then is the same animal as the 'donkey', not a different one.

Yet these objections are not quite so conclusive. On the Zechariah passage, as Meier himself admits, even the rabbis could overlook the parallelism to find two animals in the passage (albeit when they used Zechariah to identify two different Messiahs: Meier 1991: 22). Indeed, von Dobschütz regarded Matthew's use of Zechariah 9.9 as evidence in support of his Jewish, rabbinic background (von Dobschütz 1995: 34)! Nor is his treatment of Sadducees necessarily evidence for Gentile 'error'. Matthew 16.12, for example, need not be read as claiming that there was *no* substantial difference in teaching between the two parties but only that they are united in their opposition to Jesus within Matthew's narrative (for an alternative reading of 16.12 and 21.2, see Davies and Allison 1988–97: 1/32).

Nor, as we have seen in relation to the *intra/extra muros* debate, is the evidence adduced by Clark only explicable in terms of an evangelist who comes from outside the Jewish tradition. Indeed, redaction critics – generally presupposing Marcan priority – point to many of the 'Jewish' elements in Matthew coming in places where the evangelist is redacting his Marcan source rather than simply preserving inherited tradition (e.g. the polemic against Pharisees). The removal of Aramaic words (which is not in fact consistently applied across the Gospel: e.g. 6.24; 12.24; 23.8; 26.14, 36; 27.33) is evidence only that the intended audience are Greek-speakers, not that they are non-Jews; while the hints at a mission to Gentiles need not imply a rejection of Israel. Moreover Matthew contains ambiguous or even negative statements about Gentiles as well as more positive ones. When praying, disciples are not to 'heap up empty phrases as the Gentiles do' (6.7). The Twelve are explicitly told not to go in the way of the Gentiles when embarking on their mission (10.5). Rebellious believers expelled from the Church are to be treated 'as a Gentile and a tax-collector' (18.17). The disciples can expect to 'be hated by all nations [*or* Gentiles]' for the sake of Christ's name (24.9). Such stereotypical language arguably reflects a Jewish perspective on the non-Jewish world, in which the Gentile is 'the other' (see e.g. Sim 1995; Senior 1999). Moreover, as already noted, the sociological approach of Overman and Saldarini makes good sense of the anti-Pharisaic language as a reflection of heated intra-Jewish polemics.

Matthew's Roman World

Yet even if Matthew's Gospel is the work of a Christian Jew or Jewish Christian, addressing specific audiences from the same heritage, that is not all there is to be said. Significant illumination of Matthew's Gospel has certainly been achieved by reading Matthew in the light of contemporary Jewish texts and contemporary Jewish debates over Torah interpretation. However, there are limitations to concentrating solely on the Jewish world. In recent decades there has been renewed emphasis on the fact – recognized by many nineteenth-century scholars with their training in both classics and biblical studies – that ancient authors inhabited several overlapping worlds simultaneously. Thus a Jewish Matthew, writing in Greek, was already exposed to a significant degree to Greek culture, rhetoric and philosophical traditions. Moreover for good or for ill, Hellenized Jews of the first century lived in the Roman world.

Attention to the wider Roman context can provide an additional nuance to vocabulary regarded by many modern readers as purely 'religious' language. The term 'gospel' or 'good news' (Greek *euangelion*, e.g. 4.23; 24.14), for example, has strong political connotations – or better, religio-political connotations – when read alongside imperial inscriptions. The term was often used of imperial proclamations of 'good news'. The famous Priene Inscription, a Greek text extolling the virtues of the 'saviour' Emperor Augustus, declares that his birthday has heralded the beginning of 'good news' or 'gospels' for the whole world. A similar politically destabilizing message might be conveyed by the thoroughly Jewish proclamation of the 'kingdom [*or* reign] of the heavens' (e.g. 3.2; 4.17; 5.3). What first John the Baptist and then Jesus proclaim is a superior reign (Greek *basileia*) to the universal *basileia* claimed by the Roman Empire. Moreover it is God or Jesus who is true emperor or king (Jerusalem is the 'city of the great King', 5.35; Jesus is crucified as 'King of the Jews', 27.37), not the pretender enthroned in Rome. Even the religious-sounding term 'church'

(Greek *ekklēsia*, 'assembly' or 'gathering'), used by Matthew alone among the evangelists (16.18; 18.17), has political connotations in the Greek and Roman world.

Similarly, attention to the Roman context offers a different register for hearing the Gospel's Son of God language (e.g. 2.15; 3.17; 4.3; 16.16). Prioritizing the Jewish background will invite comparisons between Jesus as Son of God and Jewish claims for the king, for Israel or for a righteous or pious Israelite (e.g. Verseput 1987: 537–8). The wider imperial milieu suggests a subversive challenge to acclamations of the emperor as Son of God. As Robert Mowery has shown, Matthew uses the Greek form *theou huios* for 'son of God' (14.33; 27.43, 54, as opposed to the normal order *huios theou*), which exactly parallels the use of the term for first-century Roman emperors from Augustus to Domitian (Mowery 2002).

References to political and religious leaders throughout Matthew also alert the reader to the web of imperial influence in the world the Gospel describes, and its potential to critique the Empire's world view with its alternative vision, albeit one also framed in 'imperial' terms (see e.g. Carter 2000; Riches and Sim [eds] 2005). Some of these leaders are directly connected to Roman power: Herodian rulers such as Herod the Great (2.1–19), Archelaus (2.22), Herod Antipas (14.1–12) and Herod Philip (14.3; also alluded to in the place name Caesarea Philippi at 16.13); the various centurions encountered by Jesus (8.5–13; 27.54); the governor Pontius Pilate (27.11–26). Others are more indirect participants in Roman imperial authority: tax-collectors such as Matthew (9.9); the chief priests and elders, especially the high priest Caiaphas (e.g. 26.57–68), who exercised authority in the Jerusalem Temple by Roman consent. A further dimension of the imperial context has been proposed by postcolonial critics (see Segovia 2009). One insight of postcolonialism is that colonized groups often express their frustration with imperial rule through antagonism towards or rivalry between each other. This may shed further light on the complex tensions inscribed in Matthew's Gospel between followers of Jesus and 'the scribes and the Pharisees'.

Locating Matthew Geographically

Is it possible to be precise about the location of the evangelist and the provenance of his Gospel? According to the Preface to Jerome's commentary, Matthew's Gospel was published in Judea (Jerome 2008: 53). The reliability of Jerome's testimony is unclear. Given that he combines it with a reference to Matthew writing 'in the Hebrew language', he may have deduced it from Papias' comments about Hebrew or Aramaic Matthew. Nevertheless, the view that the Gospel was composed in the Holy Land became fairly standard. The *Opus imperfectum* claims that Matthew wrote after a persecution in Palestine (Kellerman 2010: 1/1), while Jerome's view is perpetuated throughout the Middle Ages via the *Glossa ordinaria* on Matthew.

A Palestinian provenance for the Gospel is less frequently posited in modern scholarship. There were a number of prominent Jewish-Christian communities in the early decades, for example at Caesarea Maritima, Capernaum and possibly Sepphoris. Moreover both Sepphoris and Tiberias were Galilean cities influenced by Greek culture, and with mixed Jewish–Gentile populations. Galilee was also a centre for the emerging rabbinic movement. Caesarea Maritima on Palestine's Mediterranean coast has been suggested by Benedict Viviano (Viviano 1979; though note his more cautious approach in Viviano 2007: 23). Caesarea was geographically close to Jamnia, with some historic connections to Peter (Acts 10), and a city that would become a centre of Christian learning. Others have suggested territory bordering Palestine, such as Transjordan (Slingerland 1979) and Phoenicia (Kilpatrick 1946). Back in 1957, F. C. Grant made a bid for northern Palestine, or just over the border into Syria, rather than Judea in the south (Grant 1957: 140). His main reason was the apocalyptic feel of Matthew and its similarities to *1 Enoch* (which refers to Abilene and the 'waters of Dan' and has Enoch travel south to the Holy Land).

A Syrian location has proved very popular among Matthean scholars for a number of reasons. First, several phrases unique to Matthew reflect a Syrian perspective: an explicit reference to 'all Syria' at 4.24; the description of Jesus as a 'Nazarene' at 2.23 (Syrian Christians called themselves Nazarenes); Matthew's description of the Gentile woman at 15.22 as a 'Canaanite' rather than a 'Syro-Phoenician' (Chananaia being a self-designation of the local Phoenician population). Second, Matthew's Gospel is known to Ignatius of Antioch, and there are also strong parallels with the *Didache*, believed to be a Syrian document (Luz 1989: 90–3).

Many scholars have followed B. H. Streeter's proposal of Antioch-on-the-Orontes as the setting for Matthew (Streeter 1927: 500–23; see also Sim 1998: 40–62). Streeter argued that the widespread acceptance of this Gospel by the early Church implies support by a major church in a prominent urban setting. Indeed Matthew's preference for the term 'city' (26 times in Matthew; 8 times in Mark) over 'village' (3 times in Matthew;

7 times in Mark) supports this view. Syrian Antioch suggested itself as a prime candidate, particularly given knowledge of Matthew by its bishop Ignatius. It would explain the prominence given by Matthew to the apostle Simon Peter (e.g. 14.28–33; 16.16–19), since Antiochene tradition claimed Peter as its first bishop. Antioch, as a Greek city with a significant Jewish community (see Josephus, *Ag. Apion* 2.39; *Ant.* 12.119–24; *War* 7.44–53), offered a suitable 'atmosphere' for the production of a Gospel that was profoundly Jewish, even to the extent of adopting a conservative attitude to Jewish dietary laws (Gal. 2.11–14), yet open to a Gentile mission (Acts 11.19–26). More specifically, the distinctly Matthean story of the temple tax (17.24–27) equates a 'stater' with two double-drachmas. Streeter claimed that this was only the case in Antioch and Damascus (though this claim has been challenged: e.g. Luz 1989: 91).

Antioch remains a plausible candidate. Luz's assessment is that 'Antioch is not the worst of the hypotheses' (Luz 1989: 92). However, it was not the only Syrian city where Greek was spoken and that had a thriving Jewish community. Other candidates included Damascus and Edessa (Harrington 1991: 9). Any of these fit the evidence for the 'implied readers', which Kingsbury takes as a useful index or starting point for defining the 'intended readers' of Matthew's book: followers of Jesus living in the time of the 'messianic woes' (24.8) after the destruction of Jerusalem (22.7; cf. 21.41); Greek speakers and therefore probably urban; of both Jewish and Gentile background (Kingsbury 1988: 147–60). But Benedict Viviano makes the pertinent point that the closer we locate Matthew to debates with the rabbinic developments of Jamnia, the more likely it is that the Gospel derives from northern Palestine (e.g. Caesarea Maritima, Sepphoris, Tiberias) or southern Syria (e.g. Tyre, Sidon, Damascus) rather than Antioch in northern Syria (Viviano 2007: 4).

In fact precise identification of Matthew's location adds little to the overall interpretation of the Gospel. Perhaps more important is to posit an appropriate imaginative setting. One such setting – albeit on a smaller scale – is provided by the excavated site of Capernaum on the northern shore of the Sea of Galilee. According to Matthew this became the focus of Jesus' Galilean ministry following his departure from Nazareth (4.13; 8.5; 11.23; 17.24). Visitors to the site are shown what is believed to be the remains of Simon Peter's house, now covered by a modern church. This complex of buildings was certainly used as a place of Christian worship from the fifth century and probably earlier. Most significantly, the site of Peter's house is located literally a stone's throw from a fourth- or fifth-century synagogue, perhaps constructed over the synagogue of the first century. The site at Capernaum enables the visitor to imagine Christians of Jewish origin and synagogue-frequenting Jews living and praying side by side and cheek by jowl for several centuries. If Capernaum is too small an environment to have produced the urban Gospel according to Matthew, it nonetheless serves a useful function in exemplifying the kind of ambiance that Gospel presupposes.

6

Beginnings: The Infancy Narratives

The Popularity of the Infancy Narratives

Unlike Mark and John, the Gospels according to Matthew and Luke describe events leading up to and surrounding the birth of Jesus (Matt. 1—2; Luke 1—2). Often referred to as 'infancy narratives' (though the appropriateness of this term for Matthew is sometimes disputed), these stories have had a particular impact on the Christian imagination. Matthew's version begins with a genealogy of Jesus (or rather of Joseph, the husband of Mary: 1.2–17) and an annunciation to Joseph of Jesus' birth by an angelic visitor (1.18–25). Skirting over the actual birth (referred to in passing at 1.25; 2.1), the narrative continues with the story of a miraculous star heralding Christ's coming, in which King Herod the Great (c.74–4 BCE) and a group of Eastern magi are the key players (2.1–12), culminating in the slaughter of the innocents (2.16–18) and the flight of the holy family into and their return from Egypt (2.13–15, 19–23).

The adoration of the baby Jesus by the magi, variously interpreted as kings and wise men, has proved a favourite subject for artists (e.g. Giotto, Botticelli and Rembrandt), many of whom have detected in the story subtle anticipations of the end of the Gospel, whether the passion and death of Jesus, reflected in the gift of myrrh (2.11, a spice regularly used for burial) and Herod's murderous intent (2.16), or the Great Commission to 'make disciples of all the nations' (28.19, signified by the probable Gentile origin of the magi). The connection between the birth and the death is a very ancient insight, picked up again in recent decades by narrative critics (e.g. Heil 1991). Already in the second-century *Protevangelium of James* the nativity takes place in a cave, foreshadowing Christ's tomb (*Prot. Jas.* 18.1).

The flight into Egypt has also been visualized by both Eastern and Western artists, creatively filling in the gaps left by Matthew's brief account (e.g. Giotto, Rubens and Titian). In some versions an older child identified as St James is part of the holy family (reflecting the Eastern Orthodox tradition that the 'brothers of the Lord' were children of Joseph from an earlier marriage). Christian devotion to St Joseph (e.g. Doze 1991) owes much to Matthew's portrayal of this otherwise shadowy figure who has

76

disappeared by the time Jesus begins his public ministry. The innocent children slaughtered by Herod have their own feast day and associated legends, in which Matthew's account of their deaths is sometimes read as the story of the first Christian martyrs. Finally, Matthew's genealogical interest (1.2–17), locating Jesus the Messiah within a royal family tree containing both heroes and rogues, can still be seen reflected in medieval stained glass in European cathedrals such as Chartres. These so-called 'Jesse windows', tracing Christ's ancestry back to King David and his father Jesse (1 Sam. 16), present his genealogy as a real tree, with Christ at its pinnacle (exploiting the reference to the messianic 'shoot from the stump of Jesse' at Isa. 11.1).

Genre and Relationship to Luke 1—2

But what kind of stories are these? Although attempts are sometimes made to present them as fairly straightforward historical accounts, the significant differences from Luke's Gospel (which has an incompatible genealogy, shepherds rather than magi and no account of the massacre of children or the flight into Egypt), the silence of other New Testament writings, features such as angelic appearances and dreams, and strong echoes of Old Testament narratives suggest otherwise. Michael Goulder famously described these stories as 'midrash', a Jewish term that refers to creative exegesis of Scripture (Goulder 1974: 459; see also Grant 1957: 146). This is now regarded as something of an overstatement, not least because Matthew often seems to be starting with the story of Jesus and reinterpreting the Old Testament in its light, rather than trying to explicate what prophets such as Micah, Hosea or Jeremiah meant to say (e.g. 2.6, 15, 18). As Daniel Harrington puts it: 'If someone wished to create incidents out of biblical quotations, it was possible to have done a better job' (Harrington 1991: 47; see also France 1981: 236). Indeed it is quite likely that Matthew had some sources to hand, as did Luke, rather than – *pace* Goulder – creating his 'infancy narratives' imaginatively out of the Greek Bible. A better description for Matthew's technique might be 'creative historiography', like the rewriting of biblical history in 1 and 2 Chronicles or Josephus' *Antiquities of the Jews*, which combined traditional material with a certain level of imaginative creativity to convey a theological message (Robinson 2009).

In the case of Matthew, the theological message is particularly focused on Christology: who is this Jesus, and where has he come from? In a famous article first published in 1960 (Stendahl 1995), Krister Stendahl summarized the purpose of Matthew's first two chapters as establishing who Jesus was (*Quis?* or 'Who?' in chapter 1, setting out Jesus' human and divine pedigree as son of David and Abraham, and as son of God) and where he has come from (*Unde?* or 'Whence?' in chapter 2, dominated as it is by place names). Thus Matthew 2 explains how Jesus comes from Bethlehem, the expected birthplace of a Son of David, to Nazareth. Stendahl's analysis was further refined by Raymond Brown into four questions: *Quis, Quomodo, Ubi* and *Unde* (Who? How? Where? Whence? Brown 1993: 53–4). The 'how' is explained in terms of Joseph's legal adoption of Jesus; the 'where' (Bethlehem) is distinguished from the 'whence' (from Bethlehem to Egypt, then from Egypt back into the promised land to Nazareth in 'Galilee of the Gentiles') in order to establish his identity further as the royal Messiah, the Son of David. In other words, identity and origins, and foreshadowing of what is to come (reflected in the anticipations of Jesus' passion and death), are the dominant concerns of these chapters rather than strict history.

A second question concerns whether the term 'infancy narrative' is an appropriate one for Matthew 1—2. This designation presupposes that these chapters are performing the same function as Luke 1—2. Yet the subject matter of Matthew's opening section – which in any case continues into the following chapters with the preaching of John the Baptist 'in those days', 3.1, and the baptism and temptation of Jesus, 3.13—4.11 – suggests otherwise. Unlike Luke, who tells not only of Jesus' birth but also his annunciation, circumcision, presentation in the Temple and rather precocious behaviour there as a 12-year-old (part of a trajectory that blossomed in the miraculous exploits of the child Jesus in the apocryphal *Infancy Gospel of Thomas*), Matthew has little to say of his infancy apart from his flight into Egypt.

Nor is this strictly a 'birth narrative', given that Jesus' actual birth is mentioned only briefly. Some Bibles entitle the section 1.18–25 as 'the birth of Jesus', although the translation 'birth' at 1.18 depends on what is probably a secondary reading *gennēsis* ('birth'), whereas most Greek manuscripts read *genesis* (which can mean 'origin', 'genealogy' or 'generation' as well as 'birth', cf. 1.1). In fact the theme of this passage is not Jesus' birth but the virginal conception of Jesus (at least on the normal interpretation of 'from [the] Holy Spirit' at 1.18: though see Schaberg 1987). Thus it serves to resolve the problem that Joseph's genealogy (1.2–17) is not strictly Jesus' bloodline by having Joseph legally adopt Jesus into his royal lineage. The actual birth and naming of Jesus is not referred to until verse 25. The only other birth reference is a passing one at 2.1: 'Now when Jesus was born in Bethlehem of Judea in the days of King Herod'. Rather, Matthew's focus is on surrounding events and characters that reveal Jesus' role: Herod, the magi, the slaughtered infants of Bethlehem. Therefore a preferable title for Matthew 1—2 (or the wider pre-ministry narrative of 1.1—4.11) might be 'narrative of origins', as suggested by the phrase 'account of the genealogy [or 'origin', *genesis*] of Jesus Christ' (1.1, recalling Gen. 5.1 LXX).

Finally, what is the relationship between the Matthean and Lucan accounts? The differences between them, including some significant discrepancies (e.g. the different names in their respective genealogies between David and Joseph; the statement at 2.23 that the holy family only settled in Nazareth after the birth of Jesus, contradicting Luke 1.26 and 2.4), are often appealed to in support of the Two Source Theory, which presupposes that Matthew and Luke write independently. Others, however, impressed by the many similarities between the two, argue in favour of a literary relationship between the two Gospels. Both, for example, provide a genealogy of Jesus' ancestors that includes Abraham and David, despite their differences. Both preface the birth of Jesus with an angelic annunciation story – to Joseph in Matthew, to Mary in Luke. Both locate the birth of Jesus in Bethlehem rather than Nazareth, despite Jesus being known as 'Jesus of Nazareth'. Both conclude with the holy family in Nazareth, although for Matthew this is not a return home as for Luke. Indeed the fact that these two Gospels – and only these two – choose to relate events leading up to and following Jesus' birth is regarded as highly significant. Those who posit such a view accept that Luke was not content with how Matthew went about his task, even as he accepted his basic presupposition that the gospel story demanded a 'prequel' (e.g. Franklin 1994: 353–66).

The Genealogy of the Son of David

Matthew begins his book with a genealogy (1.2–17). It serves to present Jesus as both 'son of David', a title of the royal Messiah (e.g. *Ps. Sol.* 17.21), and 'son of Abraham' (1.1). The latter has often been understood to present Jesus as the archetypal Jew, since the patriarch Abraham stood at the head of the people of Israel. However, some commentators have seen further claims implicit in the 'son of Abraham' title: whether to anticipate the inclusion of Gentiles with which Matthew's Gospel will end (28.19; cf. Gen. 17.5; 22.18) or Jesus' own sacrificial death through recalling the sacrifice of Abraham's own son Isaac (Gen. 22.1–14: Huizenga 2008).

Although readers might be tempted to skip over what appears to be a rather dull list of names, its prominent position in the text suggests that it plays an important role for the evangelist. Indeed, closer study reveals some interesting surprises. As noted above, Luke also provides a family tree for Jesus (after his account of Jesus' baptism and temptation at Luke 3.23–38), which cannot be easily reconciled with Matthew's version. Discrepancies between Matthew and Luke were a matter of considerable debate for patristic authors, who tended to resolve the difficulties in one of two ways. The first explanation appealed to the biblical concept of 'levirate marriage' whereby the brother of a married man dying without descendants was required to father a child in his stead (Deut. 25.5: e.g. Jerome 2008: 61; Simonetti [ed.] 2001: 4–5). The second attributed Luke's different genealogy to Mary, reflecting the patristic belief that Mary was also from the Davidic line (Bockmuehl 2011). Neither of these solutions is without its difficulties, nor is the alternative ingenious explanation of Luke's version found in Eusebius' *Quaestiones* 'On the Differences of the Gospels' (see Miller 2009).

Comparison with Luke highlights Matthew's neatness and fondness for triads. His genealogy is divided into three sets of 'fourteen generations'. The significance of these numbers is underscored by the artificiality of the division, for the third set actually comprises only 13 generations (Jesus included), unless Jechoniah is counted twice, once at the end of the second set and again at the beginning of the third (a point noted by ancient critics of Christianity like Porphyry: Bockmuehl 2011: 479). This suggests a specific purpose in Matthew's insistence that there are three sets of 14.

The significance of the threefold division seems clear enough. It organizes the genealogy around the highpoints and lowpoints of salvation history. It begins with Abraham, the father of the chosen people, whose story includes the unlikely promise of a son despite his great age. The first 14 generations culminate in the fulfilment of that promise in the glorious reign of King David. The second set moves from David's reign to the tragic deportation to Babylon, which brought an end to the Davidic dynasty in the southern kingdom of Judah. The third set of generations takes the reader from the depths of the exile to the restoration of David's reign with the coming of a kingly Messiah, the Son of David.

Less certain is the significance of the number 14. A plausible explanation is that it is David's number in the Hebrew alphabet (d + w + d = 4 + 6 + 4 = 14). Thus the genealogy of 'the Son of David' is shot through with David's own number. However, given that our Matthew seems to have been composed in Greek rather than a Hebrew translation, not all have found this convincing (e.g. Harrington 1991: 30). A number of commentators, both ancient and modern, note that three sets of 14 comprises six sets of seven, relating the genealogy in different ways to Jewish and Christian divisions of history between creation and the end into distinctive epochs (e.g. Simonetti [ed.] 2001: 11; Viviano 2009). One ingenious proposal picks up on the fact that Jesus the 'son of David' is also 'son of Abraham', and notes the parallels between Matthew's genealogy (where Jesus stands at the beginning of a fourth cycle of 14 generations, i.e. the forty-second generation following Abraham) and the *Book of Jubilees*, which dates the sacrifice of Isaac to the beginning of the forty-second jubilee after creation (Rosenberg 1965: 387; cf. *Jub.* 13.16; 17.15; 19.1). This Jesus–Isaac typology would then be underscored by the close verbal similarities between the angel's words in the annunciation to Joseph (1.20–21) and the announcement of the birth of Isaac to Sarah (Gen. 17.19 LXX).

Women in the Genealogy

A further puzzling feature of Matthew's genealogy is the reference to a small number of mothers alongside the fathers. Instead of the expected figures of Sarah, Rebekah and Rachel, Matthew lists Tamar (1.3; cf. Gen. 38), Rahab (1.5, probably the prostitute of Jericho: Josh. 2), Ruth (1.5) and 'the wife of Uriah' (1.6, i.e. Bathsheba, with whom King David committed adultery: 2 Sam. 11—12). Commentators struggle to find a common connection between these four, which might also link to the fifth woman mentioned, Mary the mother of Jesus (1.16). Two main explanations have proved popular across the centuries.

The first explanation treats them as non-Jews. The ninth-century Syriac commentator Isho'dad of Merv puts it thus:

> But again, because the Apostles were commanded to go forth and preach to all nations, they wished to teach us by the mention of these women, that even the Gentiles had partnership in the descent of the tribe from which the Messiah arose, and that if they repent, there is nothing to prevent them from the full remission of sins, that they may also become the Israel of God.
>
> (Gibson [ed.] 1911: 8)

Yet while the Gentile explanation chimes in with a recurring motif in Matthew's Gospel (e.g. 2.1; 8.10; 12.21; 28.19), it is clearer for some of the women than others. Rahab was from the Canaanite city of Jericho

(Josh. 2.1). Ruth was a Moabite (Ruth 1.4). The Bible is silent about Tamar's origins, although the wider literary context might suggest she was a Canaanite (Gen. 38.2). The second-century BCE *Book of Jubilees* identifies her as a non-Israelite, a 'daughter of Aram' (*Jub.* 41.4; cf. *T. Jud.* 10.1–2). Bathsheba, however, was almost certainly an Israelite. The Gentile interpretation therefore hangs on Matthew's – admittedly odd – description of her as 'the wife of Uriah', who was a Hittite (2 Sam. 12.9). To identify these four women as Gentiles, however, fails to explain any link with Mary.

A second solution is to connect these women with sexual scandal. Some commentators regard all these women as morally dubious. Thus Rahab was a prostitute (Josh. 2.1). Tamar bore children by her father-in-law Judah, who mistook her for a prostitute (Gen. 38.15). Bathsheba committed adultery with King David (2 Sam. 11). The case of Ruth is less clear: some interpreters read Ruth 3 as alluding euphemistically to seduction and fornication (see especially vv. 6–9, 14). It is a reading followed by Jerome, from which he draws a lesson about salvation:

> In the Savior's genealogy it is remarkable that there is no mention of holy women, but only those whom Scripture reprehends, so that [we can understand that] he who had come for the sake of sinners, since he was born from sinful women, blots out the sins of everyone.   (Jerome 2008: 59–60)

But such an interpretation may betray the androcentric presuppositions of commentators who promote it as much as the androcentrism of Matthew's text (what, for example, of the culpability of David in the story of Bathsheba?). A more subtle solution might be to regard them as *accused* of sexual indiscretion, and therefore relating them to Mary, suspected – wrongly in Matthew's view – of adultery due to her virginal conception (1.18, 20). This may be part of a solution. A variation on this is to emphasize the degree of irregularity in their relationships, which means that irregularity in succession is an integral part of the royal Judaic and Davidic line (Smit 2010: 205–6). Others attempt to combine both Gentile and sexual irregularity explanations by setting them in a wider context. Thus Amy-Jill Levine highlights the dominant motif of overcoming exclusion: 'the women represent people oppressed by dominant political, religious, and social systems' (Levine 1988: 62). However, one should not downplay the fact that at least three of these women were remembered as heroines in Jewish tradition. Rahab came to be portrayed as a model of faith (e.g. Heb. 11.31; *1 Clem.* 12.1) given her role in the Israelites' victory over her fellow Canaanites. Tamar was a model for proselytes since the royal tribe of Judah was perpetuated through her. The rabbis often overlooked Bathsheba's adultery because she became the mother of Solomon. The story of Ruth presented her both as Gentile great-grandmother of King David (Ruth 4.17–22) and as a model convert to Judaism (Ruth 1.16–17).

Furthermore overconcentration on the women can distract attention from other aspects of Matthew's genealogy. Equally notable are those additional explanatory comments that break the rhythmic pattern ('X was the father of Y'). John Nolland has attempted to broaden the discussion by noting that there are other annotations to Matthew's genealogy besides those referring to the mothers. As well as the addition of the women (e.g. 'by Tamar'), these include references to 'Judah and his brothers' (v. 2, highlighting the generation of the 12 patriarchs that went down to Egypt), an explicit statement that David was 'the king' (v. 6a), a division around the deportation to Babylon ('Jechoniah and his brothers': v. 11) and the extended reference to 'Mary, of whom Jesus was born, who is called the Messiah' (v. 16). Taken together these evoke 'the glories and tragedies of that story in which the purposes of God unfold' (Nolland 1997: 530). At least three of the women – Tamar, Rahab and Ruth – fit into this pattern as women from outside God's people who 'have come for refuge under the wings of the God of Israel' (Nolland 1997: 538). In addition Rahab recalls the entry into Canaan (a moment in Israel's story not otherwise mentioned in the genealogy), while 'the wife of Uriah' recalls the tragedy of David's sin.

Joseph and Mary

Central to Matthew's 'narrative of origins' beyond the genealogy itself, are the two characters of Joseph and the Virgin Mary. Yet they are characterized in very different ways. In contrast to Luke, who highlights the role of Mary, Matthew has Joseph as the key player, appearing on stage throughout the narrative of 1.18—2.23 and taking the active role. It is to Joseph, not Mary, that the annunciation of the birth of Jesus happens (1.18–25; cf. Luke 1.26–38). Joseph obeys the command of the angel of the Lord and takes Mary as his wife (1.24). He gives Jesus his name (1.25), which modern commentators – though not ancient ones – interpret as an act of legal adoption guaranteeing Jesus' Davidic ancestry. He takes Mary and the child Jesus down to Egypt and brings them up again (2.14, 21); on their return it is he who makes a home in Nazareth of Galilee (2.23). Traditional interpretation explained the differences between Matthew's and Luke's respective infancy narratives by attributing the first to Joseph's reminiscences and the second to Mary's perspective. As Raymond Brown famously noted, however, this presupposes that Mary and Joseph never spoke to one another (Brown 1993: 35)!

Two further features of Joseph's portrayal are worthy of note. The first is that he is the recipient of revelation through dreams. Dreams and the interpretation of dreams play a key role in the story of the Old Testament patriarch Joseph (Gen. 37.5–11), a possible model for Matthew's depiction of the New Testament Joseph (though see also Argyle 1956; van Aarde 2000). Through the book of Daniel (e.g. Dan. 7.1), revelation by dream also becomes an important dimension of the Jewish apocalyptic tradition. The parallels between Matthew's Gospel and Jewish apocalypses – for example interest in angels, discussion of the 'throne of glory', emphasis on the eschatological judgement and the heightened role of the heavenly Son of Man – have often been noted (e.g. Sim 1996; Rowland 2008). This interest in dreams as a vehicle of divine revelation, also found in the stories of the magi and Pilate's wife (2.12; 27.19), is a further example. The particular privilege accorded to Joseph is underscored by the fact that he alone encounters an angel of the Lord in his dreams, ruling out any ambiguity as to their heavenly origin.

Second, Joseph receives an ideal characterization as 'righteous' or 'just' (*dikaios*, 1.19). Given Matthew's interest in 'righteousness' (*dikaiosunē*, 3.15; 5.6, 10, 20; 6.1, 33; 21.32), the implied reader is to applaud Joseph's good intentions when he learns of Mary's pregnancy, and his wider role in the narrative. 'Righteousness' exceeding that of the scribes and Pharisees is demanded by Jesus of his disciples (5.20). Later in Matthew, Jesus too will be acknowledged as 'righteous' or 'innocent' by three characters in the passion narrative: Judas Iscariot, Pontius Pilate and Pilate's wife (27.4, 19, 24).

In contrast to Joseph's lead role, Mary is hardly an active participant in the drama, although she is mentioned almost as often in 1.18—2.23. Almost all the verbs describe actions done to her rather than by her. She has been engaged or betrothed to Joseph (1.18), probably from an early age. Joseph plans to dismiss or release her after discovering that she is pregnant (1.19). As a result of the angelic dream he instead 'took' her as his wife (1.25). When the magi arrive at the house in Bethlehem she and the child are the object of their sight (2.11). Following the departure of the magi she is again taken by Joseph (2.14, 21). The one exception to this passivity is that she gives birth to Jesus (1.25), but even here she is defined in terms of the female role of childbearing. Nor do the two additional references to Mary in Matthew's story (12.46–50; 13.55) significantly affect matters. In the first she remains a figure outside the house while the action takes place inside; in the second she is merely mentioned by name by her fellow townsfolk. The world described by Matthew is predominantly a man's world or at least one viewed from a male's perspective (in contrast to Mary's activity in Luke: e.g. Luke 1.29, 39, 46–55; 2.19). Feminist critics, applying a hermeneutic of suspicion to this narrative, would see here another example of Matthew's pervasive 'androcentricity' already reflected in the genealogy (Anderson 1983).

The Magi and the Star

The drama of Matthew's 'narrative of origins' is particularly powerful in the story of the magi and the star. Old Testament narratives and early Christian imagination seem to come together in this multilayered story that has profoundly influenced Christian culture. Many scholars (e.g. Brown 1993: 193–6) hear echoes of the biblical story of Balaam, the pagan prophet who uttered a blessing on Israel, prophesied that 'a star shall come forth out of Jacob' (Num. 24.17, interpreted by some first-century Jews as a prophecy of the Messiah) and was described by Philo of Alexandria as a *magos* or magician (Philo, *Life of Moses* 1.276). The connection between Balaam's prophecy and the star seen by the magi was made as early as Jerome (Jerome 2008: 64). Others look to parallels from the classical world for stars heralding the births of great leaders like Alexander the Great and the Emperor Augustus, or guiding heroes to their destination (Virgil describes how Aeneas was led by a star to the location of the founding of Rome: *Aeneid* 2.694). Countless attempts have been made to identify the star of Bethlehem astronomically (whether as a comet, planetary conjunction or supernova), while patristic discussion is open to the interpretation of the star as an angelic being (e.g. Allison 2005: 17–41), and at least one apocryphal text, the *Revelation of the Magi*, claims that it was a manifestation of Christ himself in celestial form (Landau 2008).

The original magi were the priestly caste of Persia (Herodotus, *Hist.* 1.101.132), famed as astrologers and interpreters of dreams although the word came to be used to describe 'magicians' or 'sorcerers' in general (e.g. Acts 8.9; 13.6, 8). Their Persian origin is reflected in the dress of the magi on the fifth-century door panels of Santa Sabina in Rome. In Matthew's story they are certainly from the east and bear gifts that suggest their non-Jewish origin (2.11). According to Isaiah 60.6, the Gentiles will bring gold and frankincense when they come to Jerusalem in the last days (*pace* Mann 1958, who claims that the magi were Babylonian Jews). That they follow a star points to their astrological interests.

These negative connotations of the magi (e.g. Philo, *Life of Moses* 1.92; Dan. 2.2, 10 LXX) are reflected in the earliest Christian commentary on Matthew. Ignatius of Antioch writes that it was by the star of Bethlehem that 'all magic was dissolved and every bond of wickedness vanished away' (*Eph.* 19.3; Lake 1925: 1/193), while Justin Martyr interprets the magi as turning from superstition to the adoration of the one true God (*Dial.* 78.9). There is irony, then, in that stargazing pagan magicians worship the true king of the Jews, while Herod, the upstart 'king of the Jews', and the Jewish leadership seek to have him destroyed. In the light of this, Mark Allan Powell has made a plausible case that the implied reader of Matthew could be expected to identify the magi as ignorant and foolish stargazers rather than the wise men of later tradition (what they do *not* know is more important than what they do know). But in the light of 11.25 it is to them, rather than to the wise and intelligent like King Herod and the Jewish scribes, that God reveals the Christ (Powell 2000b).

But this does not necessarily mean that later developments of the magi story are thereby illegitimate (see Brown 1999: 86–92). The number of their gifts gradually led them to be viewed as a group of three, and they were transformed into three kings, even acquiring names (the commonest are Melchior, Caspar and Balthazar), ethnic backgrounds (Persian, Indian and Arabian respectively) and ages (Melchior is traditionally an old man and Caspar a youth), with a shrine in Cologne to house their relics. This identification of the magi as kings can be traced to Tertullian (*Adversus Iudaeos* 9), although it became increasingly important in the post-Constantinian period in providing legitimation for Christian rulers (see Powell 2000a). However, possible intertextual allusions in Matthew's story mean that this reading cannot be dismissed out of hand, even if his original concern was to present the victory of the gospel over pagan magic and stargazing (e.g. Isa. 60.3, 6: 'Nations shall come to your light, and kings to the brightness of your dawn . . . They shall bring gold and frankincense, and shall proclaim the praise of the LORD'; Ps. 72.10–11: 'May the kings of Tarshish and of the isles render him tribute, may the kings of Sheba and Seba bring gifts. May all kings fall down before him, all nations give him service'). More difficult to sustain is the alternative view that the magi were 'wise men' (a translation that passed into English culture through the Authorized Version), although it is explicable given the 'gap' in the story as to the reasons for their observing the star. This interpretation does not emerge until the Renaissance, where the magi functioned as appropriate patrons for Renaissance philosophers and other scholars (Powell 2000b).

A second important feature of the magi story concerns the interpretation of their gifts: gold, frankincense and myrrh. The text does not give us much to go on, apart from potential echoes of Isaiah 60, which would interpret two of them as the eschatological gifts of the Gentiles. The possibilities are almost as numerous as interpreters. Jerome quotes Juvencus, a fourth-century Spanish Christian poet: 'Gold, myrrh, and frankincense are the gifts they bring, | To a man, to a God, and to a king' (Jerome 2008: 65). The ninth-century Assyrian bishop Isho'dad of Merv links gold to Christ's incorruptible kingdom, myrrh to 'the passion of His humanity' and frankincense to his Godhead and humanity, given that it is a 'mixed substance' (Gibson [ed.] 1911: 20). The *Opus imperfectum* also sees the connection between myrrh and Christ's death, as well as offering an allegorical interpretation of gold, frankincense and myrrh as 'reasonable faith', 'pure reason' and 'good works' respectively (Luz 1989: 138). The interpretation of the myrrh as a bitter-sweet anticipation of the passion of Jesus (found as early as Irenaeus, *Adv. Haer.* 3.9.2, and Origen, *Contra Celsum* 1.60) connects with the artistic tradition, always ready to explore the connections between the magi story and Christ's suffering and death. These links are picked up again in T. S. Eliot's *Journey of the Magi* and in several twentieth-century Jesus films (see Kreitzer 2002: 24–44).

Jesus, Israel and Moses

The Balaam story may well be an important intertext for Matthew's story of the magi – with King Herod playing King Balak to the magi's prophet Balaam (Num. 22—24). But Brown and others have also detected a deeper narrative, bubbling to the surface at strategic points throughout these two chapters: the story of Moses. Parallels between Jesus and Moses are detected, for example, in their birth of Israelite/Jewish parents; their being hidden as babies to protect them from a wicked ruler intent on destroying the male children; their movements to and from Egypt (compare e.g. Matt. 2 and Exod. 1—4). This 'typological' reading – placing Jesus' story in juxtaposition to that of Moses – is a very early way of interpreting Matthew, found already in patristic exegesis (Allison 2005: 122–5).

These Mosaic parallels are strengthened when one considers how Moses' story was embellished by Jews in the New Testament period (e.g. Philo's

Life of Moses; the *Testament of Amran* and especially Josephus' *Antiquities of the Jews*). In his *Antiquities* Josephus recounts how the Egyptian king was told of the destiny of Moses by one of his sacred scribes (*Ant.* 2.205–6; compare 2.4). Later, Moses' father was reassured in a dream that his child would escape from those seeking to destroy him, and deliver the Hebrews from their bondage in Egypt (*Ant.* 2.210–16). This latter dimension of the post-biblical story of Moses closely parallels the dreams of Joseph regarding the destiny of Jesus (1.18–25; 2.13–15, 19–23).

The slaughter of the innocents (2.16–18), echoing the slaughter of the Israelite male children by Pharaoh (Exod. 1.15–22), continues this Mosaic theme. This story has provoked a rich reception in its own right. The innocents are commemorated annually in the Christian calendar with their own feast day (28 December in the Western calendar). But the story is not without its interpretative difficulties. For some commentators Matthew seems worryingly unconcerned about the deaths of the innocents as a means by which God's Son is spared (Luz 1989: 147). Thus subsequent developments of the tradition offer more moral interpretations than the evangelist himself, such as the claim of Leo the Great (*Sermo* 37.4) that the children share in the sufferings of Christ, or the sermon for the Holy Innocents in the *Golden Legend*, which prioritizes the cruelty of Herod, and their martyrdom for Christ's sake. Yet even Matthew's interpretation of this event remains somewhat ambiguous. It may be significant, for example, that the quotation about Rachel weeping for her children (from Jer. 31.15) has a fulfilment formula that lacks a purpose clause introduced by 'in order to' and the words 'by the Lord' (2.17; cf. 1.22; 2.15).

However, Jesus is not simply Moses but one greater than Moses (e.g. 5.21–48). The journey of Jesus – down to Egypt and out of Egypt – is the reverse of that taken by Moses, who flees from Egypt, only then to return in order to liberate the people. A closer fit for many is the story of Israel, who – in the person of Jacob/Israel and his sons, and at the instigation of another dreaming Joseph (Gen. 46) – went down into Egypt and subsequently came out of Egypt at the exodus. Matthew's story therefore presents Jesus 'the Son of God' as the personification of Israel. It is made explicit in a quotation from Hosea, originally referring to God's calling his 'son' Israel out of Egypt at the exodus but now finding deeper fulfilment in the life of God's obedient Son Jesus: 'Out of Egypt have I called my son' (2.15, citing Hos. 11.1). Jesus-as-Israel is embarking on a new exodus, in which he will 'save his people from their sins' (1.21). Indeed the parallel runs into Matthew 3—4, where Jesus, as Israel or the perfect Israelite, passes through the water at his baptism (3.13–17) and then goes Israel-like into the wilderness to be tested (4.1–11).

The Function of Matthew's Infancy Story

Matthew's 'narrative of origins' has provided some of the most fertile material for the ongoing Christian imagination, shaping liturgy, art and poetry. Although scholars continue to debate the balance of tradition and redaction, historical kernel and creative midrash-like storytelling, the primary function of this opening narrative – and its continuation to 4.11 – would appear to be christological. These stories are aimed at ensuring that the reader gets right who Jesus is, in a complex web of citation, allusion and biblical echo. Jesus is the messianic Son of David and the Son of Abraham capable of bringing together Jew and Gentile in one family. He is the Son of God, conceived by a new creative act of God's Spirit, and the one who will save his people from their sins. He wears the clothing of Moses and re-enacts the great events in the story of God's people Israel.

Though more controversial, these stories may also have a secondary purpose as early Christian apologetic, responding to Jewish criticism of Christian-Jewish claims for Jesus. The heavy concentration of direct Old Testament quotations in Matthew 1—2 (five, if one includes the mysterious 'He will be called a Nazorean' at 2.23) may point in this direction. Matthew's opening chapter may be an early attempt to respond to Jewish charges of Jesus' illegitimacy (which occurs much later in rabbinic texts, and is also echoed in the *Acts of Pilate* 2.3 and in Origen, *Contra Cels.* 1.29, 32, 69). Alternatively, the Gospel infancy narratives may themselves be the origin of that charge. It is also possible that the quotation from Micah at 2.6 responds to Jewish questions as to how one known as Jesus of Nazareth could be the Davidic Messiah. That Matthew is aware of other Jewish propaganda against Christian claims is evident in his story of the guard at the tomb, which presents an alternative explanation of why Jesus' tomb was discovered empty (28.11–15).

What does seem clear is that, like the best of trailers for the latest cinematic blockbuster, this 'infancy' narrative prepares the audience for the highlights of the unfolding story. It introduces the key Matthean motif of fulfilment of Scripture. It prepares its readers for the surprising ways in which God acts to bring about his purpose (not least through the surprising additions, and omissions, in the genealogy). In particular, the end is prefigured in the beginning, whether in the violent reaction of Herod, the magi's bitter-sweet gift of myrrh or the naming of the baby Jesus as Emmanuel, 'God-with-us' (1.23), anticipating the promise of the risen Lord that 'I am with you always, to the end of the age' (28.20).

7

Jesus as Teacher: Ethics and Judgement

Jesus the Teacher?

It is one of the many paradoxes of Matthew's Gospel that it combines a strong emphasis on Jesus' teaching with an equally bold statement of the inadequacy of viewing him as a teacher. On the one hand, close comparison with Mark reveals a Matthean emphasis on a tripartite ministry of *teaching*, preaching and healing (e.g. 4.23; 9.35; contrast Mark 1.39, where Jesus went around Galilee preaching and casting out demons). Jesus can speak of himself as the one authentic teacher of his disciples ('But you are not to be called rabbi, for you have one teacher, and you are all students', 23.8), a claim supported by his five great teaching discourses (5.1—7.27; 10.5–42; 13.1–52; 18.1–35; 24.1—25.46). He teaches his disciples that, as disciples, they are not above their teacher (10.24–25). When prior to Jesus' passion the disciples are sent ahead to prepare the Passover, they are to say to the owner of the house, 'The Teacher says, My time is near' (26.18).

On the other hand, the only other characters in the story to utter the word *didaskalos* ('teacher') are those hostile to him (e.g. 9.11; 12.38; 17.24; 22.16, 24, 36) or who have not yet made the leap to authentic following (e.g. 8.19; 19.16). Redaction critics would detect in many of these examples the evangelist's distinctive hand: e.g. the question Mark attributes to the scribes of the Pharisees, 'Why does he eat with tax-collectors and sinners?' (Mark 2.16) is rephrased in Matthew as: 'Why does *your teacher* eat with tax-collectors and sinners?' (9.11, asked by 'the Pharisees'). By contrast, 26.18 notwithstanding, the disciples of Jesus and those favourably disposed to him address him not as 'Teacher' but as 'Lord', *Kurie* (e.g. 8.2, 6, 8; 8.25; 14.28; 17.4; 26.22). The one exception is Judas Iscariot, who calls Jesus 'Rabbi' (26.25, 49). Mark, by contrast, seems to regard 'teacher' as an appropriate designation for Jesus on the part of his disciples (e.g. Mark 4.38; 9.38; 10.35; 13.1). Yet although he regularly tells his readers that Jesus 'taught' (e.g. Mark 1.21–22, 27; 2.13; 4.1–2; 6.2, 6, 34; 8.31; 9.31; 10.1; 11.17–18; 12.35, 38; 14.49), there is a paucity of actual teaching preserved (notable exceptions include Mark 4.3–32; 13.5–37).

The regular punctuation of Matthew's narrative with substantial blocks of teaching (whether or not this constitutes a new Pentateuch) complements this Marcan reserve. Yet interpreters across the centuries have often been sharply divided over the interpretation of Jesus' teaching as preserved in Matthew, especially his Sermon on the Mount. Moreover many modern Western commentators have found this Gospel's strong emphasis upon judgement, and its apparently simplistic division of the world into 'good' and 'bad', 'wise' and 'foolish', especially problematic.

Jesus in the Teaching Discourses

Especially since B. W. Bacon's Pentateuchal interpretation of Matthew (Bacon 1918 and 1930), scholars have identified five major teaching blocks in Matthew (5—7; 10; 13; 18; 24—25). Together they cover major topics of relevance to followers of Jesus: the Sermon on the Mount with its concern for a pattern of living that fulfils rather than abolishes the Law of Moses and the teaching of the prophets (5.1—7.27); advice for missionaries as they are sent to the 'lost sheep of the house of Israel' (10.1–42); a series of parables exploring the nature of the kingdom of the heavens, and how human beings respond to it (13.1–52); a disparate collection of teachings for the life of the community (18.1–35, which Bacon rather optimistically labelled 'Concerning Church Administration'); teaching about the future, especially those events that can be expected to precede the End (24.1—25.46).

The stereotypical conclusion to each of these five discourses underscores their prominence in this Gospel. However, they are not the only blocks of teaching in Matthew (see e.g. 11.7–19; 12.25–45; 19.23—20.16; 21.24—22.14; 23.1–39). Indeed the fact that Bacon's schema fails to account for the woes against the scribes and Pharisees – separated from 24—25 by changes of location at 24.1 and 3 – has prompted alternative theories. Gnilka, for example, argues for six discourses in Matthew, including Matthew 23 (Gnilka 1986: 2/269, 309). Ulrich Luz finds a common thread linking the 'lesser discourses', namely Jesus' conflict with Israel. For Luz they serve to move the story of Jesus on towards its climax. By contrast the five 'big' discourses stand 'outside' the narrative, speaking to the present situation of the readers (Luz 2005b: 22–4).

Nor are all five major discourses consistent with each other. For example, a balanced concentric or ring-shaped structure may be detected in the Sermon on the Mount (5.1–2 = 7.28—8.1a; 5.3–16 = 7.13–27; 5.17–20 = 7.12 ('the Law and the prophets'); 5.21–48 = 6.19—7.11; 6.1–6

= 6.16–18), centred around the Lord's Prayer (6.7–15: Luz 1989: 212; see also Allison 2005: 173–206). On the other hand, the 'parables discourse' of Matthew 13 has rather less coherence, with interruptions (13.10, 36b) and even a change of scene (13.36a). Although these difficulties have implications for identifying the Gospel's structure, they do not detract in any way from the centrality of Jesus' teaching for Matthew's overall vision.

The location of Jesus' teaching – particularly of his programmatic Sermon on the Mount – has often been held significant for understanding his identity. For many commentators the mountain Jesus ascends at 5.1 evokes the ultimate mountain of revelation in the Bible, Mount Sinai, where Moses encountered God and received the Law. Sufficient evidence has been adduced to support a prevalent Moses–Christ typology running throughout the Gospel (see Allison 1993), and the relationship between the Mosaic Law and Jesus' teaching will be a prominent feature of Matthew 5—7 (especially 5.17–48). The Mosaic pattern already detected in the first four chapters continues here in the correct chronological order (slaughter of infants – return of the hero – passage through water – temptation/ testing in the wilderness – mountain of lawgiving: see Farrer 1966: 179–99; Allison 1999: 18).

Yet in such a multilayered, polyvalent text, the mountain motif may not be so easily reducible to one referent (see Chapter 4 above). The *Opus imperfectum* makes an explicit link with Isaiah: 'Get you up to a high mountain, O Zion, herald of good tidings' (Kellerman 2010: 1/83, citing Isa. 40.9). That this is a plausible Old Testament intertext is confirmed by the widespread use of Isaiah elsewhere in Matthew, including a direct quotation from Isaiah 40 (3.3, citing Isa. 40.3). This would then emphasize that the 'gospel' proclaimed by Jesus is a new return from Exile, the theme of this section of Isaiah. Some more recent scholars (e.g. Donaldson 1985) have also found echoes here of Mount Zion, though in its role as God's 'holy mountain' where the messianic King will be installed ('I have set my king on Zion, my holy hill', Ps. 2.6).

But even if the main Old Testament echoes are to the Moses tradition, Jesus should be understood as one 'greater than Moses'. Throughout the Sermon on the Mount, for example, Matthew's Jesus speaks with the authoritative 'I' (e.g. 'But I say to you', 5.22, 28, 32, 34, 39, 44). In the Mosaic parallel in Deuteronomy, by contrast, Moses speaks of God and the divine word in the third person (e.g. 'At that time the LORD said to me', Deut. 10.1; 'When you have come into the land that the LORD your God is giving you as an inheritance to possess', Deut 26.1; 'This very day the LORD your God is commanding you to observe these statutes and ordinances', Deut 26.16). Mosaic typology only takes us so far; the unique relationship between God and his Son invests his teaching with an authority greater than that of Moses.

A further christological dimension to Jesus as Teacher is present in Matthew's use of Jewish traditions about the personified feminine figure of heavenly Wisdom. Not only – in the reading preferred by many textual critics – can 11.19 ('Yet wisdom is vindicated by her deeds') be understood as identifying Matthew's Jesus with personified Wisdom, Jesus' invitation at 11.28–30 ('Come to me, all you that are weary and are carrying heavy burdens, and I will give you rest') is often connected with Wisdom's words (Prov. 9.5; Sir. 24.19; 51.23–27: e.g. Suggs 1970; Deutsch 1990; but against this view see Johnson 1974; Stanton 1992: 366–71). Precisely what is being claimed in connecting Jesus to Wisdom, and how central this Wisdom motif is for Matthew's Christology, are issues that continue to be debated. Some also find here another indication of Matthew's capacity for marginality: heavenly wisdom, normally the preserve of 'the wise', is hidden from them and revealed instead to uneducated and powerless 'infants' (11.25: see Rowland 2008).

The Teaching Discourses and Transparency

Christian readers of Matthew over the centuries, however, have also read Matthew's teaching discourses for the insight they shed on Christian individual and corporate life. Whereas in Mark particular emphasis lies on following Jesus through taking up the cross and embracing suffering, for Matthew following Jesus' way involves close attention to his teaching in the pattern of one's life. The post-resurrection commission of the Church contains at its heart a call to make disciples (i.e. those who learn) in order that they too might be taught to observe all that Jesus commanded his first disciples (i.e. his recorded teaching, 28.16–20). The content of the discourses, then, is of direct interest to the post-Easter community.

Several features of the Gospel serve to underscore – to use Luz's term – the 'transparency' of the discourses not simply to the original audiences of the evangelist's own time but to the Church throughout history. First, Kingsbury's narrative-critical analysis of Matthew highlights the fact that none of Jesus' major discourses are addressed to the religious leaders (Kingsbury 1988: 107; in contrast to some of the 'lesser speeches'). Instead, his teaching is addressed primarily to the disciples (5.1–2; 10.5; 13.10–17, 36–52; 18.1, 21; 24.3), and occasionally also to the crowds (who listen in to the Sermon on the Mount, 7.28–29, and hear at least some of Jesus' parables, although it is unclear exactly how many, 13.2–3, 34). But there are clues that the 'disciples' signify more than their historical referents. From his narrative-critical perspective, Kingsbury claims that Matthew's Jesus speaks 'past his story-audience' of crowds and disciples to address instead the 'implied reader' living in the period between resurrection and Parousia (Kingsbury 1988: 109). Luz similarly describes the discourses as addressed 'out of the window' of the narrative of Jesus' historical ministry, in order to address the present (Luz 2005b: 147).

In the 'Missionary Discourse' of Matthew 10, for example, although the readers are told that Jesus 'sent out' the Twelve (10.5), there is no explicit statement that this actually occurred in the story, nor do they return at a later point in the narrative (contrast Mark 6.12–13, 30; Luke 9.6, 10). This allows us to read this mission as one that is ongoing from the perspective of the evangelist. Similarly, the fourth discourse in Matthew 18 speaks of the 'church' (18.17) and gives advice for its life and organization, including a structure for excommunication (18.15–17), in a manner many find anachronistic, presupposing a post-resurrection situation. Similarly anachronistic is the teaching about fasting in the Sermon on the Mount (6.16–18), which is only appropriate for that time 'when the bridegroom is taken away from them' (9.15). References to persecution in the Missionary Discourse, including flogging in 'their synagogues' (10.17, 23; cf. 5.10–12), also appear to anticipate the later experience of missionaries.

The manner in which Jesus often speaks in the discourses also has the effect of 'generalizing' the audience (see Brown 2005). Although in the Sermon on the Mount, for example, he is directly addressing the disciples, his mode of address is often wider: 'Blessed are the poor in spirit, for *theirs* is the kingdom of heaven' (5.3; contrast Luke 6.20: 'Blessed are you who are poor, for *yours* is the kingdom of God'); 'No one can serve two masters' (6.24); 'Not everyone who says to me, "Lord, Lord", will enter the kingdom of heaven' (7.21); 'Everyone then who hears these words of mine and acts on them will be like a wise man who built his house on rock' (7.24). This shift from the second person to the third person is found in other discourses too (e.g. 10.24, 32, 37; 18.4–5; 24.36, 45). These are words not just for the small band of Christ's original disciples but for all who strive to follow him. The parallels with Moses' sermon in Deuteronomy underscore this; for Deuteronomy, although ostensibly set during the period of Israel's wilderness wanderings, is also addressed to God's people in the present.

The Sermon on the Mount

This transparency to the present is particularly exemplified in the first discourse, the Sermon on the Mount (a title given to Matthew 5—7 by St Augustine). For Augustine the Sermon contains 'a perfect standard of the Christian life', containing 'all the precepts which go to mould' such a life (Augustine 1999: 3). Its careful structure, centred around the Lord's Prayer, has already been noted. Indeed Matthew himself may be responsible for the particular form it takes, due to its concentration on important Matthean themes such as 'righteousness' and 'fulfilment', and its divergence from the nearest parallel in Luke (Luke's Sermon on the Plain at Luke 6.17–49). There is a danger, however, in separating out the Sermon from its narrative context and from the succeeding discourses. Luz reminds us, for example, that the Sermon only makes sense following Matthew 1—4, which presents Jesus' origin as Son of God who is able to speak authoritatively: teaching and Christology are interwoven in the Sermon (Luz 1989: 215).

A brief survey of the Sermon's reception history, however (e.g. Luz 1989: 218–23; Clarke 2003: 61–94), reveals that its meaning and purpose is not at all clear. For many, like Augustine, it encapsulates the 'greater righteousness' asked of followers of Christ, which is to 'exceed that of the scribes and Pharisees' (5.20). It is full of stark and uncompromising demands ('But I say to you that everyone who looks at a woman with lust has already committed adultery with her in his heart', 5.28; 'But if anyone strikes you on the right cheek, turn the other also', 5.39; 'Love your enemies and pray for those who persecute you', 5.44; 'Do not store up for yourselves treasure on earth', 6.19; 'Enter through the narrow gate', 7.13), which have appealed to many outside the Church. Mahatma Gandhi famously said that, when he read Jesus' Sermon, it went straight to his heart. As Luz has shown, even when a distinction arose in the Middle Ages between 'precepts' (to be followed by all) and certain 'counsels' for those like monastics who sought a 'higher righteousness' (Aquinas lists poverty, chastity and obedience: *Summa Theologiae* 1/II, q. 108, art. 4), this did not override the fundamental belief that the Sermon made radical demands on every Christian (Luz 1989: 219–20). Nonetheless, the recognition that some of the precepts of Jesus' Sermon might be too demanding for some is anticipated as early as the *Didache* (Allison 1999: 2): 'For if thou canst bear the whole yoke of the Lord, thou wilt be perfect, but if thou canst not, do what thou canst' (*Did.* 6.2: Lake 1925: 1/319).

One pervasive interpretation, springing from the Lutheran Reformation, is that the Sermon is a 'preparation for the gospel', given that human beings are incapable of keeping its demands and therefore led to acknowledge their need for divine grace. But critics of this 'impossible ideal' interpretation object that it reads Matthew in the light of Paul, or a particular Lutheran understanding of Paul's gospel of grace. There is no indication that Matthew thinks these demands impossible to fulfil (Luz 1989: 221), particularly if one recalls that at the heart of the Sermon is the Lord's Prayer with its urgent request for God to bring in his kingdom and a petition for the forgiveness of sins. On the contrary, it is the 'heavy burdens' of the scribes and Pharisees that are 'hard to bear' (23.4). Nor is it quite so easy, to follow another line of Reformation interpretation, to distinguish between the individual's decision to obey the Sermon's demands in the private sphere and what is possible in the public, secular sphere.

Some nineteenth- and early twentieth-century scholars (e.g. Johannes Weiss and Albert Schweitzer) understood the Sermon as proposing an 'interim ethic' – a particularly intense ethical teaching for the short period. This reflects the view that Jesus misguidedly believed the time before the End to be very short. His ethical teaching calls for an extreme heroism for extreme circumstances, representing the last opportunity for repentance. It was not intended to set out a long-term blueprint for Church life, still less an ethical programme to be adopted by society at large.

Yet the view that the Sermon on the Mount makes demands to be fulfilled by disciples has remained remarkably resilient throughout Church history. Luz, following Troeltsch, describes the theology espoused by the Sermon as an example of 'sect theology', the radical perfectionist manifesto of a minority group (Luz 1989: 219). This explains its particular appeal to marginal groups who have been its most impressive advocates: e.g. the early Franciscans, the Anabaptists, Leo Tolstoy and, in the present day, the Mennonites and the Bruderhof communities. Its centrality for the Bruderhof is summed up in the community's *Foundations of Our Faith and Calling*:

> Jesus asks us to live as citizens of his coming kingdom. It is not enough to accept him as our personal savior or to say to him, 'Lord, Lord.' We must prove our love to him in deeds, putting into practice his words in the Gospels, especially the Sermon on the Mount. (Bruderhof 2012: 3)

The cost of taking the Sermon seriously is exemplified by Dietrich Bonhoeffer, leader of the Confessing Church in Nazi Germany and twentieth-century martyr. Bonhoeffer wrote the following:

> The Sermon on the Mount is not a Word to be treated cavalierly – this, that or the other is no good, here we find an inconsistency. Its validity depends

on its being obeyed. This is not a Word to be freely evaluated, not a Word that you can take or leave. It is a compelling, dominating Word.

(quoted in Bethge 1970: 369)

This radically literal reading of the Sermon on the Mount presupposes a particular interpretation of the key word *dikaiosunē* (5.6, 10, 20; 6.1, 33), variously translated 'righteousness', 'justice' and 'piety'. In contrast to Paul, *dikaiosunē* for Matthew refers to what human beings *do* (a literal translation of 6.1 is 'Be careful not to *practise* your righteousness before people'): practical obedience to the Father's will (action that bears 'good fruit', 7.17–18). Moreover there is a connection between doing 'righteousness' and doing 'mercy' (Hinkle 1998), closely linked to the quotation from Hosea that Matthew places twice on Jesus' lips ('I desire mercy and not sacrifice', Hos. 6.6; Matt. 9.13; 12.7). 'Doing mercy' is a synonym for 'giving alms' at 6.2. Those who are blessed are those who 'hunger and thirst for *dikaiosunē*' (5.6). In modern parlance, Matthew is a Gospel for 'activists' (Viviano 2010: 344), albeit an activism grounded in the prior action of God.

The Parables in Matthew

The Parables Discourse of 13.1–53 is another important section for understanding Jesus' teaching, particularly regarding the 'kingdom of the heavens'. Coming at a later point in Matthew's Gospel than its parallel in Mark (Mark 4.1–34), some regard it as a crucial turning point in the narrative, providing a theological commentary on the growing conflict that the coming of the Messiah provokes and that will increasingly dominate the story (e.g. Kingsbury 1969). This is exemplified in the very next pericope, where Jesus is rejected by his own townsfolk in Nazareth (13.54–58).

As in the other Synoptics, Matthew's Jesus uses the parable – from the Greek *parabolē* meaning 'thrown beside'; that is, a comparison or illustration – as a fundamental mode of communication. As well as this sermon devoted to parabolic teaching, Matthew's Jesus teaches in parables in three of the four other discourses (e.g. 7.24–27; 18.12–14, 23–35; 25.1–46), as well as during his debates with the religious leaders on arrival in Jerusalem (e.g. 21.28–44; 22.1–14). Several of Matthew's parables are found in all three Synoptics (e.g. the parable of the sower), some are shared with Luke (e.g. the parable of the talents/pounds) while others (e.g. the parable of the two sons) are unique to Matthew.

The Matthean parables highlight the role of Jesus as the great teacher of the kingdom of the heavens, and the higher righteousness demanded of those who wish to enter it. The harsh demands of discipleship, as laid out in the Sermon on the Mount, are exemplified by brief parabolic sayings (e.g. 5.13, 14; 6.24; 7.13–14, 15) and at least one complete parable (the wise and foolish builders, 7.24–27). The character of the kingdom of the heavens is a particular feature of the Parables Discourse: the varied response to it in the parable of the sower (13.1–9, 18–23); the division between the righteous and the evildoers, which will only be revealed 'at the end of the age', in the parables of the weeds and the wheat and the two types of fish (13.24–30, 36–43, 47–50); its capacity to grow from the smallest of beginnings, like a mustard seed or yeast in flour (13.31–33); the ultimate value of the kingdom, to be compared with treasure hidden in a field or a pearl of great value (13.44–46). Preparation for the Church's existence in this world in between the resurrection and the 'end of the age' is offered by Jesus in the Discourse on the Church, notably the demand for forgiveness and mercy as a mark of Christ's people (18.23–35). Finally, Matthew's Jesus teaches about the coming judgement, both of Israel and of the nations, in the Eschatological Discourse.

Even in those parables shared with other Gospels, Matthew exhibits specific characteristics. Michael Goulder (Goulder 1974: 47–69) has identified significant parallels between the Matthean parables and those in rabbinic literature, a reflection of the world of formative Judaism Matthew inhabits, and of his capacity to write 'in the Hebrew style'. First, his parables tend to be indicative rather than imperative (e.g. 'The kingdom of heaven may be compared to a king', 22.2). Second, Matthew's parables, like those of the rabbis, are full of striking characters: for example, rulers, farmers and their workers, servants, bridesmaids. Whereas Mark simply notes that the kingdom is 'like a mustard seed, which, when sown upon the ground, is the smallest of all the seeds on earth' (4.31), Matthew introduces a human character: 'The kingdom of heaven is like a mustard seed that someone took and sowed in his field' (13.31). Yet the characters he introduces lack the depth and rounded character of those in the Lucan parables (e.g. Lazarus the poor man; the Good Samaritan). They tend to be stock figures described in 'dualistic' language: a wise and a foolish builder (7.24–27); wise bridesmaids and foolish bridesmaids (25.1–13); sheep and goats (25.31–46).

A further difference between Matthew and his fellow evangelists is his strong tendency towards allegory; that is, finding a point-by-point correspondence between characters and details in the parable and the real world. Scholars throughout much of the twentieth century, influenced by the German scholar Adolf Jülicher (1859–1938) and his disciples such as Joachim Jeremias (Jeremias 1954), invested much energy in attempting to 'de-allegorize' the parables in the conviction that Jesus' original parables were simple, one-point stories. Whatever the merits or otherwise of Jülicher's thesis, Matthew certainly exhibits a greater tendency towards allegorization in comparison to both Mark and Luke. Thus in his parable of the weeds and wheat (possibly a reworking of Mark's seed growing secretly: compare 13.24–30 with Mark 4.26–29), the sower, wheat, weeds, enemy, slaves and harvest time all have their own symbolic meanings.

The liking for allegory means that there is also a great need in Matthew to provide interpretations of the complex stories for his readers. Not only does Matthew's Jesus offer an interpretation of the parable of the sower (13.18–23; cf. Mark 4.14–20), he also provides interpretative keys to the parables of the wheat and tares (13.37–43), the dragnet (13.49–50) and the two sons (21.31–32), and offers short explanations of the parables of the lost sheep (18.14), the unforgiving servant (18.35), the labourers in the vineyard (20.16), the thief coming in the night (24.44) and the wise and foolish bridesmaids (25.13).

Finally, Matthew's Parables Discourse offers a very different understanding from Mark as to why Jesus taught in parables. Mark 4.11–12 has puzzled many readers, with its seeming implication that Jesus' parables are intended to prevent outsiders from understanding ('*in order that* [Greek *hina*] "they may indeed look, but not perceive"'). Matthew's Jesus, by contrast, understands the parables as an accommodation to the inability of Jesus' hearers to understand his non-parabolic teaching (literally 'For this reason I speak to them in parables, because [Greek *hoti*] seeing they do not see' 13.13). In other words, Jesus' parables are meant to *aid* understanding; though the interpretations given privately to the disciples, those to whom 'it has been given *to know* the secrets of the kingdom of heaven' (13.11; cf. Mark 4.11), are required for full understanding. The other side of this is that it heightens the complicity of the Jewish leadership in Jesus' rejection and death later in the narrative.

The Final Judgement

Matthew's Gospel has a heightened interest in the Last Judgement and corresponding fate of the righteous and the wicked. The motif of judgement 'at the end of the age' has been noted already in the Parables Discourse (13.37–40, 49–50). It will be echoed again in the parable of the forgiving master and unforgiving servant (18.35) and will come to particular prominence in Jesus' final sermon delivered on the Mount of Olives (the traditional location of the Last Judgement, Zech. 14.4), which contains the parable of the talents (25.14–30, closely related to Luke's parable of the pounds, Luke 19.12–27) and the uniquely Matthean parables of the wise and foolish bridesmaids and the sheep and the goats (25.1–13, 31–46). God the merciful Father is also the Judge (7.1), who shares that judgement with the Son of Man (13.41–42; 25.31–46), and he in turn with the Twelve (19.28). The judgement motif is present in the fiery preaching of John the Baptist ('Even now the axe is lying at the root of the trees', 3.10) and in the urgency of Jesus' own teaching. Examples include the repeated references to the 'day of judgement' (10.15; 11.22, 24; 12.36, 41, 42), to Gehenna (5.22, 29, 30; 10.28; 18.9; 23.15), to the eternal fire (18.8; 25.41) and to weeping and gnashing of teeth (8.12; 13.42, 50; 22.13; 24.51; 25.30). Parallels with the apocalyptic tradition are particularly strong here (see Sim 1996).

It is unsurprising, therefore, that Matthew's Gospel has had a particular influence on artistic depictions of the Last Judgement (surprisingly, more influential than the book of Revelation). Fra Angelico's *The Last Judgement* (1432–5; Museo di San Marco, Florence) is heavily influenced by Matthew's parable of the sheep and the goats (25.31–46), with heaven and the blessed on the right hand of the enthroned Christ and hell and the damned on his left. As if orchestrating events, the right hand of Fra Angelico's Christ points the righteous upwards towards heaven while his left hand points down towards hell. A similar pattern, though with more visual influence from Revelation, is found in Doom paintings in English medieval churches.

This emphasis on judgement has left many modern readers of Matthew feeling uncomfortable. It appears to promote a 'fire and brimstone' theology, rejoicing in the sight of enemies burning in hellfire (a similar moral objection is made to Revelation, especially Rev. 14.9–11). Some find equally problematic those passages in Matthew that may be interpreted as proclaiming divine judgement on Judaism and marking the end of the election of Israel (e.g. 21.43; 23.34–39; 27.25; see Luz 1995b: 137). But such passages are sufficiently ambiguous as to be susceptible to quite different readings (see Levine 1988, who claims that any distinctions between Jew and Gentile are obliterated by Matthean judgement passages). Moreover modern – particularly Western – squeamishness about the judgement per se may reveal as much about the interpreters and their interests as about the evangelist. The conviction that actions will be judged, that justice will ultimately be done in a world that is meaningful, is an important theological idea. Actions have consequences, and those who act have responsibilities.

Nonetheless the Matthean concept of judgement requires certain quali-
fications. First, precision over the judgement language is required. For
example, the name Gehenna, although often translated into English as
'hell' (as in the NRSV), refers to the burning rubbish heaps in Jerusalem's
Hinnom Valley, outside the safety of the city. This does not lessen the
dire warning in Jesus' Gehenna sayings: the fiery threat of the Hinnom
Valley functions as a potent symbol of fiery judgement and separation.
But it does mean that the vivid medieval images of the pangs of hellfire
such as occur in the Doom paintings recede somewhat into the background
of Matthew's text. It is also important to appreciate the genre of such
language: this is symbolic, non-literal apocalyptic language, although functioning rhetorically to promote authentic, moral living in the present (see
Byrne 2004: ix–x).

Second, judgement in Matthew is especially focused on those who pre-
sume to place themselves at the centre of things, to the exclusion of those
they have themselves judged. When Jesus encounters the faith of a Gentile
centurion, he speaks of the 'sons of the kingdom' being cast into the
outer darkness, presumably Gehenna (8.12). The 'sons of the kingdom'
here refers to the people of Israel, or more specifically those at the centre
of the land who reject the offer of the kingdom, now replaced by those
'from east and west'. The scribes and Pharisees are judged for locking
people out of the kingdom of heaven (23.13).

Moreover Matthew's Gospel combines warnings of the coming judgement with equally harsh warnings about human beings standing in judgement over others: for example, 'Do not judge, so that you may not be
judged. For with the judgment you make you will be judged' (i.e. by God,
a divine passive: 7.1–2). Judgement belongs to God, who exercises his
final judgement through the Son of Man. The essence of this judgement
is very different from human judgement, however. In the parable of the
Sheep and the Goats, those who are counted among the blessed 'sheep'
are as surprised to find themselves in that particular company as are the
accursed 'goats' (25.37–39, 44). The other side of this is that the Church
stands as much under the judgement of Christ as the rest of the world
(cf. 7.21–23).

Fra Angelico's aforementioned *The Last Judgement* engages with this
Matthean subtlety, exploiting particular gaps in Matthew's text. At a first
look, it appears that Christ himself has done the separating: his right hand,
above the righteous, is pointing upwards to heaven; his left hand, above
the damned, is hanging rather limply downwards. But on a second look, the
separation of the nations into sheep and goats seems to be self-selecting.

Those on his left apparently recoil in horror as they glimpse his right and left hands, and run towards the gates of hell as if trying to escape. For the right and left hands of Christ the Shepherd-King are hands bearing the wounds of his passion, and in them the wounds of his suffering 'brothers and sisters'. For the goats these are hands of judgement, which terrify them and cut them to the quick. For the sheep these same hands are shepherd's hands, the hands of Christ the Shepherd-King who brings back the strayed, binds up the injured, strengthens the weak and feeds them with justice (see Ezek. 34).

Matthew and the Apocalyptic Tradition

The judgement motif, with its focus on the coming Son of Man as end-time judge, is just one example of the 'apocalyptic' atmosphere that pervades Matthew's Gospel (Sim 1996; Rowland 2008). Apocalyptic refers to that stream of early Jewish and Christian religion that emphasizes the revelation of heavenly secrets to privileged human visionaries, enabling the boundary separating heaven from earth to be crossed (it contains interest in the End and the Last Judgement, but should not be defined by eschatology). Other apocalyptic motifs in Matthew include revelation by dreams, interest in angels, the 'dualism' already noted in the parables (drawing a sharp distinction between the righteous and the unrighteous) and the identification of the 'other' in the hostile polemic against the Jewish leaders. Elements of determinism in Matthew can also be explained as due to the Gospel's apocalyptic mentality: for example, 'For many are called, but few are chosen' (22.14); the motif of fulfilment (e.g. 1.23; 2.15, 18, 23), especially the foreseeing of Jesus' suffering and death (e.g. 16.21; 17.22–23; 20.18–19; 26.21–25, 34). Whereas in many apocalypses, however, heavenly mysteries are revealed to 'the wise' among God's people (e.g. Dan. 12.3; *1 Enoch* 82.3; *4 Ezra* 12.37–38; 14.45–47; *2 Bar.* 28.1), Matthew represents a subversive re-imagining of the apocalyptic tradition: the true revelation of heavenly secrets has been made, not to 'the wise and the intelligent' but to 'infants' (11.25).

Several recent scholars have drawn attention to the social function of apocalyptic, which seems to have played a particular role in theological debates about Judaism in the light of the first Jewish War against Rome and the fall of Jerusalem. They emphasize the relationship between crisis or social alienation and apocalyptic language, thus locating this dimension of Matthew's Gospel against the backdrop of painful separation from Judaism and also of Roman pogroms against Jews triggered by the Jewish War (e.g. Hagner 1985; Stanton 1992: 146–8; Sim 1996: 181–221).

If Matthew is located against the backdrop of post-70 Jewish realignment, then his Son of Man sayings are given particular significance. The fall of Jerusalem and the destruction of the Temple provoked a number of Jewish responses. While the Pharisee-led coalition of Jamnia emphasized renewed focus on study of Torah, and zealots a more revolutionary response that was to culminate in a second Jewish revolt against Rome led by bar-Kochba, some visionaries – such as the authors of the late first-century apocalypses *4 Ezra* and *2 Baruch* – hoped in direct intervention from heaven. One of Ezra's apocalyptic visions (*4 Ezra* 11.1—12.3) describes a lion, clearly the Davidic Messiah (*4 Ezra* 12.32; Gen. 49.9; Rev. 5.5), who emerges roaring from the forest to destroy a terrifying eagle, the symbol of the Roman Empire. Matthew's Jesus presents an alternative apocalyptic vision: Jesus the Son of Man is the one in whom God will definitively act to establish his victory over the forces of evil and chaos. Yet this victory is achieved not by military might but through the suffering and death he endures in Jerusalem.

The Coming Son of Man

The eschatological figure of the 'son of Man' or 'the Human One' has been mentioned several times already in relation to the judgement motif in Matthew. It is precisely as Son of Man that Jesus will sit in judgement – a particular emphasis of this Gospel, and one shared with the *Similitudes of Enoch* (e.g. *1 Enoch* 62.5; 69.27, 29). The enigmatic self-designation 'the Son of the Man' – a Semitic phrase that jars even in Greek – is found on the lips of Jesus in all four Gospels. The Son of Man sayings refer variously to Jesus' current ministry on earth (e.g. having authority on earth to forgive sins, or being lord of the Sabbath, 9.6; 12.8), his impending suffering and death (e.g. the passion predictions, 17.12, 22; 20.18) and his future coming in glory (at the Parousia, e.g. 16.27; 24.27, 30).

Many of the Son of Man references in Matthew are shared with Mark and Luke (e.g. 9.6; 12.8; 16.27; 17.22; 20.18; 26.24; 26.64), some are paralleled in Mark alone (e.g. 17.12; 20.28; 26.45) and others are shared with Luke (8.20; 11.19; 12.32, 40; 24.27, 37, 39, 44). Occasionally Matthew will make clear that Jesus is the Son of Man where this is not obvious in the parallels – at 16.13 Jesus asks his disciples who people say the Son of Man is, whereas in Mark and Luke he asks: 'Who do people/the crowds say that I am?' (Mark 8.27; Luke 9.18).

But Matthew also has his own unique references, which emphasize the future role of the Son of Man from heaven (the addition at 26.2 focuses more specifically on the Son of Man being 'handed over to be crucified'). The mission of the Twelve to Israel will not have been completed before the Son of Man comes (10.23). The interpretation of the uniquely Matthean parable of the wheat and the tares (13.36–43) identifies the sower of the good seed as the Son of Man, who will send out his angels at the Last Judgement to separate out the 'workers of lawlessness' from the righteous in his kingdom. Matthew 19.28 refers to the Son of Man seated on the throne of his glory, joined in judgement by the Twelve seated on thrones (the parallel at Luke 18.30 lacks a reference to the Son of Man). Similarly the Matthean parable of the sheep and the goats presents the Son of Man coming in glory with all the angels and taking his throne as king and judge (25.31). Meanwhile the kingdom is described as 'his kingdom' (16.28; cf. Mark 8.38; Luke 9.26), and the angels specifically 'his angels' (16.27–28; cf. Mark 8.38; Luke 9.26), further emphasizing the eschatological role of the crucified and vindicated Jesus. His self-identification with 'the least' of his brothers and sisters in the present – whether these refer to the poor and needy, members of the Church or specifically Christian missionaries (Harrington 1991: 357) – adds a further surprising dimension to this Gospel that constantly surprises.

Finally, Matthew alone of the evangelists uses the Greek word *parousia* to describe the Son of Man's coming (24.3, 27, 37, 39; it is also used in a similar way by Paul: e.g. 1 Cor. 15.23; 1 Thess. 2.19; 3.13; 4.15; 5.23). This has become a technical theological term to describe Christ's coming at the end of time ('the Parousia'), although its root meaning is 'presence' or 'arrival'. In the ancient world it often referred to the triumphant arrival of a king or emperor. It heightens the note of expectancy and readiness that has characterized the teaching of Jesus throughout Matthew. The one who teaches is also the one who judges, and who challenges his followers to a constant state of readiness, of performing that 'righteousness' that is conformity to the will of their heavenly Father.

8

Jesus as Healer and Exorcist

The Gospel Miracles Tradition

All three Synoptic Gospels agree that Jesus was remembered as an exorcist and healer. So embedded are the exorcisms and healings in the stories about Jesus, together with miraculous events such as calming a storm, walking on water and feeding multitudes, that the 'miracles tradition' cannot be so easily dismissed as a late addition to the tradition. Matthew's Gospel even reveals that Jesus' opponents accepted his ability to cast out demons, although attributing this power to Beelzebul rather than God (e.g. 9.34; 12.24–32).

This generally positive assessment of the miracle stories (see e.g. Meier 1994: 509–1038) contrasts with the scepticism of many early twentieth-century form critics. They emphasized rabbinic and especially pagan parallels to Jesus' miracles, notably the miraculous deeds attributed to Apollonius of Tyana. They regarded the Gospel miracle stories as part of the early Church's apologetic attempt to make Jesus compete with rivals. Yet the essentially Jewish context within which evangelists locate Jesus' healings and exorcisms – the in-breaking of the kingdom of God (or Matthew's preferred 'kingdom of the heavens'), as well as similarities with Old Testament stories about Elijah, Elisha and Moses – counts against a late origin influenced by paganism. Moreover the relative reserve associated with the Gospel miracle stories, with Jesus sometimes refusing to draw attention to what he does (e.g. Mark 5.37; 7.33; 8.23), or his occasional inability to heal due to lack of faith on the part of his audience (e.g. Mark 6.5; cf. Matt. 13.58), is also problematic for seeing their originating purpose as presenting Jesus as a worthy match for other miracle workers or 'sons of God'.

Matthew's treatment of the stories of Jesus as healer and exorcist – together with other stories generally referred to as 'miracles' – is distinctive in several ways. Before analysing his portrayal, however, several preliminary observations should be made. First, Matthew and the other evangelists generally avoid the language of 'miracle' or 'the miraculous' (Latin *miraculum*, roughly equivalent to the Greek *thauma*, 'wonder' or 'marvel') – although the verb 'to marvel' is used of the response of the crowds (e.g. 8.27; 9.33;

15.31). Thus to speak of the 'miracle stories' in the Gospels reflects a later categorization. The synoptic evangelists' preferred term for Jesus' healings is *dunamis*, 'power' or 'deed of power' (e.g. 11.20–23; 13.54, 58; 14.2; contrast the false messiahs and false prophets who perform 'great signs and omens', 24.24).

Indeed the term 'miracle' covers a wide variety of stories in the Gospels, generally subdivided into 'miracles of healing' and so-called 'nature miracles', the latter referring to the two sea miracles, the two miraculous feedings, the finding of the coin in the fish's mouth and the withering of the fig tree, in which Christ shows his power over nature. Even the 'miracles of healing' describe different phenomena that are explained according to different causes. Thus the exorcisms (e.g. 8.28–34; 9.32–34) presuppose possession of human beings by malevolent forces (demons or unclean spirits, cf. *1 Enoch* 15.8–11) beyond their control and from which they need to be liberated. The story of the leper (8.1–4) is strictly a cleansing; that is, the overcoming of ritual impurity that prevented the person from entering the Temple in Jerusalem and full participation in the life of the nation. Ritual impurity should not be confused with sin: for example, a pious Jew could become ritually unclean through burying his parents – a good act, yet contact with a corpse rendered one impure. The story of the woman with a haemorrhage is also often understood to be another example of ritual cleansing, although Amy-Jill Levine urges caution: 'If the woman had a sore on her leg, her breast, her nose, etc. – and all these places are possible given the semantic range of "hemorrhage" – then while she would still be ill, she would not be impure' (Levine 1996: 384). Other stories describe healings proper, including one restoration to life of a dead girl (9.18–19, 23–26). Only one, however, makes an explicit link between the condition of the sick person and sin or personal wrongdoing (the paralytic, who is told 'Your sins are forgiven', 9.2–8).

A second observation, however, is that Matthew has a distinct preference for the verb 'to heal' (*therapeuein*): 16 occurrences as opposed to five in Mark. Of these, five are in uniquely Matthean summary statements (4.23–24; 9.35; 12.15; 15.30), and one in the non-Marcan story of the centurion's servant (8.7). Whereas in Mark the Twelve are commissioned to preach and cast out demons (Mark 3.14–15), in Matthew's parallel they are also sent out to 'heal' (10.1, 8). In Matthew the question raised by Jesus regarding curing the man with a withered hand is not 'Is it lawful on the Sabbath to do good or do evil?' (Mark 3.4) but 'Is it lawful on the Sabbath to *heal*?' (12.10; see also 12.22). Matthew's version of the cleansing of the Temple includes an explicit reference to Jesus healing the blind and lame there

(21.14), a feature lacking in the Marcan parallel (Mark 11.15–17; see also Matt. 12.22; cf. Mark 3.20; Matt. 14.14; cf. Mark 6.34; Matt. 19.2; cf. Mark 10.1). Finally, his version of the story of the epileptic boy highlights the therapeutic no less than the exorcistic dimension (*therapeuein* used at 17.16, 18; cf. Mark 9.14–29).

Healings within Matthew's Story

Given his penchant for order and structure it is not surprising to find healings and other miracles grouped together in Matthew, a point noted long ago by the author of the *Opus imperfectum* (Kellerman 2010: 1/1). This is most evident in Matthew 8—9, where – as a comparison with Mark and Luke reveals – thematic order takes precedence over strict chronology. Matthew has gathered together a series of 'miracle' stories that in Mark are scattered across chapters 1, 2, 4 and 5, and added some non-Marcan healings (8.5–13; 9.27–34) and Marcan stories of conflict with religious authorities. Connecting temporal phrases (e.g. 8.18, 28; 9.1) link the individual pericopae into a coherent narrative, albeit not ironing out all the awkwardness (see Luz 2001: 1). For example, Jesus' command to the leper not to tell anyone (8.4) is odd in the Matthean context, given the presence of 'great crowds' (8.1). The major literary *inclusio* of 4.23 and 9.35 connects this section closely with Matthew's preceding discourse, the Sermon on the Mount (5—9). Further healings (e.g. the man with a withered hand, 12.9–14; the blind and mute demoniac, 12.22–23; the Canaanite woman's daughter, 15.21–28; the epileptic boy, 17.14–21; the two blind men at Bethsaida, 20.29–34) and other miracles (e.g. two miraculous feedings, 14.13–21 and 15.32–39; Jesus walking on the water, 14.22–33; the coin in the fish's mouth, 17.24–27; the withering of the fig tree, 21.18–22) occur later in Matthew's narrative, where their positioning tends to be much closer to the parallel Marcan context.

The significance of the careful thematic arrangement in Matthew 8—9, and its relationship to the Sermon, is open to several explanations. In general terms it seems to provide a confirmation of Jesus' authority to teaching on the mountain, through presenting him also as 'Messiah of deed' (Bornkamm 1982: 53). It is an explanation at least as old as Jerome's fourth-century commentary: 'In this way the words he has just spoken are confirmed among his hearers by means of miraculous powers' (Jerome 2008: 99).

But what more is being claimed? Some (e.g. Davies 1993: 68) propose a link with the ten miracles performed by Moses in Egypt (Exodus 7—12), another example of Matthew's Mosaic typology. A relevant parallel is found in *Pirke Aboth* 5.5, 8: 'Ten wonders were done for our Fathers in Egypt, and ten by the sea' (quoted in Kingsbury 1978: 561). Luke also makes a connection between the healings of Jesus and the 'wonders' performed by Moses in Egypt (e.g. Acts 2.22; 3.22), even though the latter as 'plagues' do not have therapeutic benefits for the recipients. Against this, however, is that the number ten is far from clear to many readers of Matthew 8—9, particularly given that the sequence of healings and other miracles is interrupted by stories of conflict (e.g. 9.3–6, 10–17). To achieve the number ten requires separating out the intercalated miracles of the woman with a haemorrhage and the raising of the ruler's daughter. Jerome also does this, but also distinguishes the 'many at evening' from the healing of Peter's mother-in-law, thus counting 11 miracles in these two chapters rather than 10 (Jerome 2008: 113, though he is more interested in the fact that Jesus performs 15 miracles in total). Nor does this section of Matthew's Gospel contain other clear echoes of the Moses story (Davies 1989: 86–90).

Indeed this section of the Gospel emphasizes Jesus' role as the Servant (*pais*) of the Lord (8.17). Although Moses is sometimes referred to as the Lord's 'servant', the LXX uses the term *therapeuōn* or *oiketēs* rather than *pais* (e.g. Num. 11.11; 12.7; Deut. 3.24; 34.5): the former term would have been ideal had Matthew wished to emphasize the Mosaic credentials of Jesus the Servant-healer. In an unusual New Testament interpretation of Isaiah 53 (used elsewhere to interpret Christ's saving death, e.g. Luke 22.37; Acts 8.32–33; Heb. 9.28; 1 Pet. 2.22–25), Jesus as Servant literally 'takes' or 'carries' infirmities and diseases through healing them. Another formula citation from Isaiah's Servant Songs will occur later in Matthew's narrative to underscore Jesus' Servant role: anticipating the mission to the Gentiles who will hope in the Servant's name, it is presented by Matthew as direct fulfilment of the secrecy surrounding Jesus' healing of the crowds (12.16, quoting Isa. 42.1–4). Kingsbury has attempted to subsume the 'servant' motif in Matthew under what he regards as the dominant Son of God Christology. For Kingsbury, what is said of the Servant is said elsewhere in Matthew of Jesus as the Son of God (e.g. both the baptism and the Transfiguration link Jesus as Servant with Jesus as God's Son: Kingsbury 1978: 565). Others, however, have found this a case of special pleading, in order to preserve Kingsbury's view that Son of God is the pre-eminent title for Jesus in Matthew's Gospel (see Hill 1980). In another context Kingsbury has noted that the Greek verb *therapeuein* can mean 'to serve' as well as 'heal', in order to illuminate further why Matthew presents Jesus as the Servant in this context: 'In healing, Jesus Son of God assumes the role of the servant of God and ministers to Israel by restoring persons to health or freeing them from their afflictions' (Kingsbury 1986: 70).

A variant solution to the ordering and number of the miracles in Matthew 8—9 is offered by Austin Farrer. Matthew 8—9 contains the healing of ten Israelites plus one Gentile, the centurion's servant (Farrer 1966: 38–56). Farrer achieves this number by counting individuals healed – that is, the haemorrhaging woman and the ruler's daughter, two demoniacs, two blind men – rather than the individual healing stories (and omitting the one non-healing, the miraculous calming of the storm). This then anticipates the future mission to the Gentiles. Whether this theory owes more to Farrer's ingenuity than to the Gospel's patterning remains a moot point.

Christological Focus

All these solutions have in common the conviction that there is a christological dimension to Matthew's ordering: that it serves to reveal the truth about Jesus the healer, exorcist and miracle-worker, whether as a new Moses, the healer of Israel and the nations or the Servant of the Lord. Christology may also provide a partial explanation for another distinctive feature of the healing stories in Matthew's Gospel: their striking conciseness, which is thrown into sharp relief by a comparison with their parallels in the other Gospels, especially Mark. Matthew's story of the two Gadarene demoniacs (8.28–34), for example, takes only 16 lines of Greek in the United Bible Societies' fourth edition of the *Greek New Testament*, as opposed to 38 lines for the Marcan parallel (Mark 5.1–20). The resulting lack of detail in the Matthean version makes it a far less dramatic account.

For many this phenomenon is best explained on a theory of Marcan priority, Matthew removing unnecessary detail in order to zoom in on the two main characters. However, it is an observation that stands even if another theory of synoptic relationships, such as Matthean priority, is preferred. In his account of the healing of Peter's mother-in-law (8.14–15), Matthew's is the one that reads 'him' (Jesus) rather than 'them', and omits explicit reference to the presence of Peter and his companions. Matthew's version of the woman with haemorrhages (9.20–22) dispenses with the jostling crowd, such that there is no need, as in Mark and Luke, for Jesus to ask: 'Who touched me/my clothes?' (Mark 5.30; Luke 8.45). In his account of the healing of the paralytic, he omits any reference to the sick man's friends lowering him through the roof, thus leaving the reader to puzzle over the meaning of 'When Jesus saw their faith' (9.2).

Whatever the direction of the abbreviation (Mark to Matthew; Matthew to Mark), the Matthean version seems to have a christological focus (see Held 1982). Matthew is not simply shorter for abbreviation's sake, given that he can add details to miracle stories when he wishes (e.g. he inserts sayings about discipleship into the stilling of the storm and adds a story about Peter to the walking on the water: 8.19–22; 14.28–31). Rather he avoids all unnecessary details in order to focus on Christ the healer and those in need of that healing. Jesus is the Lord who saves; these are stories of the Lord who saves. If one treats the healing stories, like the discourses, as examples of 'transparency', then they function to give Christian readers in the present confidence that they can approach the risen Lord for their own needs.

But what kind of Messiah heals the sick? Mention has been made above of the explicit links made between Jesus the healer and the Servant of the Lord, through two formula citations from Isaiah 42 and 53. But the wider context of Isaiah is also of significance for Matthew's Gospel. When later in the narrative Jesus is asked by disciples of the imprisoned John the Baptist whether he is 'the one who is to come', his response is to remind them – and the Gospel's readers – of his healing ministry in words that recall a string of Isaian passages: 'Go and tell John what you hear and see: the blind receive their sight, the lame walk, the lepers are cleansed, the deaf hear, the dead are raised, and the poor have good news brought to them' (11.5; cf. Isa. 29.18–19; 35.5–6; 42.18; 61.1). Examples of each of these miracles have occurred in the 'miracles' narrative of Matthew 8—9 (with the exception of the *deaf* hearing, although the same Greek word *kōphos* was used of the dumb demoniac in 9.32). The wider context then is the expectation of miraculous deeds in the messianic age (even if Jewish tradition was not too specific about the miracles the Messiah could be expected to perform: see Nolan 1979: 165–6).

Jesus the Healer as Son of David

One further christological connection Matthew's Gospel makes with Jesus' healings concerns the title 'son of David'. That Jesus is the Son of David is an important dimension of Matthew's story (see Verseput 1987: 533–7), having been introduced in the Gospel's opening verse. Matthew uses the term nine times (1.1, 20; 9.27; 12.23; 15.22; 20.30, 31; 21.9, 15; the title is also implied at 22.42; cf. Mark 12.35), of which seven are unique to him (only 20.30 and 31 are paralleled in Mark, 10.47, 48). The term would become an important messianic title after the New Testament period for the rabbis (e.g. *b. Sanh.* 97a–98a) but is already used of the Messiah in the first-century BCE *Psalms of Solomon* (*Ps. Sol.* 17.21; cf. *4 Ezra* 12.32; John 7.42).

The striking feature of Matthew's use of the Son of David title, like his Servant concept, is his connecting it with Jesus' healings and exorcisms (four times, as opposed to once each for Son of God and Son of Man, and three times for Lord: Baxter 2006: 38), leading to the claim that Matthew depicts Jesus as a 'therapeutic Son of David' (Duling 1977). Presuming Marcan priority, Matthew would have found justification for this in Mark's story of Bartimaeus (20.30–31; Mark 10.46–52). But he extends it so that Jesus is also acclaimed as Son of David in the earlier occurrence of two blind men (9.27–31) and by the Canaanite woman seeking healing for her daughter (15.22–28). The latter is particularly striking in having a non-Israelite use that title. The healing of the blind and mute demoniac also provokes the question from the crowds: 'Can this be the Son of David?' (12.23, although the framing of the question suggests they expect a negative answer).

Several different explanations have been given for this linking of Jesus' healings to the Son of David title. The first relates it to Jewish traditions concerning the great Son of David, King Solomon. The memory of Solomon's wisdom led to the view among some Jews that this had extended to the knowledge of how to defeat demonic powers. The first-century Jewish historian Josephus describes having witnessed an exorcism performed using incantations supposedly composed by Solomon and a ring containing under its seal a root prescribed by him for the purpose (Josephus, *Ant.* 8.44–49). Other traditions also link King Solomon to exorcisms, including Aramaic incantation bowls referring to Solomon (Fisher 1968), and the apocryphal *Testament of Solomon* (Duling 1975). This explanation has failed to convince many, however. Luz, for example, objects that the Jewish traditions about Solomon as exorcist such as the *Testament of Solomon* are late, and do not present him specifically as a healer (Luz 2005b: 86). This contrasts with Matthew's tendency to emphasize Christ's therapeutic over his exorcistic qualities (as noted by Duling 1975: 251). The story in Josephus, meanwhile, does not actually present Solomon himself as performing exorcisms. Moreover Matthew fails to mention Solomon by name in this context, whereas he has no qualms elsewhere. Such references, however, appeal not to Solomon's exorcistic qualities but to his royal ancestry (1.6–7), his glorious attire (6.29), his wisdom (12.42:

Baxter 2006: 47) and possibly also to his role as temple-builder (compare Jesus as builder of the Church at 16.18; cf. 2 Sam. 7.13–14).

An alternative solution connects Jesus' healing ministry with his role as the Davidic Shepherd. A number of scholars have explored the link between Matthew's Jesus and Ezekiel 34 (e.g. Heil 1993; Baxter 2006), where God responds to the failure of Israel's shepherd-leaders to strengthen the weak, heal the sick and seek the lost by raising up 'my servant David' who 'shall feed them and be their shepherd' (Ezek. 34.4, 23–24; see also Mic. 2.12–13; 5.2–4; Zech. 11.4–17; *1 Enoch* 85–95; *Ps. Sol.* 17.40). A good case can be made for the influence of Ezekiel 34, both thematically and in terms of verbal allusion (e.g. 9.36 = Ezek. 34.5; 25.32 = Ezek. 34.17). The combination of healing and shepherding is also found in the so-called *Messianic Apocalypse* from Qumran (4Q521: Baxter 2006: 46).

This motif of Ezekiel's Shepherd, or the Davidic Shepherd in Judaism more widely (see Chae 2006), has the merit of tying together a number of otherwise disparate threads in Matthew's Gospel: the fierce denunciation of the leaders, especially the scribes and Pharisees; the connection between the Son of David and healing; the concern for the 'lost sheep of the house of Israel' (a specific feature of the healing of the Canaanite woman's daughter, 15.24); the close proximity of healing and feeding (e.g. 14.14, 19; 15.30–31, 36), including feeding on a mountain (15.29; cf. Ezek. 34.13). Indeed one should not underestimate the political dimension of the Davidic Shepherd's quest for the 'lost sheep'. As Joel Willitts notes, all uses of the Messianic Shepherd-King tradition contained both 'protest against the present religio-political situation and idyllic visions of Messianic restoration' (Willitts 2007: 222). This warns against interpreting Matthew's Christology in exclusively 'religious' categories. More controversial is Willitts' claim that by 'the lost sheep of the house of Israel' Matthew means strictly the remnant of the northern kingdom (the ten lost tribes) inhabiting rural Galilee and its environs (Willitts 2007: 157–73).

Other Dimensions of the Miracle Stories

Christology is not the only theme to be explored in Matthew 8—9 however. In his analysis of these chapters, Held also identified the themes of discipleship (particularly in the calming of the storm, 8.23–27) and faith (e.g. 9.18–26: Held 1982). His analysis is illuminating, even if he has overstated the case in his claim (Held 1982: 241–6) that Matthew has reshaped the miracle stories so that they are closer in form to controversy and scholastic dialogues (e.g. the dialogue about divorce at 19.3–9).

Those attempting a holistic reading of Matthew, and therefore keen to locate these chapters within the wider narrative, note the motif of growing opposition to Jesus (9.2–17), not least in a group of three controversy stories only the first of which is also a healing (the healing of the paralytic, 9.2–8). Thus Kingsbury identifies the motif of 'separation from Israel' in this section (Kingsbury 1978: 568), even if the conflict only really intensifies in Matthew 12. William Thompson (Thompson 1971: 366) draws particular attention to the 'double-reaction' to Jesus' healings at 9.32–34 (picked up again at 12.23–24), which points to a division between the leadership and the people over Jesus. While the crowds marvel, with the exclamation that 'Never has anything like this been seen in Israel', the Pharisees accuse him of performing the exorcism of the mute demoniac by the 'ruler of the demons'. For Ulrich Luz this whole section contains the story of Jesus in microcosm: the Messiah's activity among his people leads to the creation of 'a community of disciples (8.18–27) whom he will lead through the storm into gentile territory (8.28–34)' (Luz 2001: 2). However, it also leads to conflict within Israel, and eventual rupture (9.32–34). This is a story that will be continued, and intensified, in the remainder of Matthew's narrative (see also Stewart-Sykes 1995).

In parallel with this often goes an alternative literary pattern to the 'ten wonders of Moses' pattern discussed above. This triadic structure (e.g. Davies and Allison 1988–97: 1/67; 2/1–5) groups the miracle stories in three sets of three: 8.1–22 (the leper, the centurion's servant, Peter's mother-in-law, rounded off with a summary of Jesus' mass healings, a formula citation and teaching about discipleship); 8.23—9.17 (the calming of the storm, the Gadarene demoniacs, the paralytic, leading into a group of conflict stories); 9.18–38 (the ruler's daughter and the woman with a haemorrhage, two blind men, the mute demoniac, concluded with a summary report). This has the merit of accounting for the pericopae of conflict in Matthew 9 as well as the miracle stories; it also reflects Matthew's use of triads elsewhere (e.g. the threefold division in the genealogy; the three temptations; the three prayers of Jesus in Gethsemane: 1.2–17; 4.1–11; 26.36–46).

Commentators are also interested in Matthew's selection of miracle stories in the first triad of chapter 8 (the leper, the centurion's slave-boy, Peter's mother-in-law). The cleansing of the leper may be positioned first as an illustration of Jesus' claim in the preceding Sermon to fulfil rather than abolish the Law and the prophets (5.17–20; see Hare 1993: 88–9). It concludes with Jesus' command to the leper to 'offer the gift that Moses commanded' (8.4). All three, moreover, present marginal figures as recipients of Jesus' healing activity: a ritually unclean male Jew, the slave of a Gentile centurion and a Jewish woman, anticipating the extent of his ministry to the 'lost sheep of the house of Israel' and its subsequent extension to include the Gentile 'dogs' (15.21–28).

The possibility that Matthew's Gospel responds directly to Jewish charges against the early Christian movement – already noted in relation to Matthew's first two chapters – is sometimes raised about the miracles tradition also. Later rabbinic tradition claims that Jesus of Nazareth was a sorcerer who led Israel astray (see Davies and Allison 1988–97: 3/654). An early version of this charge may be reflected in Matthew's resurrection narrative, where the Pharisees describe Jesus as 'that deceiver' (27.63), and in their earlier reaction to the claim that Jesus was the Son of David by attributing his powers of exorcism to Beelzebul, 'the ruler of demons' (9.34; 10.25; 12.24, 27; on this see Stanton 1992: 169–91, 232–55). There is an inherent ambiguity to Jesus' healings. They could be interpreted as signs of the Messiah (e.g. 11.2–6; cf. Isa. 35.5–6) or God's eschatological agent of the kingdom (e.g. 12.28). But they could be the works of a magician or of a deceiver possessed by the Evil One. Matthew goes out of his way to show that Jesus acts not by Beelzebul but 'by the Spirit of God' (12.28), and highlights the element of 'healing' in Jesus' ministry (through his preference for the verb *therapeuein*, 'to heal'), which distances Jesus from any charge of attempts to manipulate by magic. Applying a 'hermeneutic of suspicion', one might suspect Matthew of deliberately covering up those less palatable aspects of Jesus' healing activity that would surface in those later rabbinic charges.

This concern may explain – on a theory of Marcan priority – the omission by Matthew of two Marcan healing stories: the healing of the blind man at Bethsaida (Mark 8.22–26) and the peculiar story of the deaf and dumb man (7.31–37). The Bethsaida story has Jesus use spittle to effect the cure (as well as requiring Jesus to attempt the healing twice). In the story of the deaf and dumb man, Jesus puts spittle on the man's tongue and sticks his fingers in his ears. Both actions might suggest elements of sorcery. In their place Matthew has the healing of two blind men (9.27–31), which closely parallels his two blind men in Jericho (20.29–34), a variant of Mark's story of Bartimaeus (Mark 10.46–52), and a double-tradition story of a dumb demoniac (9.32–34; Luke 11.14–15; a doublet to 12.22–24). It is possible too that his omission of Aramaic words *Ephphatha* (Mark 7.34) and *Talitha cum* (Mark 5.41) is to avoid any suggestion to his Greek-speaking audiences that these are magical incantations.

Symbolic Interpretation of Miracle Stories

Our earlier discussion of patristic exegesis noted the tendency towards allegorical interpretations of certain stories, encouraging a quest for multivalency of meaning, albeit grounded in the literal meaning of the text. While modern critics will find some of the more detailed, point-by-point allegorizing of the Fathers problematic, some are nonetheless sympathetic to a more symbolic interpretation of certain of the miracle stories. A holistic reading of Matthew's narrative, for example, can highlight the symbolic role of the healing of two Gentiles, the centurion's servant and the daughter of the Canaanite woman (8.5–13; 15.21–28) as anticipating the post-resurrection turning point in salvation history. In contrast to the other healings, where Jesus generally touches the sick person, both of these are performed at a distance.

The two feeding miracles (14.13–21; 15.32–39) are also regularly given a symbolic interpretation. Modern as well as ancient interpreters treat the numbers (five thousand people, five loaves, two fishes, twelve baskets; four thousand people, seven loaves, seven baskets) as symbolic, as well as exploring the range of Old Testament intertexts, whether the feeding of the Israelites in the wilderness (the feeding of the five thousand occurs in 'a desert place', 14.15) or the motif of the Shepherd-King (e.g. the four thousand are fed on a mountain, 15.29; cf. Ezek. 34.13–14). A common explanation links the twelve with the tribes of Israel and the seven with the Gentile nations (see Harrington 1991: 220, 241). Thus the two events signify the feeding of the 'lost sheep' and the universal feeding of the nations respectively. The narrative context of the second, immediately after the request of the Canaanite woman that the Gentile 'dogs' be allowed to eat scraps from the Master's table (15.27), supports this reading. Indeed far from being satisfied with 'scraps', they now share fully in the bread from the table. Moreover the sequence of verbs describing Jesus' action in the miraculous feedings ('take', 'bless', 'break', 'give': 14.19; 'take', 'break', 'give', 15.36) match those of the Last Supper ('take', 'bless', 'break', 'give': 26.26). Thus the miracle also functions as a symbol of the Eucharist, by which followers of Jesus continue to be fed (15.36 includes the verb 'give thanks', *eucharisteō*). This connection has not been lost on artists, who regularly exploit the connection between the feeding of the multitudes and the Mass.

The two sea miracles – the calming of the storm and the walking on the water (8.23–27; 14.22–33) – have also frequently been given a symbolic interpretation. In a famous article, Günther Bornkamm discusses the calming of the storm as no mere 'nature miracle' but a paradigm of discipleship (Bornkamm 1982), transparent to the Church in the post-Easter period. A number of distinctive details in Matthew's version of this triple-tradition story (also recorded at Mark 4.35–41; Luke 8.22–25) support this ecclesiological interpretation. First, the pericope is introduced by sayings addressed to would-be disciples, inserted between Jesus' initial command to go over to the other side (8.18) and his getting into the boat (8.23). This juxtaposition provides a deeper resonance to the statement in verse 23 that 'his disciples followed him' (into the boat), because following Christ is a metaphor for discipleship in verses 18–22 (also 4.20, 22; 9.9; 19.21).

Second, the request of the disciples in the boat as they 'woke him up' (literally 'raised him', v. 25) is not the Marcan 'Teacher, do you not care that we are perishing?' or Luke's 'Master, Master, we are perishing!' (Mark 4.38; Luke 8.24), but 'Lord, save us! We are perishing!' The 'Lord, save us [*Kurie, sōson*]!' has the ring of a liturgical prayer, which Bornkamm interprets as the prayer of the Church to the risen Lord in its midst. Bornkamm's reading is a modern reworking of an ancient way of reading the calming of the storm. Peter Chrysologus, a fifth-century bishop of Ravenna, also offered an ecclesiological interpretation of the boat, heading towards its heavenly harbour: 'Christ gets into the vessel of his church, always ready to calm the waves of the world' (*Sermons* 50.2: Simonetti [ed.] 2001: 169). A similar symbolic reading of the boat is offered in several patristic interpretations of the second sea miracle (14.22–33; Mark 6.45–52; John 6.15–21), when the disciples in the boat encounter the Lord walking towards them on the sea. Typical is Augustine, who writes: 'Meanwhile the boat carrying the disciples – that is, the church – is rocking and shaking amid the storms of temptation, while the adverse wind rages on' (Augustine, *Sermon* 75.4: Simonetti [ed.] 2002: 11). Matthew's version of this story contains the episode of Peter attempting to emulate Jesus but sinking beneath the waves (vv. 28–31), in which he repeats the prayer of all the disciples from the previous sea miracle: 'Lord, save me [*Kurie, sōson me*]!' (v. 30). The motifs of Christology and faith, identified by Held as two of the key themes of Matthew 8—9, come to the fore again here. Hence Peter becomes a paradigm for the mixture of faith and weakness in all believers, and the story a classic example of tropology. Jerome, commenting on this passage in the light of Peter's faithful enthusiasm elsewhere in the Gospel, draws a moral lesson for all Christian readers: 'If this is so, what will Jesus say to us, who do not even have the smallest particle of this little faith?' (Jerome 2008: 176).

9

Fulfilling the Law and the Prophets

Standing on the Shoulders of Giants

In the famous rose window in the south transept of Chartres Cathedral, the four evangelists are each depicted standing on the shoulders of a prophet, as if on the shoulders of giants. Their chosen prophetic antecedent provides them with sufficient height to enable them to record the ways Christ – at least from their privileged vantage-point – meets the hopes and expectations of the ancient prophecies. Matthew's prophet at Chartres is Isaiah, in recognition of his prominent place in the First Gospel. Of the 17 quotations from Old Testament prophets in Matthew (not counting the vague 'through the prophets' at 2.23), seven are from this prophet, who is explicitly named in six of them (3.3; 4.14; 8.17; 12.17; 13.14; 15.7; Matthew also quotes from Isaiah, though without naming him, at 1.22–23). It is no surprise that in Christian tradition Isaiah comes to be viewed as 'the fifth evangelist', foretelling the 'good news' of Jesus Christ (Sawyer 1996). His writings, along with those of other prophets of ancient Israel, play a key role in a central motif of Matthew's Gospel: that of fulfilment.

Nor are the prophets the only Old Testament characters to impact on Matthew's vision, for his Jesus comes to fulfil the Law as well as the prophets (5.17). In the frescoes that adorn the walls of the Sistine Chapel in Rome, painted by a variety of eminent artists including Botticelli, Ghirlandaio and Perugino, scenes from the life of Moses on the south wall parallel scenes from Christ's life on the north, from his baptism through his Sermon on the Mount to the Last Supper. Mosaic typology has been a regular feature of our analysis of Matthew's book so far, particularly in relation to his Christology. When it comes to the theme of fulfilment it is especially the teaching contained in the books attributed to Moses that comes to the fore – though even here Meier emphasizes prophetic over Torah fulfilment (Meier 1991: 224–8).

Yet neither of these two dimensions of fulfilment – the Law or the prophets – is straightforward in Matthew's account. Matthew's choice of prophetic texts, particularly in the so-called 'formula citations', sometimes appears arbitrary or sitting fast and loose to the Old Testament text as it has come down to us in the various Greek, Hebrew and Aramaic versions.

Moreover we find ancient prophecies being read in new ways, including several that appear not to have been understood by first-century Jews as prophecies of the Messiah being read in precisely that way in the light of Jesus. Nor are things much clearer when it comes to the Law of Moses. It is unclear precisely what Jesus' relationship to the Mosaic Torah really is (Jesus' sharp rebuttal of the charge that he 'abolishes' the Law at 5.17 suggests that at least some understood his teaching as undermining it), and whether Torah observance is required of his ongoing community of followers. This chapter will explore some of these complexities and the debates they have provoked, through examination of the motif of fulfilment, the distinctive set of Old Testament quotations often referred to as the 'fulfilment quotations' or 'formula citations' and the question of the ongoing validity of the Mosaic Law for readers of Matthew.

Fulfilment

The language of 'fulfilment' is commonly regarded as a prominent feature of Matthew's redaction. The main term is the Greek verb *plēroō*, which has the various nuances of 'I fulfil', 'I complete' or 'I fill' (as in filling a bottle). A supplementary verb occasionally used by Matthew is *anaplēroō* ('fill up'), used of the fulfilment of Isaiah at 13.14. Although the term *plēroō* is present in the other Synoptic Gospels (three times in Mark; nine times in Luke, although rarely of fulfilling the Scriptures), Matthew's interest in fulfilment is striking. He uses *plēroō* no fewer than 16 times (1.22; 2.15, 17, 23; 3.15; 4.14; 5.17; 8.17; 12.17; 13.35, 48; 21.4; 23.32; 26.54, 56; 27.9), 12 of them in relation to quotations from the prophets or general fulfilment of prophetic writings, and one more concerning the fulfilment of both Torah and prophets. A similar interest in fulfilment of Scripture, as well as the words of Jesus, is found in John's Gospel (e.g. John 18.9; 19.36).

There is debate about the precise meaning of the verb *plēroō* in Matthew and whether one definition covers all those usages (leaving aside 13.48, which refers to the dragnet in Jesus' parable being 'full', and 23.32, which comes in a negative reference to the scribes and Pharisees). John Meier has rightly pointed to the preponderance of prophetic references, arguing on the basis of this that even the statement that Christ came to fulfil *the Law* and the prophets (5.17) be redefined in terms of prophetic fulfilment (Meier 1991). Yet given that what the Matthean Jesus goes on to do in 5.21–48 is precisely to tackle interpretation of *Torah* (he cites a variety of texts from the Law of Moses before offering his own definitive interpretation) and challenge certain Jewish interpretations of those Mosaic commandments (e.g. 'You shall love your neighbour *and hate your enemy*', 5.43), one may need to allow for a different nuance to 'fulfil' at 5.17 from the earlier quotations from the prophets.

In the prophetic references the emphasis is upon events of Jesus' life fulfilling specific prophetic writings: for example, his conception of a virgin, his coming out of Egypt, the slaughter of the innocents after his birth, his settling in Nazareth, his coming to Capernaum in 'Galilee of the Gentiles', his healing ministry, his low-key ministry as the Servant of the Lord, his teaching in parables, his riding as a humble king into Jerusalem, his betrayal by Judas Iscariot. The sense appears to be that, read in the right way, these prophecies point to and find their completion in what Jesus does and in what happens to him, between the cradle and the grave. The sense of *plēroō* as 'fill' may be pertinent here: whatever these prophetic passages may have meant to their prophetic authors, Matthew finds a 'fuller' meaning in the divine words spoken 'through the prophet' as God's vehicle of revelation. The prophecy from Isaiah 7.14 quoted at 1.23 is thought by many Old Testament scholars to have as its primary reference the birth of Hezekiah, who would succeed his father Ahaz as king of Judah (cf. 2 Kings 18.1). The 'virgin' (LXX; the Hebrew has 'young woman') in this case is the mother of Hezekiah, currently a young woman or 'virgin', who will – in the future from the prophet's perspective – conceive in the normal way. Yet the much later emergence of Jesus as the true royal Messiah and descendant – at least by adoption – of Hezekiah (1.9), and one born of a virgin, meant that this passage found an even greater 'fulfilment' than Isaiah of Jerusalem would ever have imagined.

Also important for understanding fulfilment in Matthew is 5.17–20, in which Matthew's Jesus vehemently denies that he has come to 'abolish' the Law or the prophets. *Pace* Meier, this suggests that prophetic fulfilment in the events of Jesus' life is not all there is to be said. Another possible dimension is that Christ 'fulfils' the Law in the sense of doing what the Law requires, as the Son of God who is utterly obedient to the Father's will. This is probably also the sense of 'it is proper for us in this way *to fulfil all righteousness*', spoken by Matthew's Jesus to John the Baptist at the River Jordan (3.15). Given that Matthew's concept of 'righteousness' means something like 'practical obedience to the will of God', Jesus' words point to his baptism as one such deed in accordance with the Father's will (i.e. that the sinless Son identify himself fully with the sinful people of Israel). The New English Bible paraphrases 3.15 as 'to do all that God requires'.

Yet 5.17–20 can also be understood to be making demands on his followers, given that Jesus warns the disciples against setting aside the smallest commandments and teaching others to do likewise. This suggests that fulfilment of the Law is a possibility for others besides Jesus, at least if the Law is read in the light of Jesus' so-called 'antitheses' ('You have heard it was said . . . But I say to you', 5.21–48), and the two commandments to love God and neighbour (22.40).

The Formula Citations

One key body of evidence for understanding the concept of 'fulfilment' in Matthew's Gospel comprises a special subgroup of Matthew's Old Testament quotations (see e.g. Brown 1993: 96–104; Luz 1989: 156–64; Senior 1997 warns against overconcentration on this subgroup, given that Matthew's use of the Old Testament is far more extensive). These are the formula citations, so called because they are each introduced with a similar formula, along the lines of 'This was to fulfil what had been spoken by the Lord through the prophet'. They are sometimes referred to as the fulfilment quotations, referring to the verb 'fulfil' found in the introductory formula. These function as a commentary on the surrounding narrative by the narrator, specifically indicating how Scripture has been 'fulfilled', 'filled up' or 'completed' in Jesus' birth, life and ministry.

There is some scholarly disagreement as to how many formula citations Matthew contains (ranging from 10 to 14, several scholars preferring 12, given its symbolic significance as the number of Israel's tribes). The disagreement is due to the fact that the precise formula – referring to fulfilment through the prophet(s) – is only found in ten cases (1.22; 2.15, 17, 23; 4.14; 8.17; 12.17; 13.35; 21.4; 27.9), but the introductions to several other Old Testament quotations are similar. Thus the chief priests and scribes at 2.5 tell Herod that the Messiah was to be born in Bethlehem 'for so it has been written by the prophet' (then citing from Mic. 5.2). The appearance of John the Baptist is accompanied by the statement: 'This is the one of whom the prophet Isaiah spoke when he said' (3.3, introducing a quotation from Isa. 40.3). At 13.14, Jesus says of those who have not been given the secrets of the kingdom: 'With them indeed is fulfilled the prophecy of Isaiah' (the verb here is *anaplēroō*). Finally, 24.15 is sometimes also grouped together with the formula citations: 'so when you see the desolating sacrilege standing in the holy place, as was spoken of by the prophet Daniel' (the explicit reference to Daniel is Matthew's own: cf. Mark 13.14; Luke 21.20). The ten formula citations all agree upon are as shown in the table overleaf.

1.23 = Isa. 7.14	God-with-us, born of a virgin (cf. 18.20; 28.20)
2.15 = Hos. 11.1	God's Son, obedient where Israel was disobedient
2.18 = Jer. 31.15	Slaughter of innocents foretold
2.23 = unknown;	Upbringing in Nazareth foretold
cf. Isa. 11.1; Judg. 13.5	
4.15–16 = Isa. 9.1–2	Messiah ministers in 'Galilee of the Gentiles'
8.17 = Isa. 53.4	The Lord's Servant bears the suffering of the sick
12.18–21 = Isa. 42.1–4	The Lord's hidden Servant, in whom the Gentiles will hope
13.35 = Ps. 78.2	Jesus' teaching in parables foretold in Scripture
21.5 = Zech. 9.9;	The humble King enters Jerusalem
cf. Isa. 62.11	
27.9–10 = Jer. 18.1–3;	Judas' betrayal foretold
32.6–15; Zech. 11.12–13	

Several features of these formula citations are noteworthy and will be dealt with in turn. First, unlike the Old Testament quotations Matthew shares with Mark (which tend to follow the LXX), these typically Matthean quotations exhibit much greater textual fluidity. Second, although a range of prophetic writings are quoted (e.g. Hosea, Zechariah, plus Micah if one includes the closely related 2.5–6, as well as the book of Psalms, suggesting that David is also viewed as a prophet, 13.35), only Isaiah and Jeremiah are mentioned by name (albeit Isaiah is not explicitly named in the better manuscripts of 1.22). These two issues will be discussed in more detail below.

One additional puzzling feature of the formula citations concerns their distribution. Rather than being evenly placed across the Gospel they are particularly concentrated towards the beginning (four out of ten in the first two chapters, along with the closely associated quotation from Micah at 2.6), while only two (21.4–5; 27.9–10) are concerned with events in the last week of Jesus' public ministry. This last point is particularly striking, given the central role often accorded to the cross of Christ in early Christian debate with the Synagogue ('a stumbling block to Jews', 1 Cor. 1.23). For this reason many scholars, notably Raymond Brown, conclude that the primary purpose was not apologetic (to defend Christian claims against counterclaims from non-Christian Jews), nor even missionary, but didactic, aimed at teaching Christian readers. However, even Brown is prepared to admit that the quotations may still have served Christians well as debating tools, albeit at a secondary level:

> Even in this situation, however, there were Christians of Jewish descent in Matthew's community who may have found such citations useful when they

were called on to defend their adherence to Jesus in the course of discussions with their Jewish neighbors who remained in the Synagogue.

(Brown 1993: 99)

An alternative explanation is that by the time Matthew was written the focus on Church–Synagogue debate had shifted from Christ's suffering and death to different issues, such as his disputed parentage or his association with Nazareth rather than David's hometown of Bethlehem.

Textual Fluidity

We begin with the variety of Old Testament versions reflected in the formula citations and related quotations. It is true that in a small number of cases these quotations follow or are very close to the LXX, which seems to be Matthew's practice in the Old Testament quotations he shares with Mark. Thus the quotation from Isaiah 7.14 at 1.23 is almost identical to the LXX, apart from 'they shall name him' instead of 'you shall name him'. The fact that the LXX has the word 'virgin' (Greek *parthenos*) better suits Matthew's story of Jesus' virginal conception than the Hebrew alternative. The quotation from Jeremiah at 2.18, despite being closer to what became the standard Hebrew version, the Masoretic Text (MT), nonetheless also exhibits some agreement with the LXX.

Others, however, diverge considerably from the LXX and from the MT. Such divergences, which in some cases appear to involve rewriting the text in order to fit the Jesus story better, may be puzzling or even shocking to modern readers. An obvious example is the citation from Micah – not strictly a formula citation given that its introduction lacks the verb 'fulfil' – attributed to the chief priests and scribes at 2.6. Not only is this a mixed text (although the main reference is to Micah 5.2, some of the wording seems to be influenced by 2 Samuel 5.2: 'It is you who will be shepherd of my people Israel') that diverges both from the LXX and the MT, but Matthew's version also transforms the meaning of Bethlehem (from Micah's 'who are one of the little clans of Judah') by the addition of 'by no means': in the light of Christ's birth there, little Bethlehem is now '*by no means* least among the rulers of Judah'.

Nor is this quotation alone in its fluidity. The quotation about the Servant (Isa. 42.1–4) at 12.18–21 has similarities with the LXX and the Targums (Aramaic translation-paraphrases of the Hebrew Bible) as well as the Hebrew (Davies and Allison follow Jerome in thinking that Matthew made his own translation from the Hebrew text: Davies and Allison

1988–97: 2/322). Another example is the formula citation attributed to Jeremiah at 27.9–10, used to comment on Judas' betrayal of Jesus for 30 pieces of silver and the purchase of the 'Field of Blood' by the chief priests and elders. This is in fact a rather complex interweaving of passages from Jeremiah and Zechariah (suggestions include Jer. 18.2; 19.11; 32.6–9 and Zech. 11.12–13). Finally there is the mysterious 'quotation' at 2.23 ('He shall be called a Nazorean'), rather vaguely explained as having been spoken 'through the prophets'. Some earlier commentators offered ingenious solutions to the difficulty that this precise prophecy is found nowhere in the canonical prophets. Thus the ninth-century exegete Isho'dad of Merv believed this citation was contained in a writing that 'perished in the various captivities' but that Matthew knew (Gibson [ed.] 1911: 21). However, even Isho'dad recognized that part of an explanation might be found in a wordplay between 'Nazorean' or 'Nazarene' and the messianic 'Branch' (Hebrew *nētzer*) of Jesse at Isaiah 11.1. This reading goes back at least to Jerome, who noted, rather more critically than Isho'dad, that Matthew 'has not taken the words, but rather the sense, from the Scriptures' (Jerome 2008: 67). As well as the Isaiah reference Jerome also proposed an etymological connection between 'Nazarene' and 'holy' (*nazir*, 'consecrated one' or 'Nazirite'), reflecting the consistent view of the Old Testament that the Lord was to be holy. Jerome's allusion here is to the story of Samson, who was to be a 'nazirite to God from birth' (Judg. 13.5).

Both explanations are regularly repeated by modern commentators on Matthew. In other words, Matthew is able to make sense of the fact that Jesus, contrary to any known messianic expectation of the time, was associated with an otherwise obscure Galilean village called 'Nazareth' (and the fact that early Christians, at least in Syria, were known as Nazarenes). He is a Nazarene, or a Nazorean, because he is the messianic Branch or *nētzer* of the line of Jesse, the father of David, or because he is the Son consecrated to his Father.

Origins of the Formula Citations

Various scholarly attempts have been made to explain the origins of the formula citations and whether they spring from the evangelist's own pen or rather reflect Old Testament quotations he inherited. Krister Stendahl famously argued that the distinctly Matthean formula citations originated in an early Christian 'scribal school' with access to a range of textual traditions, which engaged in a style of exegesis akin to that found in the Qumran *pesher* ('interpretation') or Commentary on Habakkuk (Stendahl 1954:

97–127). While the suggestion of a group of Christian Jewish scribes is an attractive one (Matthew's more positive view of scribes has already been noted), there are difficulties with his likening the process to the Qumran *pesharim*. Whereas in the Qumran examples the starting point is the biblical text, for which the author provides the definitive interpretation ('Interpreted, this concerns . . .'), Matthew's starting point seems to be the events of Jesus' life, in the light of which scriptural passages are read in fresh ways. It is difficult, for example, to explain the stories of the magi, the flight into Egypt or the slaughter of the innocents as narratives that would have developed straightforwardly on the basis of the Old Testament quotations at 2.6, 15 and 18. Indeed Stendahl modified his original position somewhat in the Preface to the second edition of his book (Stendahl 1968). By contrast Robert Gundry gave greater weight to the evangelist himself as 'Targumist', distinguishing between the largely Septuagintal Old Testament quotations specifically borrowed from Mark, and Matthew's greater freedom when importing his own, and not just in the formula citations (Gundry 1967). Likewise, Graham Stanton points to similar redactional tendencies to those found in the formula citations in Matthew's other Old Testament quotations. This supports the idea that the evangelist played a crucial role in their development (Stanton 1992: 346–63).

The complexity of the evidence favours a complex solution. First, as Stendahl noted, we must allow for a much greater range of textual traditions in Hebrew and Greek, as well as the kind of Aramaic paraphrasing that has survived in the later Targums. Second, it is possible that in some cases the evangelist or the tradition on whom he draws is working from memory rather than physical scrolls (indeed, Luz believes that Matthew's community possessed a scroll of the prophet Isaiah but no other prophetic books: Luz 1989: 157). Third, even if some of the formula citations had already been developed by others, one should not thereby rule out Matthew's own creativity in producing his own (the reworking of Micah by the addition of 'by no means' at 2.6 is a case in point). Moreover Brown is probably correct that Matthew himself has made the step of introducing the formula citations into the existing narratives of Jesus' conception, birth and infancy in order to clarify them, and to emphasize the Matthean motif of 'fulfilment' (Brown 1993: 104). Several of them (e.g. 1.22–23; 2.15, 17–18, 23) may be removed without doing undue damage to the surrounding story. This is confirmed by the two 'servant' quotations at 8.17 and 12.17–21, where the citation is not present in the parallel passage in Mark or Luke (both come at the end of editorial summaries of Jesus' ministry: cf. Mark 1.29–34; Luke 4.38–41; Mark 3.7–12; Luke 6.17–19).

Naming Prophets

Also of note is the apparent lack of consistency in naming the prophet being quoted in the various formula citations and related Old Testament quotations. In several cases the evangelist simply speaks anonymously of 'the prophet' (1.22; 2.5, 15; 13.35; 21.4) or 'the prophets' (2.23: the vagueness in this case is understandable). More interesting is the fact that two prophets are explicitly mentioned by name. The first is Isaiah, whose prominence in Matthew was recognized by the designer of the Chartres rose window. The second is the prophet Jeremiah.

Isaiah makes his first explicit appearance at 3.3, an editorial comment identifying John the Baptist as the 'voice of one crying out in the wilderness' of Isaiah 40.3 (LXX). Isaiah is mentioned again by name in the Old Testament quotations at 4.14 (announcing 'a great light' for 'Galilee of the Gentiles'), 8.17 and 12.17 (both referring to the Servant of the Lord) and 13.14 (a saying on Jesus' lips, interpreting the mixed response to his parabolic teaching). Jesus also mentions Isaiah by name at 15.7 (introducing a quotation paralleled at Mark 7.6–7). On the other hand, Matthew's introduction to the quotation about the virgin conceiving (1.22) lacks a reference to Isaiah, except in a few manuscripts (which can be explained as scribal corrections). Some manuscripts even insert a reference to Isaiah at 13.35, despite the fact that the formula citation ('I will open my mouth to speak in parables') appears to come from Psalm 78.2.

Jeremiah is named explicitly in two places. The first (at 2.17) is relatively straightforward. This introduces a passage from Jeremiah 31.15 about Rachel weeping for her children, originally describing the bitter trauma of the exile to Babylon but now interpreted as finding its fulfilment or completeness in the slaughter of the innocents by Herod. The second attribution to Jeremiah (at 27.9), providing a theological commentary on Judas' 'blood money' and the purchase of the 'Field of Blood' by the chief priests and elders, is more complex. Although various passages from Jeremiah seem to have fed into this formula citation (suggestions include Jeremiah 18—19; 32.6–9), the basic shape of this rather loose quotation appears to come from Zechariah 11.12–13, which links 'thirty shekels of silver', 'wages' or 'price' and the 'treasury in the house of the LORD'. Unsurprisingly, therefore, a small number of manuscripts and quotations in the Fathers replace 'Jeremiah' with 'Zechariah' at this point.

Why does Matthew draw attention to these two prophets and only these two? A liking for Isaiah is understandable enough, particularly if Luz is correct that Matthew's circles possessed no other scroll of the prophets.

Isaiah is a prophet of 'the gospel', using the verb *euangelizomai* ('I proclaim good news', e.g. Isa. 40.9; 52.7), which is closely related to the noun *euangelion* or 'gospel'. He is also the prophet who speaks of the shadowy figure 'the Servant of the Lord', who is important christologically for Matthew. Moreover some of the Isaianic passages quoted by Matthew have an interest in the spread of salvation to the Gentiles (e.g. Isa. 9.1–2; 42.1–9). Thus Isaiah's prophecy contains a cluster of motifs that are also characteristically Matthean.

The interest in Jeremiah can also be explained in several ways, not necessarily mutually exclusive. First, Jeremiah was the prophet who foresaw and witnessed the destruction of the Temple by the Babylonians in 587 BCE. If the scholarly consensus about the post-70 dating of the Gospel is correct, then Jeremiah may function as a prophetic paradigm for Matthew, attempting to make sense of Rome's desecration of the Second Temple in 70 CE (e.g. 22.7; 23.38; cf. Jer. 22.5). Second, Jeremiah is a prophet of hope as well as judgement. The wider context of the oracle about Rachel quoted by Matthew at 2.18 offers the promise of restoration following the trauma of her children, the tribes of Joseph and Benjamin, being taken into exile ('they shall come back from the land of the enemy; there is hope for your future, says the LORD', Jer. 31.16b–17a). Finally, it is possible that a typological relationship is implied between Jeremiah and Jesus (Winkle 1986). Jeremiah was 'the preeminent prophet of persecution and tragic rejection by his own people' (Heil 1991: 122), who in some Jewish apocryphal texts was martyred for his prophetic witness (by stoning, according to the *Lives of the Prophets*). Matthew's story of Jesus and of his followers is also one of tragic rejection and persecution at the hands of the people. Indeed the link is made explicit at 16.14: Jesus the Son of Man is thought by at least some of the people to be 'Jeremiah', even if this is inadequate for Matthew's christological vision (Jeremiah's name is absent from the parallels at Mark 8.28 and Luke 9.19).

Fulfilling the Law

Much of the preceding discussion has focused on Jesus as fulfiller of the prophets, primarily through a correlation between specific prophetic texts and events in Jesus' life and ministry. The procedure here has been to begin with the story of Jesus and read the prophetic writings afresh in the light of that story, often discovering fresh and 'fuller' meanings in the ancient prophecies as a consequence. However, Matthew's Gospel also explores the relationship between Jesus and the Mosaic Law. The classic passage here is 5.17–20, especially the opening phrase: 'Do not think that I have come to abolish the law or the prophets; I have come not to abolish but to fulfil.' The way scholars interpret this passage is often closely related to their view on the relationship between the evangelist Matthew (and Matthew's 'community' or 'communities') and the Pharisaic-led Synagogue.

As noted above, Meier proposed that the reference to 'the prophets' alongside the Law at 5.17, together with the fact that the majority of Matthew's uses of *plēroō* concern prophetic fulfilment, supported an interpretation of this passage along the same lines. Thus Jesus is claiming to have completed or brought to perfection that to which the Law and the prophets pointed. Moreover Meier saw in the parallel phrases 'until heaven and earth pass away' (v. 18a) and 'until all is accomplished' (v. 18c) not Hebrew parallelism, whereby the latter phrase is reiterating the former using different words, but a redefinition: 'all the events prophesied in the Old Testament' (Meier 1991: 230). All has now been accomplished by the death and resurrection of Jesus (the dawning of the new age, 27.51–53), such that the Torah is no longer binding in the way it was for the people of Israel. What is binding now is what Jesus commanded, 'whether or not that coincides with what Moses commanded' (Meier 1991: 234). The Jewish rite of circumcision has been replaced by baptism as the new entrance rite for God's people (28.19).

Others read the same words very differently, treating these two phrases as synonymous and stressing continuity between Moses and Christ. They emphasize verse 19, which appears to be advocating that even the smallest of the commandments be performed and taught, as well as the demand of a greater righteousness in verse 20. Thus both Mohrlang and Sim regard the whole Mosaic Law as remaining valid for Christians (Mohrlang 1984; Sim 1998), a position justified by careful attention to those passages in Matthew in which Jesus debates with the Pharisees and others over the technicalities of legal interpretation. Sim goes so far as to accord the Torah 'a central place' in the Gospel (Sim 1998: 123), a view vigorously challenged by Hagner for downplaying the element of 'newness' and discontinuity in Christ (Hagner 2003).

Older commentators were able to hold together different nuances of 5.17–20 in their interpretations. Thus the author of the *Opus imperfectum* finds in the passage both prophetic fulfilment as expressed in the formula citations (that Christ 'completes' and 'fills with deeper meaning' the words of Scripture) and an ethical demand to observe what the Law requires: 'The Law and the Prophets are both in force. They prophesy concerning

Christ and constitute the law of living. Christ fulfilled them both' (Simonetti [ed.] 2001: 97). Nor is this ethical dimension only related to Christ's personal obedience to the Father's will. He also shows his disciples how they can fulfil the Law in imitation of him: 'Even as he fulfilled every law, they too must eagerly fulfil even the least part of the law.'

For all the differences between modern scholars, most are agreed – in common with the *Opus imperfectum* – that there is a christological dimension to this question. Whether or not specific elements of the Mosaic Law continue to function for Christians, the Law is read in Matthew through the definitive interpretation offered by the Messiah Jesus. This is exemplified in the 'antitheses' (5.21–48), as well as in the Golden Rule (7.12), which parallels 5.17–20 in concentric structural analyses of the Sermon on the Mount, the priority given to the dual commandments of love of God and love of neighbour, on which 'hang all the law and the prophets' (22.40), and the emphasis on mercy rather than sacrifice in the repeated quotation from Hosea 6.6 (9.13; 12.7: Hays 2005).

The Matthean 'Antitheses'

The christological lens of Matthew's teaching about the Law finds particular expression in the so-called 'antitheses' (5.21–48), for which 5.17–20 functions as an introduction. Here Matthew's Jesus teaches his disciples the meaning of a righteousness that 'exceeds that of the scribes and Pharisees'. The title 'antitheses' reflects the 'antithetical' rhetorical structure of Jesus' words: 'You have heard that it was said . . . But I say to you'. However, this label is potentially misleading, giving the impression that Jesus' teaching is itself opposed to the Mosaic commandments to which it responds. That this is by no means the obvious sense of this section of the Sermon on the Mount is shown by Jesus' explicit claim to 'fulfil' and not to 'abolish' or 'annul'. Hence some recent scholars prefer the alternative term 'hypertheses', interpreting Jesus' words as 'going beyond' the words of Torah or contemporary scribal interpretations of Torah (Lapide 1986: 45–6).

In support of this is the observation that Matthew's Jesus begins with a quotation from the Pentateuch ('You have heard that it was said') and then offers his own more rigorous demand ('But I say to you'). In one case (5.43) the words that Jesus redefines reflect not simply Torah ('You shall love your neighbour', Lev. 19.19) but a contemporary expansion of Torah ('and hate your enemy', similar to the command to 'hate the sons of darkness' in the Qumran *Community Rule*: 1QS 1.10; 9.21).

In three of the six cases – on murder (5.21–26), adultery (5.27–30) and love of neighbour (5.43–48) – Jesus' more rigorous demand represents a clear intensification of biblical law. Scholars have identified two possible – not mutually exclusive – approaches at work here. According to the first, Matthew's Jesus is following the rabbinic practice of 'putting a fence around Torah' (Przybylski 1980: 81–3). A weightier commandment is 'fenced around' with lesser commandments in order to avoid the breaking of the former. Thus a warning against becoming angry with brother or sister prevents a situation whereby the command against murder (Exod. 20.13; Deut. 5.18) might be transgressed. A similar dynamic is at issue in lust as a prelude to adultery (Exod. 20.14; Deut. 5.17). Second, Matthew may be advocating a radicalization or 'getting to the root' (Latin *radix*) of Torah, going beyond to the deeper concern underlying the original command- ment. Thus the command to 'love your neighbour' is radicalized to include even those among one's neighbours who are enemies. For some historical critics this would have had particular poignancy for Matthew's first readers, as they were urged to love those 'enemies' close to home who flogged them in their synagogues.

The remaining 'antitheses' – on divorce, oaths, and the *lex talionis* or 'law of retribution' – are less straightforward. In 5.31–32 Matthew's Jesus effectively challenges the right of a husband to issue his wife with 'a certificate of divorce' (Deut. 24.1), except for the limited grounds of *porneia*, 'sexual immorality', perhaps adultery (for the alternative inter- pretation of the forbidden degrees of kinship as outlined in Leviticus 18.6–18, see Fitzmyer 1976). In 5.33–37 Jesus could be interpreted as undermining the Mosaic command to swear oaths by God's name (e.g. Deut. 6.13; 10.20) by refusing all oath-taking (see Moo 1984: 19–23). Finally, 5.38–42 presents him as critiquing the Mosaic commandment ensuring appropriate recompense for wrongdoing ('An eye for an eye and a tooth for a tooth', Exod. 21.24; Lev. 24.20; Deut. 19.21), through a series of non-violent yet provocative actions. Hence Meier could conclude that Matthew's Jesus on occasion makes demands that go against Mosaic demands.

Yet even in these cases Matthean 'radicalization' rather than abrogation of lesser commandments may be at work. Ruling out any oath-taking could be interpreted in terms of 'putting a fence around Torah' to prevent followers of Jesus from finding themselves in a position where they might swear 'falsely' (Lev. 19.12). Nor is being more demanding than the Law of Moses necessarily a contradiction of that Law. Divorce is certainly permitted, at least to Jewish males, by the Torah. But divorce is not a *requirement* under the Law, such that restricting it to very specific circumstances – as in Matthew's 'exception clause' – would constitute an infringement of God's command. Indeed Matthew's Jesus comes to a position on divorce close to that espoused by the 'conservative' Pharisee leader Shammai, hardly a candidate for abrogation of Torah! Jesus' teaching about turning the other cheek and going the extra mile may also be viewed as a more demanding or radical alternative to the attempt of the *lex talionis* to restrict retribution for wrongdoing.

Moreover the element of continuity between the Law of Moses and the teaching of Jesus is implicit in the narrative context of the Sermon on the Mount. W. D. Davies (Davies 1989: 107) makes the point that in positioning the Sermon on the Mount at the point where Mark has Jesus' first exorcism in the Capernaum synagogue (Mark 1.21–28), and having it provoke the same response as Jesus' teaching there ('he taught them as one having authority, and not as the/their scribes', 7.29, cf. Mark 1.22), Matthew omits to call it 'a new teaching' (cf. Mark 1.27). Jesus' teaching is not something new to replace the old Mosaic code, even if he is the true Teacher and one greater than Moses, who offers its true interpretation.

Did Matthew Expect Christians to Keep the Law?

A close comparison between Matthew and Mark supports the conclusion that Matthew's Jesus is no iconoclast when it comes to the Mosaic Law. Moreover it leaves open the possibility – hotly debated by scholars – that Matthew's Gospel expects Christians to continue to observe specific Mosaic commandments. Three pericopae, concerned with three different issues of legal interest – namely, Sabbath observance, dietary laws and grounds for divorce – may serve to illustrate the point. Although the scholarly discussion of these three passages generally presumes Marcan priority, the general conclusions hold even if Mark is a reworking of Matthew or there is a looser relationship between the two (the position, for example, of Albright and Mann 1971: cvi–cxv).

As the division between Jesus and the leaders of Israel begins to widen, Matthew describes a series of controversy stories, the first of which concerns a debate with the Pharisees provoked by Jesus' disciples plucking grain on the Sabbath (12.1–8). This story is found in all three Synoptic Gospels (also Mark 2.23–28 and Luke 6.1–5). In Mark's account the shocking pronouncement of Jesus – 'The sabbath was made for humankind, and not humankind for the sabbath' (2.27) – seems to relegate Israel's important Sabbath laws to an inferior place. Both Matthew and Luke lack this offending saying, sometimes explained, rather unnecessarily, by their having used a different version of Mark's Gospel from the one available to us. But Matthew's version has further distinctive features that emphasize respect for the Sabbath on the part of Jesus and – by implication – his followers.

First, Matthew's new setting for the story, following immediately from Jesus' invitation to those who carry 'heavy burdens' to come to him for rest (11.28), accentuates the contrast between Jesus and the Pharisees, who tie up 'heavy burdens' (23.4). Second, he provides a need for the disciples' behaviour ('his disciples were hungry', v. 1), thus making clearer how the story of David and his companions eating the showbread (1 Sam. 21.1–6) acts as a precedent. The technical 'infringement' of Sabbath law by Jesus' disciples – by Pharisaic standards, though not according to the Law itself (see Deut. 23.25) – is motivated by good cause. Third, Matthew provides an example of apparent infringement of the Sabbath that is actually commendable behaviour. By offering sacrifice on the Sabbath, thereby fulfilling God's Law, the priests in the Temple are technically breaking the Sabbath yet remain guiltless (v. 5). Finally, Matthew has Jesus quote from the prophet Hosea (v. 7, citing Hos. 6.6: 'I desire mercy and not sacrifice'), stressing the priority of mercy. The Pharisaic interpretation of the Sabbath laws, by contrast, lacks mercy and would permit the disciples to starve. This distinctive Matthean version of the story seems carefully designed to minimize any suggestion that Jesus or his disciples violate the Sabbath per se.

A similar case can be made for Matthew's version of the conflict story in which Jesus' disciples offend by not washing their hands prior to eating (15.1–20; cf. Mark 7.1–23). The issue is specifically one of adherence to Pharisaic oral tradition (even though Mark confuses matters by attributing the practice to 'the Pharisees, and all the Jews', 7.3). Moreover there are two distinctive features of Matthew's account compared to the Marcan parallel. First, Matthew lacks Mark's editorial comment, which interprets Jesus' words to mean that 'he declared all foods clean' (Mark 7.19). He seems to step back from drawing a similar conclusion, which would undercut a large section of the Law of Moses concerning kosher and non-kosher food. There is no reason, therefore, to suppose – *pace* Meier 1991 – that Matthew's first readers would take this story as justification for abandoning the food laws. Second, Matthew adds a saying at the very end of Jesus' speech (15.20: 'but to eat with unwashed hands does not defile') that clarifies that Jesus' criticism is directed at the oral 'traditions of the elders', not the Mosaic Law as such.

The third example concerns Jesus' teaching on divorce. This topic is addressed twice in Matthew (5.31–32; 19.3–9; cf. Mark 10.2–12; Luke 16.18; 1 Cor. 7.10–11). We have encountered Matthew's exception clause ('except on the ground of unchastity [*porneia*]') already in relation to the 'antitheses' or 'hypertheses'. In both passages Matthew's Jesus engages in a debate about the interpretation of Scripture also attested in traditions about two of his contemporaries, the Pharisee leaders Shammai and Hillel. Matthew's Jesus comes closest to the position of Shammai, who interpreted 'something indecent' at Deuteronomy 24.1 in terms of unchastity/adultery (*m. Gittin* 90.1). Again the concern is to present Jesus as one who interprets the Mosaic Law, indeed one who provides the full and authoritative interpretation of that Law (speaking at 5.32 with the authoritative divine 'I'), but fulfilling rather than annulling God's revelation to Moses (see Davies 1989: 105). In the cut and thrust of debates about marriage and questions of divorce, as about Sabbath observance and food, the Torah interpretation of the Messiah Jesus remains binding on his followers.

10

'Built upon the Rock':
The Gospel of the Church

The Church in Matthew

Around the ceiling of St Peter's Basilica in Rome, in letters six feet high, is a Latin quotation from Matthew's Gospel: *Tu es Petrus et super hanc petram aedificabo ecclesiam meam* ('you are Peter, and on this rock I will build my church', 16.18). Towering over the tomb of the apostle Peter, these words are a vivid testimony not only to the prominence of Simon Peter in the early Christian memory (see Bockmuehl 2012) but also to the fact that Matthew alone of the Gospels uses the term 'church' (Greek *ekklēsia*). In the passage cited in the Vatican Basilica it refers to the universal Church; its other occurrences in Matthew (twice in 18.17) seem to refer to the local congregation of Christians. This is one major reason – Matthew's popularity in the early Church is another – why Matthew has inherited the title of 'the Gospel of the Church'.

Indeed, although on the story level Matthew's Gospel recounts the earthly life and ministry of Jesus of Nazareth, many have read it as providing insight into the ongoing life of the Christian Church. Whereas Luke may well have distinguished between the period of Jesus and the period of the Church (separated by the ascension), there is no such clear distinction in Matthew, for whom the risen Christ remains rather than going away (28.20: Brown 1984: 125). The Lord abides with his Church 'to the end of the age' (28.20). Ulrich Luz's term 'transparency' describes this connection the Gospel establishes between the disciples of Jesus' pre-resurrection ministry and the post-Easter community. At times the evangelist or narrator speaks explicitly 'beyond the narrative' to address those living in a post-Easter situation ('All this took place to fulfil what had been spoken by the Lord through the prophet', e.g. 1.22; 'For this reason that field has been called the Field of Blood to this day', 27.8; 'And this story is still told among the Jews to this day', 28.15b). The teaching of Jesus arguably provides patterns for later community living (liturgical prayer: 6.9–13; the rituals of baptism and Eucharist: 26.26–29; 28.19; a mechanism for excommunication: 18.15–17). The teaching about fasting (6.16–18) seems to presuppose a later situation, given Jesus' clear statement that the wedding guests cannot fast while the bridegroom is still with them (9.14–15). Finally, as noted above, the discourses also exhibit signs of transparency to the life of the Church. It is not surprising that, in the patristic tradition that the Apostles' Creed was created by each of the Twelve dictating one of its articles, it is Matthew who is responsible for the phrase 'holy catholic church' (Clarke 2003: 139).

Israel and the Church

Matthew's claim that Jesus founds a 'Church' raises the question of the relationship of his people to the people of Israel. For although the word *ekklēsia* would have been meaningful to the wider Graeco-Roman society (where it referred to a local 'assembly' or 'gathering' for political purposes), it had particular associations for Greek-speaking Jews. In the LXX *ekklēsia* describes the 'congregation' or 'assembly' of the Lord (e.g. Deut. 9.10; 23.1; Judg. 20.2; 1 Kings 8.14; Neh. 5.13; Ps. 35.18; Ps. 149.1; Mic. 2.5), the ancient people of Israel. A similar phrase is used to describe the community at Qumran in some of its sectarian writings (e.g. 1QM 4; 1QSa 2.4; CD 7.17; 11.22; 12.6). The Lord's 'congregation' or 'church' is therefore an ancient designation for God's ancient people Israel.

The precise relationship between the ancient 'Church of the Lord' (Israel) and the Church of Jesus the Lord is somewhat ambiguous. On the one hand, references to Israel in Matthew are generally positive. 'Israel' is used to refer to the Holy Land (2.20–21; 9.33) and the people (e.g. 2.6, citing Mic. 5.2; 27.9), including Israel's 'lost sheep' (e.g. 10.6; 15.24), who have YHWH as their God and Jesus the Messiah as their king (e.g. 15.31; 27.42). On the other hand, there are passages in Matthew that may be read as advocating a replacement of Israel by Christ's Jew–Gentile Church or even by the Gentiles. Israel's faith is trumped by that of a Gentile centurion, leading to the warning that the 'heirs [literally 'sons'] of the kingdom will be thrown into the outer darkness' (8.10–12). In Matthew's version of the parable of the vineyard tenants, Jesus tells his hearers that 'the kingdom of God will be taken away from you and given to a people (*ethnos*) that produces the fruits of the kingdom' (21.43). The Greek word *ethnos* can be used in the plural, *ethnē*, to designate Gentiles. At 27.25, 'all the people' ultimately reject their king, calling for his crucifixion. Finally, in the Great Commission of 28.16–20 the restrictive mission to 'the lost sheep of the house of Israel' is apparently superseded by a universal mission to *panta ta ethnē*: 'all the nations' (including Israel), or possibly 'all the Gentiles' (excluding Israel: for debate over the meaning see Hare and Harrington 1975; Meier 1977a).

Such passages account for the pervasive reading of Matthew as advocating either a replacement of Israel by the Gentiles or of the old 'Church' of Israel by the new Jew–Gentile Church of Christ. For John Chrysostom, for example, one of the 'many things' taught by the parable of the tenants is 'the calling of the Gentiles, the casting out of the Jews' (John Chrysostom 1991: 415). More nuanced interpretations are offered by modern commentators. Thus those who advocate an *extra muros* situation (see Chapter 5 above) for Matthew's relationship with the Synagogue interpret the ecclesiological language in terms of the bitter experience of separation and consequent self-definition (e.g. Stanton 1992: 113–45). Commenting specifically on the parable of the tenants, Rudolf Schnackenburg reads the 'you' at 21.43 in the light of 27.25 ('all the people'), concluding: 'By "you" only the old Israel can be meant' (Schnackenburg 1965: 70). Nonetheless, Schnackenburg admits that the parable itself is particularly directed at the leaders. From a narrative-critical perspective Frank Matera finds in Matthew's plot a definitive rejection of Jesus by Israel, with acceptance of him by the Gentiles anticipated in the Roman soldiers at the cross, leading to a plot resolution in favour of the Gentiles in the concluding verses of the Gospel. Matera's strategy for uncovering the plot – understood as 'narrative logic' – is to start from the end of the story rather than the beginning (Matera 1987; though see Powell 1992: 190 for a denial that all story plots follow a pattern of strict causality).

Replacing the Shepherds

There is an alternative way of reading the evidence regarding the relationship between Israel and the Church. This gives precedence to the motif of the shepherd in Matthew's story. This motif has been present almost from the beginning, where the chief priests and scribes – somewhat ironically, given the way the narrative develops – quote from Micah about the ruler 'who is to shepherd my people Israel' (2.6). Jesus' claim to be sent to 'the lost sheep of the house of Israel' and his command to the Twelve to do the same (10.5–6; 15.24) explicitly casts Jesus and his disciples in the shepherd role.

Elsewhere Jesus also speaks in a shepherd-like manner: he has compassion on the crowds because they are 'like sheep without a shepherd' (9.36). In his final parable he likens the Last Judgement by the Son of Man to a shepherd separating sheep from goats (25.32). When Jesus and his disciples make their way to the Mount of Olives following the Last Supper, he quotes from Zechariah about the striking of the shepherd and the scattering of the sheep, in its present context clearly a reference to his forthcoming arrest (26.31, quoting Zech. 13.7).

Several scholars, in their different ways, have drawn attention to intertextual echoes of Ezekiel 34 in order to illuminate Matthew's narrative (e.g. Heil 1993; Baxter 2006; Willitts 2007). This prophetic text, in which God as the true shepherd castigates the failing shepherds/leaders of Israel and promises to raise up 'my servant David' as shepherd in their place, brings together several motifs found in Matthew: seeking the lost, healing and feeding. Against this background the fierce attack on the scribes and Pharisees can be understood as a critique of false shepherds who neglect to tend the flock entrusted to their care. They 'tie up heavy burdens' rather than a burden that is light and easy to bear (23.4; cf. 11.30).

Nor are the leaders contrasted only with Jesus the Davidic shepherd. The disciples are also cast in the role of shepherds sent to the lost, healing the sick and feeding the hungry (e.g. 10.6, 8; 14.19; 15.36). Reading Matthew's Gospel within such a context, the parable of the tenants becomes less a supersessionist manifesto for a predominantly Gentile Church than a story describing a change of leadership over God's people. The strong echoes of Isaiah 5.1–2 in the introduction to the parable at 21.33 invite an allegorical interpretation of the parable, in which the vineyard symbolizes 'the house of Israel' (Isa. 5.7) and the tenants the leaders entrusted with the nation's care. This is precisely how the parable is understood within the narrative: 'When the chief priests and the Pharisees heard his parables, they realized that he was speaking about them' (21.45). Nor does Matthew's additional saying at verse 43 undermine such a reading. 'The "people" producing the fruits of the kingdom' is denoted not by the plural *ethnē* ('Gentiles') but by the singular *ethnos*, which means not just 'nation' but 'company' or 'group of people'. At a climactic stage in Matthew's story the replacement of one set of leaders (the chief priests *and the Pharisees*, the latter only mentioned explicitly in Matthew's version of this parable) by another (presumably the Twelve, or the disciples) is foretold.

Built upon the Rock

A similar interpretation can be offered of that crux passage for Matthew's understanding of the Church, the story of Peter's confession at 16.13–20. Exegesis of this text is fraught with difficulties, as its chequered and often bloody reception history attests. Davies and Allison engage in classic understatement when they write of 16.18: 'The verse is among the most controversial in all of Scripture' (Davies and Allison 2004: 268).

The contrast with the parallel in Mark and Luke (Mark 8.27–30; Luke 9.18–21) is striking. Whereas in Mark, Jesus' response to Peter is a command to silence (with the implication that Peter has not understood), Matthew's Jesus utters a blessing, declaring Peter's expanded confession to be the result of divine revelation ('Blessed are you, Simon son of Jonah!'). Perhaps most striking is Jesus' statement that 'you are Peter, and on this rock I will build my church', together with the promise to Peter of 'the keys of the kingdom of heaven' (vv. 18–19). This saying treats Peter's name, *Petros*, as a pun on the Greek word for rock, *petra*.

Interpretations of this passage diverge sharply, from Origen's 'typological' interpretation that treats Peter as a 'type' of or model for all Christians, through an 'Eastern' interpretation that views the 'rock' as Peter's faith or confession, and a 'christological' interpretation that reads Matthew 16.18 in the light of 1 Corinthians 3.11 and 10.4 ('and the rock was Christ'), to the 'Roman interpretation' (that the rock is Peter and his successors) that Luz particularly associates with Leo the Great (for a more detailed discussion, see Luz 1994: 57–74).

Whatever potential for meaning the later reception of this passage would reveal, one widely recognized Old Testament influence supports the idea that Matthew's ecclesiology presupposes a change of leadership over God's people. This is the prophecy regarding the replacement of a certain Shebna by Eliakim son of Hilkiah as steward of the royal household in Jerusalem (Isa. 22.15–25). Shebna's crime is to have built himself a magnificent tomb (carved 'in the rock', v. 16). As a result God is to have him replaced as major-domo of the palace by another more trustworthy leader, Eliakim, giving him 'the key of the house of David' ('he shall open, and no one shall shut; he shall shut, and no one shall open', v. 22).

Read against this intertext, Matthew's Peter is given the keys of the kingdom in order for him to exercise the authority of the owner of the house; that is, Christ. Those who formerly held the keys – the scribes and Pharisees, who 'lock people out of the kingdom of heaven' (23.13) – have had them taken away from them. The 'power of the keys' is combined with the authority to 'bind and loose' – rabbinic language for making legal rulings that were to be binding on the whole community – now given to Peter and later in the Gospel to be shared with the other disciples (18.18). In the words of Davies and Allison, Matthew is presenting Peter as Jesus' 'chief rabbi' of the new community to replace the existing leadership, with authority to make decisions about the Torah, forbidding or permitting certain actions or occasionally for disciplinary decisions (Davies and Allison 1988–97: 2/639; see also Collins 2003: 112).

That is not all there is to be said, however. Other possible Old Testament intertexts point to newness as well as continuity. The first is the parallel between Jesus the Son of David building the Church and Solomon the Son of David building the Temple. According to Nathan's prophecy to David at 2 Samuel 7.5–16, it would be up to David's Son to build the house for the Lord that David himself desired. This was accompanied by a divine promise: 'I will establish the throne of his kingdom forever. I will be a father to him, and he shall be a son to me' (2 Sam. 7.13–14a). As Solomon built the Temple, so Jesus promises to build the Church as a 'new Temple' (a post-70 dating for Matthew gives these words particular poignancy).

The final Old Testament intertext, or set of interwoven intertexts, concerns Abraham. Davies and Allison detect striking similarities with Genesis 17 (Davies and Allison 1988–97: 2/623–4). In this passage Abram receives a new name ('Abraham'), symbolizing his role in a new people that is coming to birth. The etymology of Abraham ('father of a multitude') is explained in terms of his future offspring: 'for I have made you the ancestor of a multitude of nations' (Gen. 17.5). Peter too is given a new name as Christ's Church comes to birth – a people that will include people from many nations. A further connection between this Matthean passage that plays on Peter/rock (*Petros/petra*) and the figure of Abraham is offered by Isaiah 51.1–2. Isaiah identifies Abraham as a rock, a Petrine figure ('Look to the rock from which you were hewn, and to the quarry from which you were dug. Look to Abraham your father and to Sarah who bore you'). Peter the rock might thereby be viewed as a new Abraham, or what Alan Segal calls 'a kind of eponymous ancestor for the Matthean community' (Segal 1991: 9).

Peter, the Rock and Stumbling Stone

But even if the presentation of Peter as the rock does point to a significant role for him in salvation history as 'father' or 'chief rabbi' of a new people (and even this is controversial: see the discussion in Kingsbury 1979), does this legitimate an ongoing 'Petrine Office' such as developed in the later papacy? The answer one gives to this question is often difficult to disentangle from one's prior commitments and presuppositions. Catholic readers will probably be innately sympathetic both to a salvation-historical role for Peter and to an interpretation of Matthew 16 that accounts for the continuing ministry of the Bishop of Rome. Protestant commentators, meanwhile, may be predisposed to the interpretation of Peter as the ideal Christian.

But personal interests and commitments aside, answering this question also entails attending to the wider portrayal of Peter in Matthew's narrative. Many commentators have noted Peter's prominence in other Matthean passages: the story of Peter getting out of the boat (14.28–31), inserted by Matthew alone into the walking on the water; the explicit reference to Peter asking Jesus to explain his parable (15.15; Mark 7.17 attributed this to 'his disciples'); the uniquely Matthean discussion between Peter and Jesus over the Temple tax (17.24–27); Peter's question about the extent of forgiveness (18.21–22). In several of these examples Peter is portrayed as spokesman for the Twelve, prompting 'halakhic instruction regulating ethical behaviour' (Schweizer 1995: 156). Other minor adjustments also heighten Peter's role. In the list of the Twelve, Matthew explicitly notes that Peter is 'first' (10.2; cf. Mark 3.16). In the Transfiguration story Matthew omits the somewhat negative statement of Mark that Peter 'did not know what to say' (Mark 9.6). In addition to this, Matthew has a marked preference for his 'rocky' nickname Peter over his real name Simon (4.18; cf. Mark 1.16; 8.14; cf. Mark 1.29; 10.2; 14.28; 15.15; 16.16, 18, 22–23; 17.1, 4, 24, 26; 18.21; 19.27; 26.33–35, 37–46, 58, 69–75).

Holistic readings of Matthew's Gospel further enhance the portrayal of Peter. Attention to the use of 'rock' language invites the reader to find a literary anticipation of Jesus' blessing on Peter in the concluding parable of the Sermon on the Mount (the invitation to all disciples to hear Jesus' words and act on them, like 'a wise man who built his house on rock', 7.24; Collins 2003: 103). Matthew 11.25–27 is another literary preparation for Peter's confession, identifying him as one of the 'infants' to whom it has pleased the Father to reveal the Son (Luz 2005b: 4).

There is another side to the Matthean portrayal of Peter, however. As well as additions of Petrine references in Matthew there are also Marcan references that Matthew lacks. In his study of Peter in Matthew's Gospel, Arlo Nau treats four such 'Marcan omissions' – which in his view present Peter at his most 'positive' – as evidence for what he sees as Matthew's redactional tendency to denigrate as well as praise Peter's character (Nau 1992). The first is the story of Peter's mother-in-law, where in Matthew's version both Simon Peter and his associates disappear from the scene (8.14–15; cf. Mark 1.29–31). Similar is the story of the official's daughter, where again Matthew lacks Mark's explicit reference to 'Peter, James, and John, the brother of James' (9.23; cf. Mark 5.37). Third, in the story of the cursing of the fig tree, whereas Mark explicitly notes that Peter saw that the fig tree had withered and 'remembered' Jesus' prior words, Matthew attributes this more generally to 'the disciples' (21.20; cf. Mark 11.21). Most decisive for Nau, however, is the fourth example, from the resurrection narrative. Mark's explicit promise of a resurrection appearance to Peter in Galilee – 'But go, tell his disciples *and Peter*' (Mark 16.7; cf. Luke 24.34; John 21.4–8; 1 Cor. 15.5) – has become in Matthew 'Then go quickly and tell his disciples' (28.7).

Yet these 'omissions' are not as damaging to an enhanced Matthean portrayal of Peter as Nau suggests. First, the streamlining of miracle stories at 8.14–15 and 9.21–23 (as noted in Chapter 8 above) serves not so much to denigrate Peter as to emphasize Christ's role as healer. This christological focus means that even Peter and his companions need to be expunged from the narrative. Yet even here Peter's role is indirectly given prominence: in Matthew's version the house is 'Peter's house' (8.14) rather than 'the house of Simon and Andrew' (Mark 1.29). Nor is it the case that the omission of Peter's name from the fig-tree story necessarily denigrates him, given that the disciples are 'amazed' (21.20), which implies lack of understanding. Admittedly, the omission of Peter at 28.7 is more problematic, at least in so far as it fails to distinguish Peter from the wider body of disciples to which he belongs.

Perhaps better examples of a more ambivalent portrait of Peter are to be found in Matthew's 'additions'. Both Nau (Nau 1992: 112–14) and Mark Goodacre (Goodacre 2006) point to an often overlooked Matthean insertion, coming immediately after the positive scene of Peter's confession, at the point when Jesus says to him 'Get behind me, Satan!' In Matthew's version Jesus adds: 'You are a stumbling block [Greek *skandalon* = 'stumbling stone'] to me' (16.23; cf. Mark 8.33). There is dramatic irony in the swift change of the rock on which the Church is built into a stone that causes people to stumble. But it is of a piece with the ambivalent portrayal of Peter in all the Gospels, strong and yet weak, prominent among the Twelve during the ministry and yet tragic in his threefold denial of Jesus in the passion.

Peter's Multifaceted Role

Moreover the *role* Peter's character performs in Matthew's story is multi-faceted, offering support for the quite different theological assessments Christian history has drawn. In some cases Peter functions as a type of the Christian, positively and negatively (for this view of Peter as representative disciple, see e.g. Gundry 1994: 182–3, 330–7). The pericope inserted into the walking on the water (14.28–31) perhaps best exemplifies this: Peter as both the model of courageous faith and of wavering faith (Strecker 1963: 205).

This is a very early interpretation of the pericope, which often goes hand in hand with an interpretation of the boat from which Peter steps as a symbol of the Church (Augustine's commentary on this passage has already been quoted in Chapter 8 above). It is exemplified visually in a mosaic now over the main entrance to St Peter's Basilica in Rome, a reconstruction of Giotto's *Navicella* ('the little boat') that graced the façade of the original St Peter's. Giotto has captured the moment where Peter's faith wavers, and he begins to sink. The boat behind Peter is a symbol of the Church, the 'barque of Peter', tossed around by the storms of an often hostile world. Hilary of Poitiers also holds to this symbolic, ecclesial interpretation. Hilary interprets the fact that Christ walks on the water 'in the fourth watch of the night' to refer to his fourth 'coming' at the End (following his 'coming' in the Law, the prophets and the Incarnation): 'For the fourth time, then, he will return to a roving and shipwrecked church' (Simonetti [ed.] 2002: 12).

Other examples support the idea that Matthew looks back to the key role Peter played in the apostolic 'first generation', rather than viewing him merely as a type of the Christian. Yet even here many of the things said of Peter are also said of the other disciples, counting against a unique Petrine role. Jesus utters a blessing on the disciples (13.16–17) even before he blesses Peter (16.17). They confess Jesus as 'son of God' in the boat (14.33) prior to Peter's declaration that he is 'the Son of the living God' (16.16). The authority to 'bind' and 'loose' (16.19) is extended to all the disciples at 18.18. Here Peter seems to be portrayed as one among the disciples, the 'first' of the Twelve but not distinct from them.

Yet not everything said to Peter is paralleled in statements about the other disciples. The presentation of Peter as the rock is unique to him, as is the granting to him of the keys to the kingdom of heaven, which cannot straightforwardly be subsumed under the authority to 'bind and loose'. Streeter famously found in this passage the memory of Peter's foundational role in the church in Antioch, as the *pontifex* or 'bridge-builder' who held together the various Christian factions, from the Pauline 'radicals' to the conservative 'Jacobite' party. This was a key plank in his view that Matthew's Gospel, in bringing together the 'Pauline' Gospel of Mark with more cautious Jewish-Christian 'M' traditions, represents Antioch's 'Petrine compromise' (Streeter 1927: 500–23; for a more 'Jacobite' alternative for Matthew's church, see Sim 1998: 106).

Other New Testament scholars are more open to the possibility that the evangelist, writing 20 years or so after Peter's death (on the consensus dating of the Gospel), envisaged an ongoing embodiment of Peter's ministry as 'rock' (e.g. Davies and Allison 1988–97: 2/651; Viviano 2007: 167–9). This dimension is also present in Giotto's *Navicella*, where the 'terrestrial' Peter on the Sea of Galilee is supported by the prayers of the heavenly Peter in the clouds above the boat. For Giotto the storm and the assurance of calm continues not simply for the Church on earth but particularly for Peter's successors, the bishops of Rome.

The Church and the Nations

The idea that Matthew sees in the Church not a definitive rejection of Israel in favour of the Gentiles, or of a new Jew–Gentile entity, but rather a regathering of Israel under a changed leadership (in which Peter plays a key role), is not incompatible with the acknowledgement of a significant mission to Gentiles. Avoiding the later language of supersessionism (which Matthew, if a Jew, would surely have found unintelligible), one might speak instead of the Church as the scattered community of Israel gathered together around Jesus the Messiah and Shepherd-King, to which the Gentiles have now been joined. This opening to Gentiles was hinted at from the start of Matthew's story, with Jesus' designation as the 'son of Abraham' (1.1), possibly in the women named in the genealogy (1.3, 5, 6) and the offering of gifts to the baby Jesus by the Gentile magi (2.1–12). As the story unfolds, the stories of the centurion's servant and the Canaanite woman's daughter (8.5–13; 15.21–28) illustrate the capacity of non-Jews to exhibit the degree of faith expected of the people of Israel. The hints become explicit in the Great Commission, where the Eleven, having been so far restricted to 'the lost sheep of the house of Israel' (10.6), are sent to make disciples of 'all the nations' or 'Gentiles' (28.19). Whether Matthew is writing to audiences who have embarked enthusiastically on a mission to Gentiles or need persuasion that such is in accordance with the will of Jesus, the direction of the narrative is quite clear.

But this raises another 'salvation-historical' question besides that of the historic role of Peter and the other disciples: how does Matthew divide up the history of salvation, and is there a crucial shift brought about by the death and resurrection of Jesus, so as to explain the transition from a community narrowly focused on Jews to one that embraces Gentiles (Meier 1991)? Or should one resort to theories of rather poor editing of contradictory traditions by an editor who is more tradent than evangelist?

Those who offer a solution in terms of salvation history do so in different ways. Strecker posits three 'epochs' in Matthew's account of the history of salvation, similar to Hans Conzelmann's view of three periods in Luke–Acts: a time of preparation for Israel, which began with Abraham; the 'time of Jesus', a time of revelation and ethical teaching, where the mission was restricted to 'the lost sheep of the house of Israel'; the time of the Church, which is to engage in a universal mission until the close of the age (28.20). For Strecker the key period is the time of Jesus, now past, thus leading him to give priority to Christology over ecclesiology (Strecker 1995). Others (e.g. Kingsbury 1976: 1–39) posit a two-stage view of salvation history, claiming that Matthew is less clear than Luke – with his second volume, the Acts of the Apostles – that the time of the Church is a different epoch from that of Jesus. Indeed, the promise of the Matthean Jesus to remain with his disciples rather than withdraw from them until the End blurs any clear distinction between pre-Easter and post-Easter.

John Meier is less concerned with the broad sweep of the history of salvation than the particular circumstances of Jesus' life, death and resurrection. Without being dogmatic about specific 'periods', Meier nonetheless sees the death-resurrection of Jesus – as essentially a single salvific event – as a crucial turning point. Picking up on the Jewish apocalyptic idea that the 'present evil age' – dominated by the powers of evil, sin and injustice – would eventually give way to the 'new age' of God's salvation, Meier believes that for Matthew this turning point in history was brought about by the death and resurrection of Christ (Meier 1975 and 1991). This is symbolized by the dramatic 'apocalyptic' signs surrounding Jesus' death (the rending of the Temple curtain; an earthquake; the splitting of rocks and the emergence of saints from their tombs, 27.51–53) and resurrection (another earthquake, and the descent of an angel of the Lord, 28.2). However, for Meier, Matthew continues to hold to an 'already and not yet' view of eschatology: the new age has 'invaded' but not finally replaced the old age, while the Great Commission of 28.16–20 is a 'proleptic Parousia' rather than the final coming of Christ, which remains in the future. What it allows for is a universal mission to the nations that the constraints of the Mosaic Law in Jesus' earthly ministry did not make possible.

Meier's theory is a strong one, given the dramatic – and somewhat awkward – 'in-breaking' of the eschatological 'resurrection of the dead' to coincide with Jesus' death and resurrection in Matthew's account. It explains why the prophetic writings about the conversion of the Gentiles (including Isaiah's prophecy that the 'nations' will bring gifts of gold and frankincense, Isaiah 60.3, 5–6, anticipated in the story of the magi, 2.1–12) are now being fulfilled. Moreover his acknowledgement that this turning point does not mean the complete arrival of the 'new age' but an 'overlapping of the ages' meets the objection that Christ's abiding presence blurs any clear distinction between the time of Jesus and the time of the Church. But it is not a necessary corollary of Meier's thesis that the transition in salvation history means a rejection of Israel or a replacement of one mission (an 'exclusivist' one to Israel) with another (Meier, indeed, argues that the ongoing mission is to 'all the nations', including Israel, Meier 1977a; for the alternative translation of (*panta ta ethnē* at 28.19 as 'all the Gentiles', see Hare and Harrington 1975).

Amy-Jill Levine highlights the anti-Jewish implications of treating 10.5b ('Go nowhere among the Gentiles, and enter no town of the Samaritans') negatively (Levine 1988). For Levine this should not be viewed as deriving from a exclusivist 'Jewish-Christian' source, or representing a view that jars with the evangelist's overall vision, but as complementary to the universal commission to 'make disciples of all the nations' (28.19). The two commissions – to Israel and to the nations – reflect the Pauline 'to the Jew first and also to the Greek' (Rom. 1.16). Far from displacing the mission to Israel's lost sheep, the Great Commission enables the Gentiles to share the privileges on an equal footing with the Jews in the post-resurrection era of the Church. The Gospel's salvation-historical viewpoint, in other words, has two axes: a temporal axis (the mission is now expanded to include Gentiles, while the first mission to the 'lost sheep' remains operative) and a social axis (the continuity with Jewish tradition, combined with signs of tension with the leadership of the Synagogue).

Levine's reading, influenced by both feminist criticism and deconstruction, gives a more central role to those texts about the 'lost sheep' (10.5b–6; 15.24) that are peripheral to other scholarly interpretations. Her reading of the Gospel places faithful Gentiles like the magi, the centurion and the Canaanite woman not in opposition to the 'faithless Jews' but in the company of faithful Jews such as the holy family, or marginal Jews like the leper, and Peter's mother-in-law (and in contrast to the elite, both Jewish and Gentile). The 'lost sheep of the house of Israel' are specifically 'the people betrayed by and distanced from their leaders and the structures of patriarchy these leaders uphold' (Levine 1988: 14) rather than the whole people of Israel.

Community Organization

Matthew does not only think about the Church on the big scale, the scale of the history of salvation and the unfolding divine plan. His structured, pragmatic approach also means that his Gospel provides concrete advice for the ongoing life of the Christian community, and instructions as to its organization and administration.

Matthew is particularly 'transparent' to ecclesial organization in his fourth main discourse, which Bacon labelled 'Concerning Church Administration', also known as the Ecclesiological or Communitarian Discourse (Thompson 1970: 2). This block of teaching provides instructions about true greatness within the community (18.1–5), concern for 'these little ones' (18.6–14), whether that means specifically children or those who have learned how to 'become like children', that is, fellow Christians (implied by the qualifying phrase 'who believe in me' in verse 6), a procedure for community discipline (18.15–17) and a Christian ethos ordered by forgiveness and mercy (18.21–35). Some commentators (e.g. Martinez 1961) treat this discourse as addressed specifically to those who exercise leadership within the Church. Others, not least on literary grounds (for example, comparison with Matthew 10, which is specifically addressed not to 'the disciples' but to the Twelve), read this passage transparently as speaking to all Christian disciples – to use anachronistic language, laity as well as clergy (e.g. Thompson 1970: 71–2). Either way it sets out a 'blueprint' for the ideal community of the followers of Jesus, living the values of the coming kingdom of the heavens.

Matthew 18.15–17 is particularly instructive for Matthew's interest in the structures of ecclesial life. It appears to provide a mechanism for community discipline and possible excommunication, akin to the processes used by the Qumran Community (cf. e.g. 1QS 5.24—6.2; CD 9.2–3). Some would locate this passage against the backdrop of Matthew's debate with 'formative Judaism', representing a Christian-Jewish parallel to disciplining procedures developing in the Pharisaic-led synagogues, possibly reflected in the *Birkath ha-Minim*. Whether or not one can be so precise historically, sociologically it reflects the dynamic of a group in transition, needing to strengthen its community boundaries.

The liturgical and ritual life of the circles in which Matthew moved has also left its mark on Matthew's text. The liturgical ring of the Matthean version of the Lord's Prayer (6.7–13), together with close parallels with developing Synagogue prayers, may reflect the actual liturgical practice of Matthean Christians. The Great Commission explicitly advocates the initiation rite of baptism for new disciples (28.19, with a 'trinitarian' wording found in several other Christian texts from Syria: *Did.* 7.1; Ignatius, *Magn.* 13.2; *Odes of Solomon* 23.22), whether this replaced circumcision (so Meier 1991) or served as an addition to it (so Sim 1998). The parallels with the initiation rites for members of the Qumran Community and followers of John the Baptist might favour the latter view. Matthew's story of the Last Supper at 26.26–29 also seems to reflect liturgical practice, in this case the Eucharist (Matthew's version, unlike Mark's, contains explicit rubrics to 'eat' and to '[d]rink of it', 26.26, 27; cf. Mark 14.22, 23).

Serving the Church: Disciples, Prophets, Scribes

Some scholars have also attempted to piece together a picture of the ecclesial offices known to the Matthean congregations. This is only partially successful, given that this is not Matthew's primary intention and therefore the evidence is only piecemeal. Several note the prominence given to Peter and the Twelve, whether as 'historic' figures of a foundational past or exemplifying roles that continue in subsequent generations. Michael Goulder, for example, picking up on the idea of Peter as a 'chief rabbi', suggests that the Twelve function as a kind of 'Christian Sanhedrin', offering definitive interpretations of Jesus' commandments (Goulder 1997: 22; he restricts the authority to 'bind' and 'loose' to them).

In addition, commentators identify 'scribes' and 'prophets' as important offices in Matthew's vision of the Church (e.g. Schweizer 1995). Matthew's more nuanced depiction of 'the scribes' (e.g. the scribe 'trained for the kingdom of heaven' at 13.52; the scribe who desires to follow Jesus at 8.19–20) is understood in part to reflect the ongoing presence of Christian-Jewish scribes within his own circles (one may read *'their* scribes' at 7.29 as contrasted with *'our* scribes'). Some detect scribal activity in the formula citations with their often-complex mixture of textual traditions (e.g. Stendahl 1954). Others point to the need of the fledgling Christian community for its own scribes or authoritative interpreters of the Law, so as to compete effectively with rival Pharisaic claimants to the inheritance of Israel.

If scribes reflect a settled form of community life, Matthew also envisages wandering prophets, moving from place to place. The warning of false prophets who 'come to you in sheep's clothing' (7.15) presupposes that true prophets are the norm. Acts attests to the church in Syrian Antioch having its own community prophets (e.g. Agabus, Acts 11.27). The early Christian conviction that the expected gift of the last days, the Spirit of prophecy, had now been poured out led to a strong prophetic dimension within the Church (e.g. 1 Cor. 12—14).

But community prophets appear to have coexisted alongside itinerant prophets. The warning given by Matthew's Jesus echoes a concern found in the *Didache*: the need to discern true from false prophecy among wandering prophets. The *Didache's* pragmatic approach – to assume that the prophet is authentic, and therefore to be given board and lodging, with the desire to stay for three days, or a request for money, as evidence of a false prophet (*Did.* 11.3–6) – parallels Matthew's ethical criterion: prophets are to be judged by their fruits (7.16).

Finally, the harsh polemic against outsiders – specifically the 'scribes and Pharisees' – may also have an internal, ecclesial dimension. The woes against the scribes and Pharisees are often explored, appropriately enough, for the light they shed on bitter debates between Church and Synagogue at the time of the evangelist. Sociological scientific critics, as we have seen, find the hermeneutical key for such language in the self-definition of followers of Jesus, distancing themselves from fellow Jews and delegitimizing the authority of their rival leaders (e.g. Freyne 1985; Saldarini 1991: 44; Malina and Neyrey 1998).

But it would be misleading to conclude that identifying the historical *Sitz im Leben* of this chapter explains its function within Matthew's narrative. Presuming that the earliest audiences of Matthew's Gospel were members of the church rather than of Pharisee-led synagogues, these woes may function less as polemic against contemporary Jewish leaders as warning for those exercising authority within the Christian community. Once again, attention to earlier 'pre-critical' commentators is instructive. The main interest of the *Opus imperfectum*, for example, is in the implications of these woes for the contemporary priesthood, whose role is analogous to that of the scribes and Pharisees: 'see then how you sit on Moses' seat, because the seat does not make the priest, but the priest makes the seat' (Kellerman 2010: 2/343). Similarly, Origen interprets Matthew 23 as pertaining to the 'good pastor', who ought to be demanding in things pertaining to himself and 'gentle and ready to make allowances' towards those entrusted to his care (Simonetti [ed.] 2002: 165). In this, the leaders of the Church emulate the Lord of the Church, the Shepherd-King, whose yoke is easy and whose judgement is merciful.

11

Endings: The Passion and Death of Jesus

Preparation for the Passion

The final three chapters of Matthew's Gospel (26—28) recount the sequence of events surrounding Jesus' passion, death and resurrection. Contrary to B. W. Bacon's theory of Matthew as a new Pentateuch (Bacon 1930), this section is no mere epilogue but an integral and climactic part of the unfolding story. Even if, as scholars have often proposed, the passion story was the earliest part of the Gospel tradition to be produced in written form (perhaps in a liturgical setting), Matthew has woven it carefully into his overall narrative. His story is punctuated with foreshadowings of the cross, from the interpretation of Jesus' name ('he will save his people from their sins', 1.21) and Herod's failed attempt to destroy him as an infant (2.16), through the attempts of the leadership to 'destroy' him (12.14) and the arrest, death and burial of John the Baptist (14.3–12), to the succession of passion predictions (16.21; 17.22–23; 20.18–19).

The parallels between the passion story and the story of Herod and the magi are particularly striking. In both narratives Jesus is described as 'king of the Jews' (2.2; 27.11, 29, 37), whom Jewish leaders seek to kill. In both, Gentiles receive revelation by dreams (2.12; 27.19) and come to faith as a consequence of strange phenomena (a star, 2.2, 9; an earthquake, tombs splitting and the tearing of the Temple curtain, 27.51–54). In both, Jerusalem is the setting for the rejection of Jesus, the 'chief priests and scribes of the people' of the infancy story paralleling the 'chief priests and elders of the people' or occasionally the chief priests, scribes and elders, in the passion narrative (2.4; 26.3, 47, 57; 27.1, 41). Just as the holy family flee into Egypt 'by night' (2.14), so Jesus will be betrayed and arrested during the night (26.47–56). Moreover the two narratives are linked by the only two formula citations to mention Jeremiah (commenting on the slaughter of the innocents at 2.17; of Judas' betrayal of the shepherd at 27.9), remembered as a persecuted prophet.

This narrative coherence has been explored recently and very effectively by scholars using the tools of narrative criticism (e.g. Heil 1991; Donaldson

1999). However, it is not a new insight. As noted in Chapter 6 above, older commentators, including artists, often saw anticipations of the passion earlier in Matthew's story. Mabuse's *Adoration of the Kings* (1500–15; National Gallery, London) includes a small dog beneath the Virgin and Child, chewing on a bone. This is widely acknowledged as a symbol of Christ's forthcoming death, since artists often place a skull and bones at the foot of the cross. In Dürer's 1504 *Adoration of the Magi* (Uffizi, Florence), the container of myrrh is topped by a serpent, symbolizing death and destruction (Zuffi 2003: 91–3). This detail reflects an interpretation of the myrrh brought by the magi as a preparation for burial. An earlier example is a fourteenth-century ivory diptych from either France or Germany (Metropolitan Museum of Art, New York), in which the adoration of the infant Jesus by the magi is juxtaposed with a crucifixion scene, the king kneeling in the left-hand panel paralleled with another worshipping figure – possibly the centurion – beneath Christ's cross in the right-hand panel. Caravaggio is one example of an artist who exploits the connections between the beheading of John the Baptist and the passion of Jesus. The executioner who holds John's head in his *Salome with the Head of John the Baptist* (*c*.1607; National Gallery, London) appears again as one of Christ's torturers in his *Christ at the Column* (Musée des Beaux Arts, Rouen) and *The Flagellation of Christ* (Museo di Capodimonte), painted around the same time.

Literary and Dramatic Features

However, the passion story proper begins in Matthew 26, linked to Jesus' preceding ministry of preaching, teaching and healing with the stereotypical phrase 'When Jesus had finished saying *all* these things' (26.1, echoing Moses' final words to Israel at Deut. 31.1 and 32.45). Temporal expressions become increasingly important: 'You know that after two days the Passover is coming' (26.2); 'On the first day of Unleavened Bread' (26.17); 'When it was evening' (26.20); 'When they had sung the hymn' (26.30); 'When morning came' (27.1); 'From noon on [literally 'from the sixth hour'], darkness came over the whole land until three in the afternoon [literally 'until the ninth hour']' (27.45); 'When it was evening' (27.57). This precision contrasts with the lack of interest in specific dates and times earlier in the Gospel.

Such time references, which continue into the story of the resurrection (28.1, 11), invest the events leading up to Jesus' suffering and death with particular solemnity, contributing as they do to the 'slowing down of the narrative'. This measured pace – with moments of tension and pathos – invites imaginative participation as the reader follows Jesus on his journey to Golgotha hour by hour, almost moment by moment. Moreover the explicit connections with the Jewish religious calendar hint at a deeper theological significance to the events being described. The disciples prepare the Last Supper on the 'first day of Unleavened Bread' (26.17). Jesus' Last Supper with his disciples (26.20–30) is the Passover meal (contrast John, where Jesus dies before Passover begins, John 19.14). Matthew's story implies that Jesus is acting out a new Passover and new exodus, where God's people will be saved from death, liberated from a slavery greater than Israel's enslavement to the Egyptians and bound by a renewal of the covenant originally established by Moses at Sinai (e.g. 26.28; cf. Exod. 24.8). The implied reader may recall the interpretation of Jesus' name ('for he will save his people from their sins', 1.21).

The drama of Matthew's passion story has particularly lent itself to performance, a reminder of the extent to which every reading or hearing of the text is a fresh revelatory encounter (see Lash 1986: 37–46). The Matthew Passion has been performed liturgically during the Christian Holy Week, acted out dramatically in passion plays and medieval mystery plays, meditated upon devotionally and rendered musically (see the survey in Luz 2005a: 305–28). The most famous musical interpretation of Matthew's story is probably Bach's *The St Matthew Passion*, which prioritizes particular characters and moments of the narrative. Bach has, for example, recreated a profound sense of horror on the part of Judas, with the growing realization that he has betrayed innocent blood (cf. 27.4). His remorseful cry is matched, and contrasted, with the chorus of the chief priests: 'But what is that to us? See thou, see thou to that, see thou to that.' Rushing scales represent musically his throwing down of the 30 pieces of silver in the Temple (27.5), in the bass aria: 'Give, O give me back my Lord, give me, give, O give me back my Lord. See the silver, price of blood at your feet in horror pour'd.'

Bach has also highlighted the prominent role Matthew's Gospel gives to the wife of Pontius Pilate, who warns her husband of a dream she has received about Jesus (27.19). Her cry to Pilate contrasts sharply with the thunderous cry of the crowd calling for the release of Barabbas. Bach provides an equally dramatic change of tone at the moment of Jesus' death. In the Matthean account it is accompanied by spectacular events such as an earthquake and the opening of tombs (27.51–54). Bach allows them to 'crash' into each other in his powerful musical interpretation of this climactic scene.

Matthew's Sources

What are Matthew's sources for his account of Jesus' passion? The traditional attribution of the Gospel to the apostle Matthew held that the evangelist was eyewitness to most of the events he describes up until the arrest of Jesus, though dependent upon the testimony of others for the meetings of the Jewish leaders, the appearance before Pilate and the death and burial. Yet readers of Matthew are often struck by the closeness of his version to that in Mark, in order, content and vocabulary (according to one estimate, approximately four-fifths of Matt. 26—27 is identical to the Marcan parallel: Senior 1975: 1). A synoptic comparison of the two reveals this starkly, especially when Luke and John are also brought into the equation.

Variations between Matthew and Mark in pericope after pericope are often minor differences in wording. Virtually nothing of Mark's version is missing from Matthew's (he lacks the puzzling episode of the naked young man and Mark's statement that Jesus was crucified at the third hour, i.e. 9 a.m.: Mark 14.51–52; 15.25). In addition, Matthew contains unique details about minor characters (e.g. Judas Iscariot and the 30 pieces of silver, the dream of Pilate's wife and Pilate washing his hands: 27.3–10, 19, 24–25) and about the dramatic events that accompany Jesus' death (27.51–53).

The striking agreements point in the direction of a literary relationship between Matthew and Mark. Proponents of Marcan priority are often confident that Mark is Matthew's only written source for this section of the Gospel (e.g. Dahl 1995: 54), into which a small number of – probably oral – traditions and elements of Matthean redaction have been inserted. Raymond Brown has proposed that Matthew has drawn upon popular Christian folk traditions rather than written sources for the insertions, given how they differ from his 'conservative' changes to his sources elsewhere (Brown 1994: 755).

Advocates of Matthean priority, by contrast, point to those features of Matthew's passion account that suggest a greater 'closeness' to the Palestinian Jewish environment within which the passion traditions first developed. The story of the death of Judas, for example, is unlikely to be straightforward Matthean redaction, given that it contains an aetiological explanation of the 'Field of Blood' near Jerusalem (27.8; cf. Acts 1.19). It seems to reflect an interpretation preserved by early Christians living in or close to the holy city. Moreover even proponents of Marcan priority have detected the more 'Semitic feel' of Matthew's version, perhaps pointing to the bilingual or trilingual context within which Matthew's Gospel was composed (for examples, see Dahl 1995: 58).

On balance, source-critical analysis favours Marcan priority (though some scholars find the minor agreements between Matthew and Luke against Mark, notably 26.68; Luke 22.64, problematic for the Q hypothesis). Distinctive Matthean elements seem to break the flow of the narrative – notably the story of Judas' return of the silver pieces at 27.3–10 – and may be removed without doing much violence to the storyline. However, a solution to the Synoptic Problem is not required in order to hear the distinctive voice of Matthew's passion story. Juxtaposing Matthew and Mark, the following emerge as recurring motifs in the former: fulfilment of Scripture; a heightened role for the Jewish leadership in Jesus' death; a focus on what the passion story reveals about Jesus; the didactic function of certain minor characters.

Matthew and Mark on the Passion

Matthew's closeness to Mark's passion narrative is reflected in the overall feel of the narrative. Both Mark and Matthew emphasize the darkness of the story, with the note of abandonment and loneliness. Jesus has been abandoned by his male disciples (26.31, 56). Although the women are present at his crucifixion they are looking on 'from a distance' (27.55), while those near the cross taunt him, including both of the bandits crucified with him (27.38–44; contrast the story of the penitent thief at Luke 23.39–43). Jesus' dying words are the so-called 'cry of dereliction', 'My God, my God, why have you forsaken me?' (27.46). Even the cosmos reflects this mood, as the earth is shrouded in darkness for three hours (27.45).

Matthew also shares with Mark the concern for the fulfilment of the Jewish Scriptures. It is unsurprising historically that the earliest Christians made sense of the brutal death of Jesus, and its accompanying events, through the language of the Old Testament. Israel's sacred writings provided Jews, including Christian Jews, with the lens through which to view the world and interpret what is observed. This would have been the case even for those Jews present on the day of Jesus' crucifixion, whether they regarded Jesus positively or negatively – as a righteous sufferer or a cursed figure who 'hangs on the tree' (Deut. 21.23; cf. Gal. 3.13). This means that fact and interpretation are intimately interwoven, rather than the latter necessarily being a second-stage imposition on the former.

However, Matthew is even more explicit than Mark in drawing attention to scriptural fulfilment (even though the verb 'fulfil', Greek *plēroō*, only occurs at 26.54, 56 and 27.9, only the last of which introduces a 'formula citation'). This has been something of a leitmotif for his Gospel from the infancy narrative onwards. As the story of Jesus' earthly life draws to a close, Matthew is keen to show the essential continuity between Jesus' end in suffering and death and the life and ministry preceding it. This is reflected in more explicit allusions to Old Testament passages concerning the suffering of the righteous, continuing Matthew's trait of clarifying what often remains implicit or even ambiguous in Mark's account.

The Portrayal of Jesus

In line with Matthew's tendency elsewhere in his Gospel, the Matthean passion narrative heightens the reverential portrayal of Jesus. A comparison of the Gethsemane story in Matthew (26.36–46) with the parallel in Mark (14.32–42) serves as an illustration. Matthew emphasizes the filial obedience of God's Son – a feature already prominent in the temptation narrative, where Jesus is tempted to trust that God would send his angels to take care of him (4.6). Now in Gethsemane, Jesus as the obedient Son again refuses to put his Father to the test, although he knows that he could send 12 legions of angels (approximately 72,000!) to deliver him (26.53). A further reminder of Christ's obedience in the wilderness will occur at Matthew's crucifixion scene, where the crowd echoes the words spoken to Jesus by the devil: 'If you are the Son of God, come down now from the cross' (27.40; cf. 4.3, 6).

Unsurprisingly, Jesus' prayer of anguish in Gethsemane echoes the prayer he taught his disciples, the Lord's Prayer. He tells his disciples to watch and pray so that they may not enter 'into temptation' (26.41; cf. 6.13). Jesus himself prays with petitions from the Lord's Prayer: 'My Father' (26.39); 'your will be done' (26.42). It is as though Matthew is warning his readers of the risky consequences of praying the Lord's Prayer, with its petition that God may cause his kingdom to come and that God's will may be done on earth (by humans) as in heaven. Jesus' life, and his death, is in perfect conformity with the Father's will.

At least three overlapping scriptural 'types' are present in Matthew's story of Jesus' passion and death. First, Matthew shares with Mark traditions from the Psalms about the righteous sufferer (especially e.g. Ps. 22 and Ps. 69). In his tendency to clarify, Matthew's echoes of such 'psalms of lament' are more explicit. For example, whereas in the crucifixion scene Mark has Jesus being offered 'wine mixed with myrrh' (Mark 15.23), which might be a narcotic to dull the pain and therefore a kindly act (Harrington

1991: 395), for Matthew he is given 'wine mixed with gall' – an act of treachery (27.34). This is a clear reference to the enemies of the innocent sufferer in Psalm 69.21: 'They gave me poison [LXX 'gall'] for food, and for my thirst they gave me vinegar to drink.' The justification for Matthew interpreting the 'I' of the psalms of Jesus is the ancient presumption of Davidic authorship. Thus they are appropriately understood as the words of the Son of David. This Davidic emphasis is important, given the un-Davidic character of his death. As Margaret Davies writes: 'Jesus' fate was so unlike that of David, and so much more like that of a prophet' (Davies 1993: 177).

Second, Matthew heightens the attention to Jesus as the Servant of Isaiah. This shadowy figure has served as a model for Jesus earlier in the Gospel, though there it was – unusually in the New Testament – connected to Jesus' healing ministry and the hope he offers for the Gentiles (8.17, citing Isa. 53.4; 12.17–21, citing Isa. 42.1–4, 9). Here we find the more traditional connection between the Servant and the suffering Jesus. Matthew heightens the motif of Jesus' silence before Pilate by including an additional reference ('he did not answer', 27.12), recalling the statement about the Servant that 'he did not open his mouth' (Isa. 53.7).

Third, Jesus' role as Son of God comes to the fore. The mocking of Jesus in Matthew's version (27.42–43) reflects not only the wording of Psalm 22.7–8; it also recalls the taunt of the righteous man in the Wisdom of Solomon, who is explicitly identified as the Son of God (Wis. 2.18: 'for if the righteous man is God's son, he will help him, and will deliver him from the hand of his adversaries'). Here the emphasis is upon Jesus as the perfectly obedient Son of God.

But attentiveness to intertextual 'echoes', especially of the Old Testament, suggests other possibilities too. Earlier in the passion narrative Matthew's Jesus – like Mark's – has already explicitly quoted from the prophet Zechariah: 'I will strike the shepherd, and the sheep of the flock will be scattered' (26.31, an adaption of Zech. 13.7). Zechariah has also been quoted a few chapters earlier by the evangelist himself at Jesus' triumphal entry into Jerusalem (21.5, citing Zech. 9.9). Moreover the Mount of Olives has featured prominently in the lead-up to Jesus' passion (21.1; 24.3; 26.30). Zechariah 14.4 envisages the eschatological coming of the Lord on the Mount of Olives. All this justifies treating Zechariah as an important intertext for Matthew's passion story and strengthens the possibility that Zechariah's smitten shepherd – according to Horbury (1998) one of five key motifs in Jewish messianism – is christologically important for the First Gospel. The shepherding motif has already been identified above as a central one for Matthew, tying together the Gospel's interest in Christology and ecclesiology.

Another intertextual possibility occurs in Matthew's story of Judas – a Greek form of the Hebrew name Judah – and the 30 pieces of silver. This may recall the biblical story of Joseph, who was handed over for 20 pieces of silver by his brother Judah (Gen. 37.25–28; cf. 12.49; 26.14–15). The connection is already made by patristic commentators. Jerome, for example, exploits the discrepancy between the LXX version of Genesis, most commonly known to his readers, and the Hebrew text – what he calls *hebraica veritas*, 'the Hebrew truth' – with its closer resonance for the Matthean narrative: 'Joseph was sold not for twenty gold pieces, as many think, in accordance with the LXX, but, according to the Hebrew truth, for twenty silver pieces. For the slave could not have more value than the Master' (Jerome 2008: 295). This would make the Old Testament patriarch Joseph a type of Jesus (see Argyle 1956; van Aarde 2000), and not simply his adopted father Joseph the dreamer (1.20; 2.13, 19).

The Role of Israel's Leaders and Anti-Judaism

Matthew's general characterization of the leaders of Israel has been discussed in Chapter 4 above. Their depiction in his passion story is in accordance with this broader portrayal of the leadership as negative figures who are antagonistic towards Jesus. Whereas in Mark the chief priests, elders and scribes seek testimony against Jesus, in Matthew's version the chief priests and the whole Sanhedrin explicitly seek 'false testimony' (26.59; cf. Mark 14.55). Matthew's expanded story of Judas' betrayal introduces the theme of blood money, heightening the negative role of the chief priests (26.14–16; 27.3–10). Matthew has broadened the alliance of Jewish leaders – 'chief priests and elders' as opposed to the chief priests alone – persuading the crowds to ask for Barabbas' release in place of Jesus', adding a further sinister note: 'and to have Jesus killed [*or* destroyed]' (27.20; cf. Mark 15.11). Their complicity in Jesus' death is also evident in their response to Judas' return of the 30 pieces of silver and declaration of his sin: 'What is that to us? See to it yourself' (27.4). Ironically, by these words the chief priests implicitly reject their priestly ministry of announcing the forgiveness of sins.

Moreover Matthew's story distances the positive figure of Joseph of Arimathea from the Jewish leadership. Whereas Mark has no qualms about describing him as a member of the Sanhedrin (15.43), Matthew simply calls him 'a disciple of Jesus' (27.57). On the other hand, there are some puzzles, notably the complete absence from the passion narrative of the Pharisees, who were last mentioned at 23.29 and only reappear after Jesus' death at 27.62. This is particularly surprising given that the Pharisees appear as major antagonists throughout Matthew's story of the ministry (e.g. 3.7; 9.11, 14, 34; 12.2, 14, 24, 38; 15.1, 12; 16.1; 19.3; 21.45; 22.15, 34, 41; 23.2).

The invisibility of the Pharisees aside, Matthew's passion story has heightened Jewish responsibility for Jesus' death in a manner that historians would consider to skew the historical balance between Jewish politico-religious leaders and the Roman authorities led by Pilate. The tragic consequences of this in the reception of Matthew's Gospel are only too evident. Visual depictions of the events of Good Friday, including in Stations of the Cross used for public devotion in Catholic churches, often resort to crude caricatures. A sharp distinction is often drawn between the Western European appearance of Jesus, his mother and his followers and the sinister portrayal of the Jewish leadership as stereotypical Semites. Even if the Jewish leaders function in part as a foil to the character of Jesus, throwing 'into relief the integrity and majestic authority of Jesus as the Messiah and suffering Son of Man' (Senior 1998: 377), that is not all there is to be said.

Most disturbing in terms of its negative effects is the saying attributed to 'all the people' (*pas ho laos*) at 27.25: 'His blood be on us and on our children'. Although Luz claims that treatments of this verse in the history of interpretation are relatively brief and casual (Luz 2005a: 506; see also Lovsky 1987), a good number of them perpetuate the idea that the Jewish people throughout history remain responsible for Christ's death. Origen interprets this to mean that the blood of Jesus will come over succeeding generations of Jews 'until the end' (Origen, *Commentary on Matthew* 124). Similar sentiments occur in Jerome's commentary: 'This imprecation upon the Jews continues until the present day. The Lord's blood will not be removed from them' (Jerome 2008: 313). Images of the passion in medieval art often present Jesus' tormentors in the clothing of Jews of the Middle Ages, thus 'contemporizing' these first-century events to convey the enduring consequences of the bloodguilt (see Schreckenberg 1996). There were alternative views, however, which laid greater stress on divine forgiveness (Luz 2005a: 507).

Modern readers might employ a number of strategies for dealing with this verse. One might be to conclude that the sentiments expressed by Origen or Jerome approximate to Matthew's own, but that this needs to be rejected in favour of a reading that provokes love. A more nuanced approach might emphasize that all Matthew's polemic reflects the marginal voice of a threatened minority against the dominant Synagogue, which comes to sound very different when that minority has become the dominant power (Rowland 2008: 209–10). Or it might seek to locate this verse within a wider account of Matthean theology. Thus John Meier interprets 27.25 as describing a shift in the divine plan from one *laos* to another, a transferral from the Jewish people to Christ's 'people' the Church (Meier 1991: 199–200; see also Fitzmyer 1965).

However, as we have seen, Matthew's view of the people of Israel is open to other possible readings. On the one hand, this verse takes utterly seriously the fact that in the death of Jesus innocent blood is being shed, and 'according to biblical tradition (cf. especially Deut. 21.1–9), when innocent blood is shed the guilt must fall somewhere' (Byrne 2004: 201). Yet on the other hand, the possible historical parameters – the recent memory of the fall of Jerusalem on a standard scholarly dating of Matthew – constrain the verse's referents. If 'all the people' are the Jewish people rejecting their Messiah at the instigation of their leaders, their 'children' are the generation of Jerusalem's fall at the hands of the Romans in 70 CE. Following prophetic precedent (e.g. Jer. 12.7), the evangelist interprets these events witnessed by the children as divine judgement on the city for its rejection of the Messiah – see the echo here of 23.35: 'so that upon you may come all the righteous blood shed on earth'. Thus from the temporal perspective of the evangelist and his readers, the judgement is now past.

There is, moreover, one further dimension. Taking a broad narrative-critical view, the implied reader hears the reference to Jesus' blood as an echo of the previous reference to that blood in the previous chapter. In Matthew's version of the Last Supper alone, Jesus speaks of his blood as shed 'for the forgiveness of sins' (26.28). There may be irony here, but a hopeful note nonetheless. John Paul Heil expresses it succinctly: 'The Jewish people's acceptance of the full responsibility for the price/value of Jesus' blood ironically places them and all their future generations within the embrace of the forgiveness that the atoning blood of Jesus offers to all' (Heil 1991: 124; see also Cargal 1991, who interprets the words of the people as a double entendre).

Didactic Function of Characters

A constant feature of the Christian retelling of the passion story – whether in the liturgy of Holy Week or the performance of passion plays such as at Oberammergau in Bavaria – is the identification of the worshippers or audience with characters within the story. Readers across the centuries have experienced the power of the narrative to draw them in, as they identify with specific individuals and groups, feel antipathy towards others and question their own fickle response to the unfolding passion events, as if standing on shifting sands. In practice this has had the effect of mitigating some of the potential excesses of Matthew's depiction of the Jewish leaders, for the Christian worshippers are bidden to identify their own sinful selves among the chief priests, scribes and other characters who call for Jesus to be crucified. This experience of actual readers of the Gospel, caught up in a web of guilt and innocence, courage and cowardice, calls for a more nuanced reading than the neater reaction expected by the narrative critic of the 'implied reader', who might be expected to feel straightforward antipathy towards the Jewish leadership and ambivalence towards the wavering disciples.

Interest in the didactic value of characters in the passion story, then, is a well-honed instinct among Matthew's interpreters across the centuries. In Mark, Simon Peter is a particular figure for empathy and identification, in his combination of weakness and desire to follow Jesus and the pathos of his repentance following failure (e.g. 14.72). Matthew's Gospel shares many of the same characters (e.g. the wavering Peter, 26.33–35, 40, 58, 69–75; the sympathetic figure of Simon of Cyrene, compelled to carry Jesus' cross, 27.32; the women followers, who remain when the male disciples have deserted: 27.55–56). However, his narrative places particular focus on three characters: Judas Iscariot, one of Jesus' chosen Twelve, Pontius Pilate, the Roman governor and Pilate's wife, who is not mentioned in the other Gospels.

Judas is increasingly viewed as a negative figure in the Gospel tradition (e.g. 'It would have been better for that one not to have been born', 26.24); indeed, for John he becomes associated with Satan and the darkness rather than the Light of the World (13.2, 30). Yet whereas Matthew's story portrays him negatively in comparison to the other disciples, there is ambiguity in its overall depiction. On the one hand, Leslie Houlden can describe Matthew's Judas as an individual who gets his just deserts, whose 'repentance' is 'sterile remorse' leading him to despair (Houlden 1987: 46–7). This negative assessment of Judas reflects ancient readings of Matthew's portrait. Jerome writes of Judas that 'he was not only unable to amend the crime of betrayal, but to the first act of wickedness he added as well the sin of his own suicide' (Jerome 2008: 309). Similarly Luz interprets the story of the 30 pieces of silver as Matthew portraying Judas as 'avaricious and greedy' (26.15) (Luz 1995b: 133), although Luz acknowledges that it is the chief priests, elders and Pharisees rather than Judas himself who are the real villains of the narrative.

Yet others come to quite different conclusions by placing more emphasis on this last point, namely that the major contrast in Matthew's expanded narrative about Judas (26.14–16; 27.3–10) is not between Judas and the other disciples but between Judas and the chief priests and elders. Whereas Judas 'repented' (27.3, though the verb here is a different one from the 'repent' demanded by John's and Jesus' preaching, 3.2; 4.17), returning the 30 pieces of silver and confessing Jesus' innocence, their response is a non-committal 'What is that to us?' (27.4). Judas' request for money, moreover, is nowhere explicitly connected to 'greed' (contrast John 12.6). It may rather be an indication that Matthew's Judas acknowledges the value of Jesus' life (30 shekels of silver being the wages of the shepherd: Zech. 11.12).

Second, Matthew's story of Judas' death – compare the rather different account in Acts 1.16–20 – is also open to a different reading. That he hanged himself is interpreted as the result of his recognition of guilt, an act of remorse following his public confession that he has 'sinned by betraying innocent blood' (27.4). In his holistic, narrative-critical reading, for example, Heil concludes: 'But Judas did repent and confess his sin, so that he can ultimately receive the forgiveness to be effected for the sins of all by the innocent "blood" of Jesus (26.28)' (Heil 1991: 121). This more hopeful interpretation prioritizes the motif of 'blood' and its effects throughout the passion story (26.28; 27.4, 6, 8, 24), and the more optimistic reading already offered above in relationship to the difficult verse 27.25.

Both intertextual and intratextual concerns offer further nuances to Matthew's portrayal of Judas. A striking Old Testament intertext is the death of King David's counsellor Ahithophel, who hanged himself following his complicity in Absalom's betrayal (2 Sam. 17.23). This provides an additional dimension to the story of Jesus' ascent to the Mount of Olives, following the Last Supper (26.30). Like his father David (2 Sam. 15.14, 23, 30), Jesus the Son of David also leaves Jerusalem for the Mount of Olives as a consequence of an act of betrayal. Another set of intertexts is implicit in Jerome's comment on the fact that the chief priests used the blood money to buy the potter's field as a burial place for foreigners (27.7). Jerome seems to have made a connection with those Old Testament passages in which God is described as the potter (e.g. Isa. 45.9; Jer. 18.5–11), a connection suggested by Matthew's explicit reference to Jeremiah: 'Now it is called the potter's field because our Potter is Christ' (Jerome 2008: 310).

Meanwhile some Christian artists have detected another connection to the Judas story within Matthew's Gospel itself, though this time by way of contrast. A small ivory panel from *c*.420, now in the British Museum, juxtaposes Judas hanging from a noose with Christ hanging on the cross. The contrast is between death and life. Judas is clearly dead, his head upturned and eyes closed. Christ on the cross is alive and serene, gazing out at the viewer (Harries 2004: 10–13).

The two other characters with heightened roles in Matthew's passion story have also provoked interest and debate. Matthew alone among the evangelists records how Pontius Pilate, the Roman governor, washed his hands in water and declared himself 'innocent of this man's blood', which provoked the response of the people: 'His blood be on us and on our children!' (27.24–25). In a passion narrative replete with contrasts, this is generally read as comparing Pilate positively to the Jewish crowds. That the pagan Pilate performs a ritual that, according to Deuteronomy 21.6–9, Israel was meant to perform in order to distance herself from bloodguilt, accentuates the contrast. Yet even here the text contains gaps and ambiguities that allow for a more nuanced reading: what indication, for example, does the implied author provide of this character's motives? The fact that, despite his declaration of Jesus' innocence, Pilate immediately hands Jesus over to be crucified does not allow him to be exonerated from all culpability. In the apocryphal *Mors Pilati*, the corpse of Pilate is thrown into a succession of rivers after his death but rejected by the waters due to the disturbance of evil spirits.

Less ambiguous is the one character in the passion story unique to Matthew: the unnamed figure of Pilate's wife, who stands in that line of characters, both Jewish (Joseph, 1.20; 2.13, 19) and Gentile (the magi, 2.12), who receive revelation by dreams. She too declares Jesus to be 'innocent'. Building on this brief but sympathetic portrayal in Matthew, Christian tradition developed a legend describing her conversion to Christ and providing her with the name Matthew failed to give (Claudia Procla or Procula). Such was her fame, indeed, that she was canonized by the Eastern Orthodox Church and by the Ethiopian Church, which also recognizes her husband as a saint. Even in the West she is remembered favourably, appearing as a major figure in the York mystery plays. Jerome claims that divine revelation frequently came to Gentiles through the vehicle of dreams and that Pilate and his wife together represent 'the testimony of the Gentile people' (Jerome 2008: 311). Only rarely does a reception of this passage contradict the generally positive reading of Matthew's reference: Langland's *Piers Plowman* (18.300–10) offers the alternative explanation that her dream was demonically inspired (Clarke 2003: 227).

Christ and Caesar

Attention to these two Roman characters in Matthew's passion narrative is a reminder of that other overlapping world the Gospel inhabits, which can often be neglected due to concentration on the anti-Jewish potential of that narrative. Rome and Roman authority is an ever-present factor in the Gospel, even though 'Rome' is never explicitly mentioned. Moreover the ambiguity of Pilate's role in Matthew's story – despite his wife's clear warning as a consequence of her dream, Pilate fails to have 'nothing to do with' him (see 27.19) – highlights Rome's ambiguity.

The political – or religio-political – dimensions of much of Matthew's 'theological' language have been noted already in this book. The 'kingdom of the heavens' contrasts with the *basileia* or rule of imperial Rome (see Pennington 2009). The 'gospel' (*euangelion*) that Jesus proclaims and that is enshrined in Matthew's book (e.g. 4.23; 9.35; 24.14; 26.13) contrasts sharply with the 'gospels' concerning the emperor. In the passion narrative the subversion of this imperial world view can be seen to come to a climax, given that the issue at stake in the trials of Jesus concerns whether or not he is the royal Messiah, the 'king of the Jews' (e.g. 26.63, 68; 27.11, 17, 22, 29, 37, 42). Some readers find in Matthew a problematic adoption of the gospel of imperial propaganda, replacing one kind of power associated with the emperor with a heavenly variation of the same, without offering a systematic critique of its imperializing tendencies (e.g. Dube 2000). Jesus, after all, knows that he can call on a mighty heavenly army comprising more than 'twelve legions of angels' should he wish (26.53). Others, such as Carter, find a genuine subversion here: 'The life-giving and just power of God's empire conflicts with and challenges the hierarchical, exploitative, and oppressive practices of Rome's empire and the allied religious elite' (Carter 2000: 498). Indeed the juxtaposition of the passion narrative with the vision that immediately precedes it is shockingly dramatic and ironic. Having described Jesus the Son of Man as universal king and judge (25.31–46), the Gospel now describes the story of Jesus the suffering Son of Man appearing before the judgement seat of Caesar's representative in order to face execution (27.19).

A further point at which Caesar breaks through into the story of Jesus is in the response of the Roman centurion 'and those with him' to Jesus' death. The way Matthew's word order – 'God's Son' (*theou huios*) rather than 'son of God' (*huios theou*) – echoes that found in Greek inscriptions acclaiming emperors from Augustus onwards has been commented upon by scholars (Mowery 2002). Warren Carter notes how this imperial title reflects Caesar's role as the agent of Jupiter, on whose behalf he ruled on earth (Carter 2000: 40). In Matthew's story the true Son of God is the powerless, crucified Son of Man rather than the pretender seated in Rome.

The circumstances surrounding Jesus' death bear this out. What prompts the acclamation of Jesus as God's Son is not how Jesus died – as in Mark (15.39) – but the rending of the Temple curtain and those additional events described by Matthew alone: an earthquake, the opening of the tombs and the raising of 'many bodies of the saints' (27.51–53). These are generally interpreted as eschatological events, heralding the beginning of the End (e.g. Meier 1975; though see Troxel 2002 for an alternative interpretation). Expected cosmic phenomena were often associated with the deaths of great figures in the ancient world. Virgil links the assassination of Julius Caesar with the eruption of Mount Etna, an earthquake in the Alps and the appearance of comets (Virgil, *Georgics* 1.472–90). The Roman historian Cassius Dio claims that a comet heralded the death of the Emperor Claudius, together with the mysterious opening of the Temple to Jupiter Victor and a shower of blood (Dio, *History* 60.35.1). Matthew's account of Jesus' death is coloured by the language of Jewish apocalyptic. The death of Christ is nothing less than the dawn of the new age – to be inaugurated by the resurrection of the dead – that would cause all associated with the 'present evil age', the empire of Rome included, to shudder in its wake.

12

Endings and New Beginnings: The Resurrection of Jesus

Visualizing the Resurrection

In the Museo Civico of the town of Sansepulchro ('holy sepulchre') in Tuscany there is a famous depiction of the resurrection of Christ by the fifteenth-century artist Piero della Francesca. Clearly influenced by the narrative of Matthew, the fresco depicts the glorious Christ having emerged from his grave-like tomb. At his feet lie guards 'like dead men' (or rather like deep sleepers), reflecting the impact of the 'angel of the Lord' in Matthew's resurrection story. In the background the dead wood of the leafless trees on the left contrast with the spring-like trees to the right, a symbol of that new life Christ's resurrection brings.

Della Francesca's *Resurrection* captures powerfully the literary brilliance of Matthew's resurrection account, which falls neatly into three parts (28.1–10; 28.11–15; 28.16–20). As in the passion narrative, Matthew is remarkably close to Mark in his story of the discovery of the empty tomb by the women (28.1–8; cf. Mark 16.1–8), although he combines this with a brief appearance of the risen Jesus as the women leave the tomb (28.9–10; in Mark's parallel, Jesus is conspicuous by his absence). But Matthew goes his own way in what follows. In the second part (28.11–15) he continues the story of the guard at the tomb begun at 27.62–66, picking up on and challenging a rival Jewish explanation of why Jesus' tomb was found empty. Finally he describes an appearance of the risen Lord on a mountain in Galilee and his commission of the 11 disciples (28.16–20).

Despite the prominent role of an earthquake and the descent of an 'angel of the Lord', Matthew shares the reserve of the other canonical evangelists about the resurrection itself. There is no attempt to describe Jesus emerging from the tomb, unlike the apocryphal *Gospel of Peter* with its dramatic description of the stone rolling away by itself and the emergence of three giant figures – the risen Lord supported by two angels – from the tomb (*Gos. Pet.* 33–44). By contrast Matthew's interest is not on the resurrection itself but on its aftermath, its effects in this world and especially on his disciples.

Critical Questions

The Gospel resurrection narratives raise a wealth of issues, literary, historical and theological. On the literary level, how do these various accounts relate to one another? Do they reflect standard source-critical explanations or at this point do the evangelists go their own way in drawing upon independent traditions, including popular Christian legends or even their own imaginations? Interestingly both Matthew and Luke agree up to the point at which Mark ends – presupposing an original ending at Mark 16.8. Their subsequent stories of Jesus' appearances to his disciples betray no knowledge of each other, Matthew – apart from Jesus' brief appearance report at the tomb – recording a tradition associated with Galilee (Matt. 28.16–20), Luke knowing of a succession of appearances all of which occur in and around Jerusalem (Luke 24.13–53). The Galilee tradition is implied at Mark 16.7 and confirmed in John 21 (though with an appearance by the lake rather than on a mountain), while John 20 shares with Luke a tradition of Jerusalem appearances.

A second literary question concerns genre. Which kind of stories are these, particularly those that seem to contain legendary elements? They are very different from the stories recounted so far in the Gospels, even the Transfiguration, which is sometimes described as a 'displaced' resurrection appearance. Matthew's version is the most 'legendary' of all four, incorporating an earthquake and the descent of an angel of the Lord. These are two points at which his Gospel touches the distinctive world view of the Jewish and early Christian apocalypses, suggesting that the apocalypse genre might be in part instructive for reading Matthew's account.

Interwoven with these literary issues are historical questions. What really happened on that first day of the week and the days that followed, or is that now impossible to unravel from the rich tapestry of myth, memory and liturgical re-enactment bequeathed to us in the resurrection narratives? Or is this the wrong kind of question to be asking of stories that describe what is essentially 'trans-historical', an event taking the crucified Jesus not back into history but beyond history into the life of God?

A further historical question concerns how best to account for the significant discrepancies, both minor and major, between the Gospel accounts. The four accounts of the empty tomb are replete with minor discrepancies – such as over the timing of the women's arrival at the tomb, how many women were present, their intention in coming to the tomb and their reaction to what they saw and heard. These discrepancies are sometimes explained as the expected results of different eyewitnesses remembering differently and somewhat unreliably. Yet the probable literary dependence of both Matthew and Luke upon Mark – or indeed any other theory of literary dependence – renders such an explanation deficient. Deliberate redactional changes are a more plausible explanation. Major discrepancies between the various appearance narratives are even more problematic historically.

In addition, scholars debate when the story of the empty tomb made its entrance into the Gospel tradition. Some highlight the fact that the empty tomb is not explicitly mentioned by Paul at 1 Corinthians 15.3–8, though it may be implicit in Paul's juxtaposition of 'was buried' and 'was raised'. Others, including feminist scholars, employ a hermeneutic of suspicion in support of the antiquity of the empty tomb tradition. For some its attribution to inadmissible witnesses – the women – counts in its favour, although the claim that Jewish Law forbade women giving valid testimony is largely dependent upon a passage in Josephus (*Ant.* 4.219). For others the story would originally have been preserved in the 'private' sphere of women's storytelling circles, only gradually emerging in the official 'public' kerygmatic tradition of the male disciples (Osiek 2001).

Finally the resurrection narratives raise theological questions. What are these stories attempting to articulate about the faith of the early Church? What does it mean to speak of resurrection in general and the resurrection of Christ in particular? How far do the various narratives reflect the theological outlook of the individual evangelists – a question particularly related to the various post-Easter 'commissions' in the Gospels, where redactional interests are most clearly to the fore?

What Might Resurrection Mean?

One important context for understanding the latter set of questions is the meaning of resurrection in first-century Judaism. The resurrection of the dead seems to have developed relatively late as a doctrine among Jews. In the first century it was held by the Pharisees but not the Sadducees, given that it was not unambiguously taught in the Pentateuch (e.g. Mark 12.18; Acts 23.6–8). The Essenes might have held to a form of it, although Josephus claims that they believed in the immortality of the soul (*War* 2.154). But the biblical antecedents were not substantial. Certain Old Testament passages could be read as referring metaphorically to the resurrection of the nation (e.g. Ezek. 37.1–14; Isa. 25.8; 26.19; Hos. 6.1–2;

Job 19.25). There were also texts that referred to the exaltation to heaven of particularly righteous human beings, such as Enoch (Gen. 5.24) and Elijah (2 Kings 2.1–12). The peculiar ending of Deuteronomy, with its claim that although Moses was buried, 'no one knows his burial place to this day' (Deut. 34.6), led at least some Jews to conclude that Moses too had been assumed into heaven, a belief that may be implicit in the presence of both Moses and Elijah at the Transfiguration of Jesus (Matt. 17.3). Exaltation to heaven, however, describes a rather different category from resurrection from the dead.

The earliest unambiguous reference to resurrection seems to be in the book of Daniel: 'Many of those who sleep in the dust of the earth shall awake, some to everlasting life, and some to shame and everlasting contempt' (Dan. 12.2). This passage in Daniel reflects the crisis of the Maccabean period in the second century BCE, when Jews, including young Jews, began to be martyred for their fidelity to the faith ('resurrection' is also found in 2 and 4 Maccabees, some of the earliest examples of Jewish martyr literature). This connection with dying for the faith explains the first association resurrection seems to have had for Jews: resurrection meant vindication. Resurrection from the dead, despite the fact that one's earthly life had been cut short, represented God's 'yes' to the 'no' implicit in the often early deaths of pious Jews (which might be taken as a sign of divine judgement).

Second, especially in the apocalyptic tradition, the resurrection of the dead – in particular the resurrection of the righteous – was associated with the 'end of this age' (e.g. Isa. 26.19 LXX; *1 Enoch* 51.1–5; 62.13–15; *Apoc. Ad. Ev.* 13.3–4; 41.2–3; *T. Jud.* 25.4; *4 Ezra* 7.28–32). This is a key plank in Meier's salvation-historical thesis outlined in Chapter 10 above: that the last days would be heralded by the resurrection of the dead (Meier 1975 and 1991).

But there is a third aspect to resurrection: however 'corporeal' it is, and even when it presupposes resurrection to life in the land of Israel, it is not resuscitation or reanimation. Hence the evangelists make a qualitative distinction between restoration to mortal life – essentially the reanimation of a corpse – and the resurrection as it pertains to Jesus. Characters such as the official's daughter, the son of the widow of Nain, and Lazarus of Bethany (9.18–19, 23–26; Luke 7.11–17; John 11.1–44) had been restored temporarily to the life they had before and would have to face death again. Jesus, on the contrary, had passed through death into the imperishable life of God, freeing him from the constraints of mortal existence, including time and space – hence he is able to abide with his disciples 'until the end of the age'.

167

Discovering the Empty Tomb

The first type of resurrection story, found in all four canonical Gospels, concerns the discovery of the empty tomb. As in the passion narrative there are significant similarities between Matthew and Mark. Both describe how the tomb of Jesus is discovered empty, on the first day of the week (that is, after the Sabbath), by a group of women. In both the women encounter a figure in white who announces the resurrection of Jesus. Neither evangelist attempts to describe the resurrection event itself – unlike the legendary *Gospel of Peter* – but only its after-effects on those left behind. Both agree, however, that the women are commanded to tell his disciples that Jesus is risen and that he precedes them to Galilee. Finally both recount how the women, having heard these words, leave the tomb.

Despite the similarities between Mark and Matthew, however, there are also differences, such as the timing of the women's arrival, their number, their reason for going to the tomb and their response to what they heard. Most striking is the clarity of Matthew's version and its emphasis upon divine revelation unmistakably breaking through. Matthew's clarity contrasts sharply with Mark's account, dominated by Marcan themes of mystery, secrecy, fear and disobedience, and noted for its unsatisfactory ending. Mark's account contains a discrepancy between the number of women present at Jesus' burial (two) and those who come to the tomb on the first day of the week (three). Matthew has two women on both occasions. Mark tells us that the women came to anoint Jesus' body, not only a foolish act – given the heavy stone over the tomb's entrance – but also potentially faithless, for Jesus had been anointed for his burial prior to his death (Mark 14.8). For Matthew the women have simply come to 'see' the tomb, possibly reflecting the Jewish custom of watching at a tomb to avoid a loved one being buried alive (Longstaff 1981).

Matthew also clarifies Mark's mysterious young man in white (Mark 16.5). His white clothing identifies him as an 'angel of the Lord', a particularly exalted angel (cf. Gen. 16.7; 21.17; 22.11; Exod. 3.2), whose appearance 'like lightning, and his clothing white as snow' is reminiscent of Jesus at the Transfiguration (28.3; cf. 17.2). He thereby functions as a trustworthy heavenly mediator, providing a commentary on why the tomb is empty that is as reliable for the implied reader as editorial comments from the narrator himself. This angel is also responsible for rolling away the stone from the tomb's entrance, hinting that the resurrection of Jesus requires divine intervention – the passive 'he has been raised' is a divine passive (28.6).

Finally Matthew's version reinterprets the crippling fear of the women that in Mark's account prevented them from announcing the resurrection. For Matthew they are gripped with 'fear and great joy' (28.8). Their fear is holy fear, the awe and reverence appropriate to an encounter with the divine. Their response is a positive one, which contrasts with the later appearance to the male disciples on the mountain, where 'some doubted' (28.17). Moreover Matthew's story continues beyond Mark's to show that the message was delivered. In terms of plot resolution, many readers find this a much more satisfying ending than Mark's characteristically enigmatic one.

As in his passion narrative, here too Matthew includes his own special material. The 'great earthquake' (*seismos megas*, 28.2) not only reflects the mood of heavenly intervention, and matches the fact that the guards 'shook' (*eseisthēsan*, 28.4), it also connects the scene with the previous earthquake at the death of Jesus, thus strengthening Meier's claim that the two moments represent a single eschatological event (Meier 1975).

Matthew is also alone in providing a brief appearance of the risen Lord to Mary Magdalene and 'the other Mary' as they depart from the tomb (though its matter-of-fact character – 'suddenly Jesus met them', verse 9 – contrasts sharply with the otherworldly appearance of the angel whose words he largely duplicates). One puzzle is Matthew's explicit statement, without explanation, that the women 'took hold of his feet' (28.9). A possible solution is to read this in the light of John 20.17, where Mary is rebuked for wanting to hold on to Jesus, thus preventing him from ascending to his Father. Yet there is no hint of a rebuke in Matthew's account, where the women's action is combined with an act of worship. A better solution is to see this as part of an apologetic against the rival claim that the risen Jesus was only a phantom or a ghost. It is a common feature across cultures that ghosts lack feet (Davies and Allison 2004: 543).

The Role of the Guard

The recumbent soldiers in Piero della Francesca's *Resurrection* recall the second major unit in Matthew's resurrection narrative: the story of the guard at the tomb, which is also unique to him. At the end of the previous chapter the chief priests and the Pharisees – the latter having been absent throughout the passion narrative – request a guard of soldiers to prevent Jesus' disciples stealing his body (27.62–66). Matthew returns to the story at 28.11–15, with the result that the two parts of the story bracket the discovery of the empty tomb.

One consequence of this guard story is to give the empty-tomb narrative a more central role. Matthew stresses a higher degree of certainty about the tomb's location. Given that it is Joseph of Arimathea's 'own new tomb' (27.60), he could locate it. The women also knew where it was since they had been present when Jesus' body was laid to rest, and they came again to 'see' it (27.61; 28.1). Now even his enemies knew where the tomb was, given that they were guarding it to prevent any danger of grave robbery.

This focus on the tomb almost certainly has an apologetic purpose. It directly challenges an alternative explanation that Matthew tells his audience is recounted among Jews 'to this day', namely that his disciples stole his body during the night. This rival explanation is attributed not to the truth but to a lie propagated through bribery. A similar charge is known to the second-century Christian author Justin Martyr. In his *Dialogue with Trypho* 108, Justin's fictional Jewish opponent Trypho speaks of Jesus as:

> a Galilean deceiver, whom we crucified, but his disciples stole him by night from the tomb, where he was laid when unfastened from the cross, and now deceive men by asserting that he has risen from the dead and ascended to heaven.   (Justin Martyr 1996: 253; cf. *T. Levi* 16.3)

Yet readers should not be too swift to dismiss the story as 'mere' apologetic, even if there are difficulties with affirming its historicity (Brown 1994: 1310–13; for a defence of historicity, see Craig 1984). Sensitivity to narrative might reveal more than a purely historical analysis would yield. Davies and Allison point to a set of striking literary parallels in Matthew's resurrection story that serve to contrast the guard at the tomb with the women (Davies and Allison 1988–97: 3/659). Not only are both groups present at the tomb of Jesus (28.1, 4); they both also see the angel of the Lord (28.2–3) and experience fear (28.4, 8). Moreover both leave the tomb to recount what has happened (28.8, 11) and are told by others what they are to say (28.7, 10, 13–14). The difference is that the women tell the truth while the guards tell a lie. Truth and falsehood emerge as key themes in this resurrection story, as they have in the previous story of the passion (where the leaders have sought 'false' testimony against Jesus, 26.59).

Appearance Stories

Matthew's appending the resurrection appearance to the women to the end of his empty-tomb story obscures the fact that these are two different kinds of resurrection story – the other evangelists clearly distinguish between empty-tomb narratives and appearance narratives, even if John also has an appearance to Mary Magdalene close to the tomb (John 20.11–18; cf. Mark 16.9–11). This distinction is clear in Matthew's second appearance story, which takes place on a mountain in Galilee (28.16–20).

On Marcan priority, Matthew would almost certainly have found Mark's truncated ending unsatisfactory, particularly given Mark has anticipated a resurrection appearance in Galilee (14.28; 16.7). Thus like Luke and the authors of the various alternative endings of Mark, he supplies the gap, drawing upon a tradition about an appearance to the male disciples in Galilee though also betraying knowledge of an appearance to female disciples in Jerusalem. As already noted, the Gospels provide a wide variety of stories about the appearance of the risen Jesus to his followers, only some of which may be harmonized. John is particularly puzzling in this regard, containing internal inconsistencies: having appeared to the disciples twice in Jerusalem in the space of a week (John 20.19–29), Jesus then appears to them by the Sea of Galilee (21.1–8). This is doubly odd, first because the disciples in Galilee appear to have returned to their old occupation of fishing, despite being commissioned by Jesus in Jerusalem (20.22–23), second because they fail to recognize the risen Lord by the lakeside, having seen him twice in his risen form in Jerusalem (21.4).

Yet the various resurrection appearance stories are also distinctive for another reason. They exhibit a strange combination of strangeness and matter-of-factness. The everyday statement Matthew uses to describe the women's encounter with the risen Christ ('Jesus met them', 28.9) contrasts sharply with his description of the otherworldly angel of the Lord ('His appearance was like lightning, and his clothing white as snow', 28.3), or even with Jesus on the Mount of Transfiguration ('his face shone like the sun, and his clothes became dazzling white', 17.2). Yet he is also the object of worship. A similar combination is found in the appearance on the mountain in Galilee. Although Daniel's vision of 'one like a son of man' is in the background, there is no dramatic description of Christ's appearance. That the Eleven worship him implies recognition of his divine status (although the disciples have already worshipped him in the boat at 14.33). But that is not made explicit, either here or in the statement that Jesus 'came' or 'approached' (although the fact that he is the subject of this verb, whereas elsewhere in the Gospel people 'approached' him, e.g. 8.2, 5, 19; 9.20, may hint at the divine initiative).

In other resurrection appearance stories the combination of familiarity and strangeness is even more pronounced. In John, Mary Magdalene does not recognize Jesus until he speaks her name, as if to highlight his altered state (20.14, 16). In Luke, on the road to Emmaus the eyes of the two disciples are initially prevented from recognizing him (24.16, 31). Yet the presence of wounds in his hands, feet and side (Luke 24.39–40; John 20.20, 27) emphasize both that this unrecognized figure is the same Jesus who was crucified and that he is not a ghost (Matt. 28.9; Luke 24.39, 42–43). He is the same and yet different; belonging to this world and yet breaking in from the world to come. This mixture of the down to earth and the heavenly is well exemplified in Stanley Spencer's *The Resurrection, Cookham* (1924–7; London, Tate Britain), in which Spencer's own parish church at Cookham becomes the backdrop to the resurrection of the dead, Christ enthroned in the church porch and Spencer himself and his fiancée Hilda part of the action.

But the resurrection appearance stories do not simply reveal the nature of Jesus' resurrection body; they also function to prepare the readers for what happens after they have finished reading the Gospel. At the heart of most of the appearance stories is a commission (e.g. Matt. 28.10, 19–20; Mark 16.15–18; Luke 24.45–49; John 20.17, 21–23). The precise wording in each Gospel is highly redactional, reflecting what each evangelist sees as at the heart of the gospel message (thus for Matthew it is making disciples who are to be taught; for John it concerns the forgiving or retaining of sins; for Luke this forgiveness of sins is to be preached to all the world, beginning from Jerusalem). But in all, an intimate connection is drawn between the resurrection of Christ and the mission of his followers. The risen Jesus comes in order that the Church might be sent out.

A final motif common to several appearance stories is that of the meal, which many commentators read as a reference to the presence of the risen Lord in the Eucharist. The Emmaus story climaxes with an explicit reference to recognizing Jesus 'in the breaking of the bread' (Luke 24.30, 35). Later in Jerusalem the risen Jesus eats in his disciples' presence (Luke 24.41–43). In John's account of the lakeside encounter the breakfast of bread and fish recalls the earlier account of the feeding of the 5,000, with its strong eucharistic resonances (John 21.9–14; cf. John 6.12–13, 53–56). This way of reading the resurrection narratives invites participation on the part of the ecclesial reader, closing the historical gap between the first disciples in the days after Jesus' death and the contemporary liturgical life of the community. It is an approach to the appearance stories well exemplified in a homily of John Chrysostom, although here he extends the eucharistic dimension to include Matthew's story of the women grasping Jesus' feet at Matthew 28.9:

Perchance some of you would wish to be like them, to hold the feet of Jesus;
ye can even now, and not His feet and His hands only, but even lay hold
of that sacred head, receiving the awful mysteries with a pure conscience.

(John Chrysostom 1991: 527)

The 'awful mysteries' to which Chrysostom refers are the body and blood
of the Eucharist, which his congregation is about to receive.

Tying the Threads Together

Matthew's final resurrection appearance lacks a eucharistic reference,
although the commissioning motif is strong. In literary terms it represents
the climax of the resurrection narrative and indeed of the whole Gospel
(although feminist critics warn that unduly separating 28.16–20 from
the remainder of chapter 28 risks an androcentric interpretation that
places the commissioning of the 11 male disciples above what is said
of the women disciples in earlier scenes: Wainwright 2009: 103). Moreover
it represents a satisfying coming together of a number of Matthean themes:
Jesus as a new Moses; the revelatory character of mountains; the importance of Jesus' teaching; the central role of 'Galilee of the Gentiles' (on the
mixture of tradition and redaction in 28.16–20, see Meier 1977b).

The precise interpretation depends upon which Old Testament intertexts
a reader prioritizes. Again the rich intertextual character of Matthew's
narrative offers a range of possibilities. The Moses-Jesus typology is
suggested by echoes of the end of Deuteronomy, where Moses tells
the assembled Israelites to teach the words to their children 'so that they
may diligently observe all the words of this law' (Deut. 32.46), before
ascending Mount Nebo, to the top of Pisgah, where the Lord showed him
the extent of the promised land (Deut. 34.1–3). This is neatly paralleled
in Jesus' command on this mountain that new disciples are to be taught
to observe 'everything that I have commanded you' (28.20). However, Jesus
is no mere Moses. The words to be observed are Jesus' own teachings.
Moreover his final words, 'I am with you always', echo God's words to
Joshua as he is commissioned as Moses' successor: 'I will be with you'
(Deut. 31.23; cf. Matt. 28.20).

But as well as Deuteronomy there are verbal echoes of Daniel 7 LXX,
which would characterize this scene as the return of the crucified and
vindicated Son of Man. In the LXX version of Daniel it is said of the 'one
like a son of man' that 'to him was given authority, that all peoples, nations,
and languages should serve him' (Dan. 7.14 LXX). As Son of Man, the risen

Jesus has received 'all authority in heaven and on earth' (Matt. 28.18; note the allusion to the devil's offer of 'all the kingdoms of the world' on another mountain, 4.8–9).

Third, some scholars stress the verbal connections with the decree of King Cyrus of Persia at the end of 2 Chronicles, allowing for the exiles to return to Jerusalem and rebuild the Temple:

> Thus says King Cyrus of Persia: The LORD, the God of heaven, has given me all the kingdoms of the earth, and he has charged me to build him a house at Jerusalem, which is in Judah. Whoever is among you of all his people, may the LORD his God be with him! (2 Chron. 36.23)

In this case Jesus may be presented as a new Cyrus, whom Isaiah refers to as God's 'Messiah' or 'anointed' (Isa. 45.1). Alternatively this intertext may be recalling Chronicles' great hero the wise Son of David, King Solomon, who built the first Temple. Thus Jesus is another Solomon in his role as builder of the Church. Yet even this is insufficient, for Jesus has already said that 'something greater than Solomon is here!' (12.42).

The Solomonic echo is a reminder that Matthew's Gospel has had much to say about the Church, both explicitly and in its implicit use of transparency. Finally in this climactic passage, the Church comes into its own. As the risen Jesus meets his disciples he puts in train the final plan for this renewed community, rooted in the ancient *ekklēsia* of Israel but open to the other nations of the world – an openness anticipated in Jesus' title of 'son of Abraham' (1.1). This community is identified in this climactic scene as a community of disciples, those who learn from Jesus and strive to observe all his commandments. At the very end of the Gospel, where one might expect the risen Jesus to 'go ahead' (cf. Mark 16.7) or 'ascend' (cf. Luke 24.51; John 20.17), Matthew presents him as the one who stays. Matthew's risen Son of Man is the abiding divine presence, the Shekinah, 'with you always, to the end of the age' (28.20; cf. 18.20). Here we find the Gospel's last and greatest *inclusio*, taking the reader back to the beginning and the first prophecy quoted from Isaiah: '"and they shall name him Emmanuel", which means, "God is with us"' (1.23, citing Isa. 7.14).

13

Conclusions: Interpreting Matthew Today

This exploration of Matthew's Gospel and the myriad ways readers across centuries and cultures have interpreted it has made no claim to be exhaustive, nor to offer definitive solutions to the complex scholarly debates surrounding its interpretation. The more modest purpose has been to open up some of the questions posed by, and to, this multifaceted text, and some of the different strategies interpreters have used to provide some answers. Given the tendency of much critical scholarship – at least until recently – to dismiss or denigrate older, that is pre-Enlightenment, interpretations of Matthew, or to regard the Gospel as a retrograde rewriting of the original 'radical' Gospel of Mark, a deliberate decision has been taken in this book to explore the strengths as well as the weaknesses of alternative interpretations across the centuries. This reflects one recent trend in biblical scholarship in favour of reception, not for purely antiquarian interests but out of the conviction that it can enhance understanding (see especially Luz 1989, 1994, 2001, 2005a and 2005b).

At the end of our journey of exploration, what might be said about the contemporary task of reading and interpreting Matthew? I want to suggest four overlapping areas for further reflection and study. The first is a growing awareness that a text is capable of meaning several things, and that to posit multivalency of meaning is not to succumb to the heresy of 'eisegesis' ('reading into' a text) as an uncritical alternative to solid 'exegesis' ('reading out of' a text). In part this is a recognition that authorial intention – in the case of our text, what the evangelist Matthew or the implied author wished to convey – is only one dimension to what a text means. Although I have made certain judgements in this book about probable authorial concerns, I have also been aware that reconstructing those concerns is highly unstable and affected in no small part by the vantage point from which each of us reads, with its mixture of unique perspective and blind spots. In the case of Matthew, being precise about authorial concerns is hampered by what John Riches calls the 'tensiveness' of his text (Riches 2000: 322).

Moreover texts take on a life of their own once they leave the hands of their original authors, and readers and audiences are notoriously unpredictable when they read or hear a text – the complex responses of Christian hearers of the passion narrative, for example, frustrates the neat attempts of narrative critics to define how ideal readers should react to particular character groups within the story.

But even within the narrower concerns of the historical critic, multivalency may be a feature of the meaning intended by the original author. The range of possible intertextual allusions proposed in the previous chapter for the Great Commission – Deuteronomy, Daniel and 2 Chronicles – illustrates the point. Should one restrict authorial intention to only one of these? Or if we permit all three, does one take precedence over the others or is there a more dynamic interplay between them? Moreover given that no human interpreter can keep the full implications of all three in his or her mind simultaneously, can any one account of 'what Matthew wanted to convey' ever be up to the task? Contemporary Matthean interpreters could profitably reflect on the full implications of Dale Allison's observation that Matthew's Gospel is 'intertextually, intratextually, and theologically dense' (Allison 2005: 125).

Second, given the multivalency of a text like Matthew, as well as its widely acknowledged complex patterning and its interweaving of narrative with discourse and of history with transparency, a variety of interpretative methods is called for. Surveys of different scholarly approaches often speak as if they are hermetically sealed from each other and mutually exclusive, a danger present even in this book. Yet in practice holistic readings of Matthew such as found in narrative criticism are often illuminated by the types of questions provoked by historical-critical methods and vice versa. Further, awareness of perspective and the power of the interested reader to shape what a text might mean, together with exposure to challenging, unfamiliar or half-forgotten readings of familiar passages that reception history makes possible, all add to the interpretative mix. This has been reflected in the eclectic approach to reading Matthew found here.

Third, one of the outcomes of reception-historical study has been to bring into sharper focus the fact that texts and their interpretations have consequences. Interpreting the Bible, especially the Gospels, calls for responsibility on the part of those who interpret, not least because how one reads may have life or death consequences. The tragic 'history of effects' of 27.25 ('His blood be on us and on our children') is an obvious case, even if Ulrich Luz is correct that many receptions of this verse have been brief and casual (Luz 2005a: 506). The historical sensitivity and sociological awareness of recent Matthean scholarship has provided a new context for reassessing such a passage, its meanings and manifold effects, and there are positive signs that this is already bearing fruit in contemporary Jewish–Christian dialogue.

But there is further fruitful exploration to be done. In a world where religion and religious communities are increasingly polarized and polemical name-calling abounds, reflection upon the polemical language Matthew's text directs towards the 'scribes and Pharisees', its probably historical cause and its sociological function might contribute fruitfully to the debate and to a wiser and more truthful religious discourse.

Finally, several of the approaches to Matthew explored in this book invite a greater degree of participation on the part of the reader than the 'detached' interpretations of historical criticism, with its clear distinction between 'meaning' and 'application'. Both narrative criticism and pre-critical approaches are interested in the didactic function of characters in the story and the capacity of readers – implied or real – to identify with or dissociate themselves from different character groups. The liturgical commemoration of St Matthew and the associated hagiographical legends exploit particular aspects of Matthew's Gospel for the demands they make on the Christian worshipper.

Moreover Matthew's strong ethical focus, albeit one grounded in a belief in the prior action of the God of Israel, calls for action on the part of the reader: not simply to 'hear these words of mine' but also to 'act' upon them (7.24). Benedict Viviano may not be overstating the case when he categorizes Matthew's Gospel thus:

> Matthew is a gospel for 'do-ers', activists, people who are incensed about big problems in the world like genocide, ethnic cleansing, institutionalized racism, systemic rape practices, child abuse, sweatshop labor conditions, unemployment, war and peace, and clean water and air. (Viviano 2010: 344)

This is very different from the often negative assessment of Matthew as overly moralizing or obsessed with internal ecclesiastical affairs. Others will find in the same Gospel a harsh prophetic critique of human pretence or of misguided motivation, whether in the religious (symbolized by broad phylacteries and long tassels, 23.5) or the political sphere. None of these responses is without support from Matthew's text, but none of them provides the complete picture either. They are testimony to the complex, tensive and multivalent character of this Gospel that combines continuity with discontinuity, fiery judgement with limitless mercy, radical demands with ecclesial order – in short, a work like that of a householder 'who brings out of his treasure what is new and what is old' (13.52).

Bibliography

Abel, E. L., 1971. 'Who Wrote Matthew?' *NTS* 17: 138–52.

Albright, W. F. and Mann, C. S., 1971. *Matthew: Introduction, Translation, and Notes*. Anchor Bible; Garden City, NY: Doubleday.

Allen, W. C., 1907. *A Critical and Exegetical Commentary on the Gospel According to St Matthew*. Edinburgh: T. & T. Clark.

Allison, D. C., 1987. 'The Son of God as Israel: A Note on Matthean Christology', *Irish Biblical Studies* 9: 74–81.

Allison, D. C., 1993. *The New Moses: A Matthean Typology*. Edinburgh: T. & T. Clark.

Allison, D. C., 1999. *The Sermon on the Mount: Inspiring the Moral Imagination*. Companions to the New Testament; New York: Crossroad.

Allison, D. C., 2005. *Studies in Matthew: Interpretation Past and Present*. Grand Rapids, MI: Baker Academic.

Anderson, J. C., 1983. 'Matthew: Gender and Reading', *Semeia* 28: 3–27.

Anderson, J. C., 1987. 'Mary's Difference: Gender and Patriarchy in the Birth Narratives', *Journal of Religion* 67: 183–202.

Anderson, J. C., 1995. 'Life on the Mississippi: New Currents in Matthaean Scholarship 1983–1993', *Currents in Research: Biblical Studies* 3: 169–218.

Argyle, A. W., 1956. 'Joseph the Patriarch in Patristic Teaching', *Expository Times* 67: 199–201.

Augustine, 1996. *Our Lord's Sermon on the Mount*, in P. Schaff (ed.), *Nicene and Post-Nicene Fathers. First Series: Volume VI*. Edinburgh: T. & T. Clark/Grand Rapids, MI: Eerdmans: 3–63.

Bacon, B. W., 1918. 'The "Five Books" of Matthew Against the Jews', *The Expositor* 15: 56–66.

Bacon, B. W., 1930. *Studies in Matthew*. London: Constable & Co.

Barth, G., 1982. 'Matthew's Understanding of the Law', in G. Bornkamm, G. Barth and H. J. Held, *Tradition and Interpretation in Matthew*. 2nd enlarged edn, trans. P. Scott; London: SCM Press: 58–164.

Bauckham, R., 2006. *Jesus and the Eyewitnesses: The Gospels as Eyewitness Testimony*. Grand Rapids, MI and Cambridge: Eerdmans.

Bauckham, R. (ed.), 1998. *The Gospels for All Christians: Rethinking the Gospel Audiences*. Edinburgh: T. & T. Clark.

Baxter, W., 2006. 'Healing and the "Son of David": Matthew's Warrant', *NT* 48: 36–50.

Bethge, E., 1970. *Dietrich Bonhoeffer: A Biography*. London: Collins.

Blair, E. P., 1960. *Jesus in the Gospel of Matthew*. New York: Abingdon.

Bockmuehl, M., 2011. 'The Son of David and his Mother', *JTS* 62: 476–93.

Bockmuehl, M., 2012. *Simon Peter in Scripture and Memory: The New Testament Apostle in the Early Church*. Grand Rapids, MI: Baker Academic.

Bibliography

Bornkamm, G., 1982. 'The Stilling of the Storm in Matthew', in G. Bornkamm, G. Barth and H. J. Held, *Tradition and Interpretation in Matthew*. 2nd enlarged edn, trans. P. Scott; London: SCM Press: 52–7.

Bornkamm, G., Barth, G. and Held, H. J., 1982. *Tradition and Interpretation in Matthew*. 2nd enlarged edn, trans. P. Scott; London: SCM Press.

Brown, D., 1999. *Tradition and Imagination: Revelation and Change*. Oxford and New York: Oxford University Press.

Brown, J. K., 2005. 'Direct Engagement of the Reader in Matthew's Discourses: Rhetorical Techniques and Scholarly Consensus', *NTS* 51: 19–35.

Brown, R. E., 1984. *The Churches the Apostles Left Behind*. New York: Paulist Press.

Brown, R. E., 1993. *The Birth of the Messiah*. Updated edn; Anchor Bible Reference Library; New York and London: Doubleday.

Brown, R. E., 1994. *The Death of the Messiah: From Gethsemane to the Grave*. 2 vols; Anchor Bible Reference Library; New York and London: Doubleday.

Brown, R. E., 1997. *An Introduction to the New Testament*. Anchor Bible Reference Library; New York and London: Doubleday.

Bruderhof, 2012. *Foundations of Our Faith and Calling*. Rifton, NY and Robertsbridge: The Plough Publishing House.

Bultmann, R., 1963. *The History of the Synoptic Tradition*. Trans. J. Marsh; Oxford: Blackwell.

Butler, B. C., 1951. *The Originality of St Matthew: A Critique of the Two-Document Hypothesis*. Cambridge: Cambridge University Press.

Byrne, B., 2004. *Lifting the Burden: Reading Matthew's Gospel in the Church Today*. London: St Pauls.

Cargal, T. B., 1991. '"His Blood Be Upon Us and Upon Our Children": A Matthean Double Entendre?', *NTS* 37: 101–12.

Carson, D. A., 1982. 'The Jewish Leaders in Matthew's Gospel: A Reappraisal', *JETS* 25: 161–74.

Carter, W., 2000. *Matthew and the Margins: A Sociopolitical and Religious Reading*. Maryknoll, NY: Orbis.

Carter, W., 2001. *Matthew and Empire: Initial Explorations*. Harrisburg, PA: Trinity Press International.

Carter, W., 2009. 'Matthew 1—2 and Roman Political Power', in J. Corley (ed.), *New Perspectives on the Nativity*. London and New York: T. & T. Clark: 77–90.

Cave, C. H., 1963. 'St Matthew's Infancy Narrative', *NTS* 9: 382–90.

Chae, Y. S., 2006. *Jesus as the Eschatological Davidic Shepherd*. WUNT, 2nd series, 216; Tübingen: Mohr Siebeck.

Clark, K. W., 1947. 'The Gentile Bias of Matthew', *JBL* 66: 165–72.

Clarke, H., 2003. *The Gospel of Matthew and Its Readers*. Bloomington and Indianapolis: Indiana University Press.

Cohn-Sherbok, D., 1992. *The Crucified Jew*. London: HarperCollins.

Collins, R. F., 2003. *The Many Faces of the Church: A Study in New Testament Ecclesiology*. New York: Herder & Herder.

Bibliography

Combrink, H. J. B., 1983. 'The Structure of the Gospel of Matthew as Narrative', *Tyndale Bulletin* 34: 61–90.

Craig, W. L., 1984. 'The Guard at the Tomb', *NTS* 30: 273–81.

Crossley, J. G., 2004. *The Date of Mark's Gospel: Insight from the Law in Earliest Christianity*. JSNTSS 266; London and New York: T. & T. Clark.

Dahl, N. A., 1995. 'The Passion Narrative in Matthew', in G. N. Stanton (ed.), *The Interpretation of Matthew*. 2nd edn; Studies in New Testament Interpretation; Edinburgh: T. & T. Clark: 53–67.

Daley, B. E., 2003. 'Is Patristic Exegesis Still Usable? Some Reflections on Early Christian Interpretation of the Psalms', in E. F. Davis and R. B. Hays (eds), *The Art of Reading Scripture*. Grand Rapids, MI and Cambridge: Eerdmans: 69–88.

Davies, M., 1993. *Matthew*. Readings; Sheffield: JSOT Press.

Davies, W. D., 1989. *The Setting of the Sermon on the Mount*. Brown Judaic Studies 186; Atlanta, GA: Scholars Press (originally published 1964).

Davies, W. D. and Allison, D. C., 1988–97. *The Gospel According to Saint Matthew*. 3 vols; ICC; Edinburgh: T. & T. Clark.

Davies, W. D. and Allison, D. C., 2004. *Matthew: A Shorter Commentary*. London and New York: T. & T. Clark.

Deutsch, C., 1990. 'Wisdom in Matthew: Transformation of a Symbol', *NT* 32: 13–47.

Donaldson, T. L., 1985. *Jesus on the Mountain: A Study in Matthean Theology*. JSNTSS 8; Sheffield: JSOT Press.

Donaldson, T. L., 1999. '"For Herod had arrested John" (Matt. 14:3): Making Sense of an Unresolved Flashback', *Studies in Religion/Sciences Religieuses* 25: 35–48.

Doze, A., 1991. *Discovering Saint Joseph*. Slough: St Paul Publications.

Drury, J., 1985. *The Parables in the Gospels: History and Allegory*. London: SPCK.

Dube, M. W., 2000. *Postcolonial Feminist Interpretation of the Bible*. St Louis: Chalice.

Duling, D. C., 1975. 'Solomon, Exorcism and the Son of David', *HTR* 68: 235–52.

Duling, D. C., 1977. 'The Therapeutic Son of David: An Element in Matthew's Christological Apologetic', *NTS* 24: 392–410.

Dunn, J. D. G., 2011. *Jesus, Paul, and the Gospels*. Grand Rapids, MI and Cambridge: Eerdmans.

Edwards, R. A., 1985. *Matthew's Story of Jesus*. Philadelphia, PA: Fortress Press.

Ellis, P. F., 1974. *Matthew: His Mind and His Message*. Collegeville, MN: Liturgical Press.

Epp, E. J., 1999. 'The Multivalence of the Term "Original Text" in New Testament Textual Criticism', *HTR* 92: 245–81.

Esler, P. F., 1994. *The First Christians in Their Social Worlds: Social-Scientific Approaches to New Testament Interpretation*. London and New York: Routledge.

Esler, P. F., 1998. 'Community and Gospel in Early Christianity: A Response to Richard Bauckham's *Gospels for All Christians*', *SJT* 51: 235–48.

Bibliography

Eusebius, 1995. *The Church History*, in P. Schaff and H.Wace (eds), *Nicene and Post-Nicene Fathers. Second Series: Volume I*. Peabody, MA: Hendrickson: 73–387.

Evans, C. A., 2012. *Matthew*. New Cambridge Bible Commentary; Cambridge: Cambridge University Press.

Farmer, W. R., 1964. *The Synoptic Problem: A Critical Analysis*. New York: Macmillan.

Farrer, A., 1955. 'On Dispensing with Q', in D. E. Nineham (ed.), *Studies in the Gospels: Essays in Memory of R. H. Lightfoot*. Oxford: Blackwell: 55–88.

Farrer, A., 1966. *St Matthew and St Mark*. 2nd edn; London: Dacre Press.

Fenton, J., 1959. 'Inclusio and Chiasmus in Matthew', in *Studia Evangelica I*. Texte und Untersuchungen 73; Berlin: Akademie-Verlag: 174–9.

Fisher, L., 1968. 'Can This Be the Son of David?', in F. T. Trotter (ed.), *Jesus and the Historian*. Philadelphia, PA: Westminster Press: 82–97.

Fitzmyer, J. A., 1965. 'Anti-Semitism and the Cry of "All the People" (Mt. 27:25)', *TS* 26: 667–71.

Fitzmyer, J. A., 1976. 'The Matthean Divorce Texts and Some New Palestinian Evidence', *TS* 37: 197–226.

Foster, P., 2004. *Community, Law and Mission in Matthew's Gospel*. Wissenschaftliche Untersuchungen zum Neuen Testament 2. Reihe 177; Tübingen: Mohr Siebeck.

France, R. T., 1979. 'Herod and the Children of Bethlehem', *NT* 21: 98–120.

France, R. T., 1981. 'The Formula-Quotations of Matthew 2 and the Problem of Communication', *NTS* 27: 233–51.

France, R. T., 1989. *Matthew: Evangelist and Teacher*. Exeter: Paternoster Press.

France, R. T., 2007. *The Gospel of Matthew*. NICNT; Grand Rapids, MI and Cambridge: Eerdmans.

Franklin, E., 1994. *Luke: Interpreter of Paul, Critic of Matthew*. JSNTSS 92; Sheffield: Sheffield Academic Press.

Freyne, S., 1985. 'Vilifying the Other and Defining the Self: Matthew's and John's Anti-Jewish Polemic', in J. Neusner and E. S. Frerichs (eds), *'To See Ourselves as Others See Us': Christians, Jews, 'Others' in Late Antiquity*. Studies in the Humanities; Chico, CA: Scholars Press: 117–43.

Gibson, M. D. (ed.), 1911. *The Commentaries of Isho'dad of Merv, Bishop of Hadatha (c. 850 A.D.) in Syriac and English. Volume I: Translation*. Horae Semiticae No. V; Cambridge: Cambridge University Press.

Gnilka, J., 1986. *Das Matthäusevangelium*. 2 vols; HTKNT; Freiburg: Herder.

Goodacre, M., 1998. 'Fatigue in the Synoptics', *NTS* 44: 45–58.

Goodacre, M., 2002. *The Case Against Q: Studies in Markan Priority and the Synoptic Problem*. London: T. & T. Clark.

Goodacre, M., 2006. 'The Rock on Rocky Ground: Maṭthew, Mark and Peter as Skandalon', in P. McCosker (ed.), *What Is It That the Scripture Says? Essays in Biblical Interpretation, Translation, and Reception in Honour of Henry Wansbrough OSB*. LNTS; London and New York: Continuum: 61–73.

Goodacre, M., 2008. 'Mark, Elijah, the Baptist and Matthew: The Success of the First Intertextual Reading of Mark', in T. Hatina (ed.), *Biblical Interpretation in Early Christian Gospels. Volume 2: Matthew.* LNTS 310; London and New York: T. & T. Clark, 73–84.

Goulder, M. D., 1974. *Midrash and Lection in Matthew.* London: SPCK.

Goulder, M. D., 1985. 'A House Built on Sand', in A. E. Harvey (ed.), *Alternative Approaches to New Testament Study.* London: SPCK: 1–24.

Goulder, M. D., 1997. 'Matthew's Vision for the Church', in M. Bockmuehl and M. B. Thompson (eds), *A Vision for the Church: Studies in Early Christian Ecclesiology.* Edinburgh: T. & T. Clark: 19–32.

Grant, F. C., 1957. *The Gospels: Their Origin and Their Growth.* London: Faber & Faber.

Green, H. B., 1968. 'The Structure of St. Matthew's Gospel', in *Studia Evangelica IV.* Texte und Untersuchungen 102; Berlin: Akademie-Verlag: 47–59.

Gundry, R. H., 1967. *The Use of the Old Testament in St. Matthew's Gospel.* Brill: Leiden.

Gundry, R. H., 1994. *Matthew: A Commentary on His Handbook for a Mixed Church under Persecution.* 2nd edn; Grand Rapids, MI: Eerdmans.

Hagner, D. A., 1985. 'Apocalyptic Motifs in the Gospel of Matthew: Continuity and Discontinuity', *Horizons in Biblical Theology* 7: 53–82.

Hagner, D. A., 1993. *Matthew 1—13.* Word Biblical Commentary 33A; Dallas, TX: Word.

Hagner, D. A., 2003. 'Matthew: Apostate, Reformer, Revolutionary?' *NTS* 49: 193–209.

Hare, D. R. A., 1993. *Matthew.* Interpretation; Louisville, KY: Westminster John Knox Press.

Hare, D. R. A., 1998. 'Current Trends in Matthean Scholarship', *Word and World* 18: 405–10.

Hare, D. R. A. and Harrington, D. J., 1975. '"Make Disciples of All the Gentiles" (Mt. 28:19)', *CBQ* 37: 359–69.

Harries, R., 2004. *The Passion in Art.* Ashgate Studies in Theology, Imagination and the Arts; Aldershot: Ashgate.

Harrington, D. J., 1991. *The Gospel of Matthew.* Sacra Pagina 1; Collegeville, MN: Liturgical Press.

Hauerwas, S., 2006. *Matthew.* SCM Theological Commentary on the Bible; London: SCM Press.

Hays, R. B., 2005. 'The Gospel of Matthew: Reconfigured Torah', *HTS* 61(1&2): 165–90.

Heil, J. P., 1991. 'The Blood of Jesus in Matthew: A Narrative-Critical Perspective', *Perspectives in Religious Studies* 18: 117–24.

Heil, J. P., 1993. 'Ezekiel 34 and the Narrative Strategy of the Shepherd and the Sheep Metaphor in Matthew', *CBQ* 55: 698–708.

Held, H. J., 1982. 'Matthew as Interpreter of the Miracle Stories', in G. Bornkamm, G. Barth and H. J. Held, *Tradition and Interpretation in Matthew.* 2nd enlarged edn, trans. P. Scott; London: SCM Press: 165–299.

Bibliography

Hill, D., 1980. 'Son and Servant: An Essay on Matthean Christology', *JSNT* 6: 2–16.

Himmelfarb, M., 1991. 'The Temple and the Garden of Eden in Ezekiel, the Book of the Watchers, and the Wisdom of ben Sira', in J. Scott and P. Simpson-Housley (eds), *Sacred Places and Profane Spaces: Essays in the Geographics of Judaism, Christianity, and Islam*. Westport, CT: Greenwood Press: 63–78.

Hinkle, M., 1998. 'Learning What Righteousness Means: Hosea 6:6 and the Ethic of Mercy in Matthew's Gospel', *Word and World* 18: 355–63.

Horbury, W., 1998. *Jewish Messianism and the Cult of Christ*. London: SCM Press.

Houlden, J. L., 1987. *Backward into Light: The Passion and Resurrection of Jesus according to Matthew and Mark*. London: SCM Press.

Huizenga, L. A., 2008. 'Matt 1:1: "Son of Abraham" as Christological Category', *Horizons in Biblical Theology* 30: 103–13.

Jacobus de Voragine, 1941. *The Golden Legend*, trans. G. Ryan and H. Ripperger. New York, London and Toronto: Longmans, Green and Co.

Jeremias, J., 1954. *The Parables of Jesus*. London: SCM Press.

Jerome, 2008. *Commentary on Matthew*, trans. T. P. Scheck. The Fathers of the Church 117; Washington, DC: Catholic University of America Press.

John Chrysostom, 1991. *Homilies on the Gospel According to St Matthew*, in P. Schaff (ed.), *Nicene and Post-Nicene Fathers. First Series: Volume X*. Edinburgh: T. & T. Clark/Grand Rapids, MI: Eerdmans.

Johnson, L. T. and Kurz, W., 2002. *The Future of Catholic Biblical Scholarship: A Constructive Conversation*. Grand Rapids, MI: Eerdmans.

Johnson, M. D., 1974. 'Reflections on a Wisdom Approach to Matthew's Christology', *CBQ* 36: 44–64.

Justin Martyr, 1996. *Dialogue with Trypho*, in A. Roberts and J. Donaldson (eds), *The Ante-Nicene Fathers. Volume I*. Edinburgh: T. & T. Clark/Grand Rapids, MI: Eerdmans: 194–270.

Keck, L. E., 1986. 'Towards the Renewal of New Testament Christology', *NTS* 32: 362–77.

Kellerman, J. A. (trans.), 2010. *Incomplete Commentary on Matthew (Opus imperfectum)*. 2 vols; Ancient Christian Texts; Downers Grove, IL: IVP Academic.

Kennedy, G. A., 1984. *New Testament Interpretation through Rhetorical Criticism*. Chapel Hill: University of North Carolina Press.

Kiley, M., 1984. 'Why "Matthew" in Matt 9,9–13?' *Biblica* 65: 347–51.

Kilpatrick, G. D., 1946. *The Origins of the Gospel According to St Matthew*. Oxford: Clarendon Press.

Kingsbury, J. D., 1969. *The Parables of Jesus in Matthew 13: A Study in Redaction-Criticism*. London: SPCK.

Kingsbury, J. D., 1976. *Matthew: Structure, Christology, Kingdom*. London: SPCK.

Kingsbury, J. D., 1978. 'Observations on the "Miracle Chapters" of Matthew 8—9', *CBQ* 40: 559–73.

Kingsbury, J. D., 1979. 'The Figure of Peter in Matthew's Gospel as a Theological Problem', *JBL* 98: 67–83.

Kingsbury, J. D., 1984. 'The Figure of Jesus in Matthew's Story: A Literary-Critical Probe', *JSNT* 21: 3–36.

Kingsbury, J. D., 1986. *Matthew as Story*. Philadelphia, PA: Fortress Press.

Kingsbury, J. D., 1987. 'The Developing Conflict between Jesus and the Jewish Leaders in Matthew's Gospel: A Literary-Critical Study', *CBQ* 49: 57–73.

Kingsbury, J. D., 1988. *Matthew as Story*. 2nd edn; Philadelphia, PA: Fortress Press.

Kingsbury, J. D., 1995. 'The Developing Conflict between Jesus and the Jewish Leaders in Matthew's Gospel: A Literary-Critical Study', in G. N. Stanton (ed.), *The Interpretation of Matthew*. 2nd edn; Studies in New Testament Interpretation; Edinburgh: T. & T. Clark: 179–97.

Knowles, M., 2004. 'Reading Matthew: The Gospel as Oral Performance', in S. E. Porter (ed.), *Reading the Gospels Today*. Grand Rapids, MI/Cambridge: Eerdmans: 56–77.

Kreitzer, L. J., 2002. *Gospel Images in Fiction and Film: On Reversing the Hermeneutical Flow*. London and New York: Sheffield Academic Press.

Krentz, E., 1964. 'The Extent of Matthew's Prologue: Toward the Structure of the First Gospel', *JBL* 83: 409–14.

Lake, K., 1925. *The Apostolic Fathers with an English Translation*. 2 vols; Loeb Classical Library; London: Heinemann/New York: G. P. Putnam's Sons.

Landau, B., 2008. 'The *Revelation of the Magi* in the *Chronicle of Zuqnin*', *Apocrypha* 19: 182–201.

Lapide, P., 1986. *The Sermon on the Mount: Utopia or Program for Action?* Maryknoll, NY: Orbis.

Lash, N., 1986. *Theology on the Way to Emmaus*. London: SCM Press.

Levine, A.-J., 1988. *The Social and Ethnic Dimensions of Matthean Salvation History: "Go Nowhere Among the Gentiles . . ." (Matt. 10:5b)*. Studies in the Bible and Early Christianity 14; Lewiston, NY, Queenston, Ontario and Lampeter: Edwin Mellen Press.

Levine, A.-J., 1996. 'Discharging Responsibility: Matthean Jesus, Biblical Law, and Hemorrhaging Woman', in D. R. Bauer and M. A. Powell (eds), *Treasures New and Old: Recent Contributions to Matthean Studies*. SBL Symposium Series; Atlanta, GA: Scholars Press: 379–97.

Levine, A.-J. (ed.), 2001. *A Feminist Companion to Matthew*. Sheffield: Sheffield Academic Press.

Longstaff, T. R. W., 1981. 'The Women at the Tomb: Matthew 28:1 Re-Examined', *NTS* 27: 277–82.

Lovsky, F., 1987. 'Comment comprendre "son sang sur nous et nos enfants"?', *Études théologiques et religieuses* 62: 343–62.

Luz, U., 1989. *Matthew 1—7: A Commentary*. Edinburgh: T. & T. Clark.

Luz, U., 1994. *Matthew in History: Interpretation, Influence, and Effects*. Minneapolis, MN: Fortress Press.

Luz, U., 1995a. 'The Disciples in the Gospel according to Matthew', in G. N. Stanton (ed.), *The Interpretation of Matthew*. 2nd edn; Studies in New Testament Interpretation; Edinburgh: T. & T. Clark: 115–48.

Luz, U., 1995b. *The Theology of the Gospel of Matthew*. New Testament Theology; Cambridge and New York: Cambridge University Press.

Luz, U., 2001. *Matthew 8—20*. Hermeneia; Minneapolis, MN: Fortress Press.

Luz, U., 2005a. *Matthew 21—28*. Hermeneia; Minneapolis, MN: Fortress Press.

Luz, U., 2005b. *Studies in Matthew*. Grand Rapids, MI/Cambridge: Eerdmans.

McNeile, A. H., 1928. *The Gospel According to St. Matthew: The Greek Text with Introduction, Notes, and Indices*. London: Macmillan.

Malina, B. J., 1981. *The New Testament World: Insights from Cultural Anthropology*. Atlanta, GA: John Knox Press.

Malina, B. J. and Neyrey, J. H., 1998. *Calling Jesus Names: The Social Value of Labels in Matthew*. Sonoma, CA: Polebridge Press.

Malina, B. J. and Rohrbaugh, R. L., 2003. *Social Science Commentary on the Synoptic Gospels*. 2nd edn; Minneapolis, MN: Fortress Press.

Mann, C. S., 1958. 'Epiphany – Wise Men or Charlatans?' *Theology* 61: 495–500.

Martinez, E. R., 1961. 'The Interpretation of HOI MATHĒTAI in Matthew 18', *CBQ* 23: 281–92.

Massaux, E., 1990–3. *The Influence of the Gospel of Saint Matthew on Christian Literature before Saint Irenaeus*. 3 vols; ed. A. J. Bellinzoni; trans. N. J. Belval and S. Hecht; New Gospel Studies 5/1–3; Macon, GA: Mercer University Press.

Matera, F. J., 1987. 'The Plot of Matthew's Gospel', *CBQ* 49: 233–53.

Meeks, W. A., 1985. 'Breaking Away: Three New Testament Pictures of Christianity's Separation from the Jewish Communities', in J. Neusner and E. S. Frerichs (eds), *'To See Ourselves as Others See Us': Christians, Jews, 'Others' in Late Antiquity*. Studies in the Humanities; Chico, CA: Scholars Press: 93–115.

Meier, J. P., 1975. 'Salvation-History in Matthew: In Search of a Starting-Point', *CBQ* 37: 203–15.

Meier, J. P., 1977a. 'Nations or Gentiles in Matthew 28:19?', *CBQ* 39: 94–102.

Meier, J. P., 1977b. 'Two Disputed Questions in Matt 28:16–20', *JBL* 96: 407–24.

Meier, J. P., 1980. 'John the Baptist in Matthew's Gospel', *JBL* 99: 383–405.

Meier, J. P., 1991. *The Vision of Matthew: Christ, Church, and Morality in the First Gospel*. New York: Crossroad.

Meier, J. P., 1994. *A Marginal Jew: Rethinking the Historical Jesus. Volume Two: Mentor, Message, and Miracles*. Anchor Bible Reference Library; New York and London: Doubleday.

Metzger, B., 1971. *A Textual Commentary on the Greek New Testament*. London and New York: United Bible Societies.

Miller, G. D., 2009. 'Trying to Fix the Family Trees of Jesus', *Scripture Bulletin* 39: 17–30.

Minear, P. S., 1974. 'The Disciples and the Crowds in the Gospel of Matthew', *Anglican Theological Review* Supplementary Series 3: 28–44.

Bibliography

Minear, P. S., 1984. *Matthew: The Teacher's Gospel*. London: Darton, Longman & Todd.

Mohrlang, R., 1984. *Matthew and Paul: A Comparison of Ethical Perspectives*. Cambridge: Cambridge University Press.

Moo, D. J., 1984. 'Jesus and the Authority of the Mosaic Law', *JSNT* 20: 3–49.

Moule, C. F. D., 1966. *The Birth of the New Testament*. 2nd edn; BNTC; London: A. & C. Black.

Mowery, R. L., 1997. 'From Lord to Father in Matthew 1–7', *CBQ* 59: 642–56.

Mowery, R. L., 2002. 'Son of God in Roman Imperial Titles and Matthew', *Biblica* 83: 100–10.

Müller, M., 1999. 'The Theological Interpretation of the Figure of Jesus in the Gospel of Matthew: Some Principal Features in Matthean Christology', *NTS* 45: 157–73.

Nau, A. J., 1992. *Peter in Matthew: Discipleship, Diplomacy, and Dispraise*. Good News Studies 36; Collegeville, MN: Michael Glazier.

Nicholls, R., 2008. *Walking on the Water: Reading Mt. 14:22–33 in the Light of Its Wirkungsgeschichte*. Biblical Interpretation Series 90; Leiden and Boston: Brill.

Nickelsburg, G. W. E., 1981. *Jewish Literature Between the Bible and the Mishnah: A Historical and Literary Introduction*. London: SCM Press.

Nolan, B. M., 1979. *The Royal Son of God*. Orbis biblicus et orientalis 23; Freiburg: Universitätsverlag.

Nolland, J., 1997. 'The Four (Five) Women and Other Annotations in Matthew's Genealogy', *NTS* 43: 527–39.

O'Day, G., 2001. 'Surprised by Faith: Jesus and the Canaanite Woman', in A.-J. Levine (ed.), *A Feminist Companion to Matthew*. Sheffield: Sheffield Academic Press: 114–25.

O'Kane, M., 2005. 'The Artist as Reader of the Bible: Visual Exegesis and the Adoration of the Magi', *Biblical Interpretation* 13: 337–73.

O'Leary, A. M., 2006. *Matthew's Judaization of Mark Examined in the Context of the Use of Sources in Graeco-Roman Antiquity*. LNTS 323; London and New York: T. & T. Clark.

Origen, 1994. *Commentary on Matthew*, in A. Menzies (ed.), *Ante-Nicene Fathers: Volume IX*. 4th edn; Peabody, MA: Hendrickson.

Osiek, C., 2001. 'The Women at the Tomb: What Are They Doing There?', in A.-J. Levine (ed.), *A Feminist Companion to Matthew*. Sheffield: Sheffield Academic Press: 205–20.

Overman, J. A., 1990. *Matthew's Gospel and Formative Judaism: The Social World of the Matthean Community*. Minneapolis, MN: Fortress Press.

Parker, D. C., 1997. *The Living Text of the Gospels*. Cambridge: Cambridge University Press.

Parker, D. C., 2012. *Textual Scholarship and the Making of the New Testament*. Oxford: Oxford University Press.

Bibliography

Patte, D., 1987. *The Gospel According to Matthew: A Structural Commentary on Matthew's Faith*. Philadelphia, PA: Fortress Press.

Pennington, J. T., 2009. *Heaven and Earth in the Gospel of Matthew*. Grand Rapids, MI: Baker Academic.

Powell, M. A., 1992. 'The Plot and Subplots of Matthew's Gospel', *NTS* 38: 187–204.

Powell, M. A., 2000a. 'The Magi as Kings: An Adventure in Reader-Response Criticism', *CBQ* 62: 459–80.

Powell, M. A., 2000b. 'The Magi as Wise Men: Re-examining a Basic Supposition', *NTS* 46: 1–20.

Powell, M. A., 2001. *Chasing the Eastern Star: Adventures in Biblical Reader-Response Criticism*. Louisville, KY: Westminster John Knox Press.

Powell, M. A., 2009. 'Literary Approaches and the Gospel of Matthew', in M. A. Powell (ed.), *Methods for Matthew*. Methods in Biblical Interpretation; Cambridge: Cambridge University Press: 44–82.

Przybylski, B., 1980. *Righteousness in Matthew and His World of Thought*. SNTSMS 41; Cambridge: Cambridge University Press.

Riches, J. K., 2000. *Conflicting Mythologies: Identity Formation in the Gospels of Mark and Matthew*. Edinburgh: T. & T. Clark.

Riches, J. K. and Sim, D. C. (eds), 2005. *The Gospel of Matthew in Its Roman Imperial Context*. Early Christianity in Context; London: T. & T. Clark.

Robinson, B. P., 2009. 'Matthew's Nativity Stories: Historical and Theological Questions for Today's Readers', in J. Corley (ed.), *New Perspectives on the Nativity*. London and New York: T. & T. Clark: 110–31.

Rosenberg, R., 1965. 'Jesus, Isaac, and the Suffering Servant', *JBL* 84: 381–8.

Rowland, C., 2008. 'Marginalia in Matthew', in P. Lampe, M. Mayordomo and M. Sato (eds), *Neutestamentliche Exegese im Dialog: Hermeneutik – Wirkungsgeschichte – Matthäusevangelium. Festschrift für Ulrich Luz zum 70. Geburtstag*. Neukirchen-Vluyn: Neukirchener Verlag: 197–211.

Saldarini, A. J., 1991. 'The Gospel of Matthew and Jewish-Christian Conflict', in D. L. Balch (ed.), *Social History of the Matthean Community: Cross-Disciplinary Approaches*. Minneapolis, MN: Fortress Press: 36–59.

Saldarini, A. J., 1994. *Matthew's Christian-Jewish Community*. Chicago and London: Chicago University Press.

Saldarini, A. J., 1995. 'Boundaries and Polemics in the Gospel of Matthew', *Biblical Interpretation* 3: 239–65.

Sanders, E. P. and Davies, M., 1989. *Studying the Synoptic Gospels*. London: SCM Press/Philadelphia, PA: Trinity Press International.

Sawyer, J. F. A., 1996. *The Fifth Gospel: Isaiah in the History of Christianity*. Cambridge: Cambridge University Press.

Schaberg, J., 1987. *The Illegitimacy of Jesus*. San Francisco: Harper & Row.

Schnackenburg, R., 1965. *The Church in the New Testament*. Freiburg/London: Herder/Burns & Oates.

Bibliography

Schnackenburg, R., 2002. *The Gospel of Matthew*. Grand Rapids, MI and Cambridge: Eerdmans.

Schreckenberg, H., 1996. *The Jews in Christian Art: An Illustrated History*. London: SCM Press.

Schüssler Fiorenza, E., 1983. *In Memory of Her: A Feminist Theological Reconstruction of Christian Origins*. New York: Crossroad.

Schweizer, E., 1995. 'Matthew's Church', in G. N. Stanton (ed.), *The Interpretation of Matthew*. 2nd edn; Studies in New Testament Interpretation; Edinburgh: T. & T. Clark: 149–77.

Segal, A. F., 1991. 'Matthew's Jewish Voice', in D. L. Balch (ed.), *Social History of the Matthean Community: Cross-Disciplinary Approaches*. Minneapolis, MN: Fortress Press: 3–37.

Segovia, F. F., 2009. 'Postcolonial Criticism and the Gospel of Matthew', in M. A. Powell (ed.), *Methods for Matthew*. Methods for Biblical Interpretation; Cambridge and New York: Cambridge University Press: 194–237.

Senior, D., 1975. *The Passion Narrative According to Matthew: A Redactional Study*. BETL 39; Leuven: Leuven University Press.

Senior, D., 1996. *What Are They Saying about Matthew?* New edn; New York: Paulist Press.

Senior, D., 1997. 'The Lure of the Formula Quotations: Re-assessing Matthew's Use of the Old Testament with the Passion Narrative as a Test Case', in C. M. Tuckett (ed.), *The Scriptures in the Gospels*. BETL 131; Leuven: Leuven University Press: 89–115.

Senior, D., 1998. 'The Gospel of Matthew and the Passion of Jesus: Theological and Pastoral Perspectives', *Word and World* 18: 372–9.

Senior, D., 1999. 'Between Two Worlds: Gentiles and Jewish Christians in Matthew's Gospel', *CBQ* 61: 1–23.

Sim, D. C., 1995. 'The Gospel of Matthew and the Gentiles', *JSNT* 57: 19–48.

Sim, D. C., 1996. *Apocalyptic Eschatology in the Gospel of Matthew*. SNTSMS 88; Cambridge: Cambridge University Press.

Sim, D. C., 1998. *The Gospel of Matthew and Christian Judaism: The History and Social Setting of the Matthean Community*. Studies of the New Testament and Its World; Edinburgh: T. & T. Clark.

Sim, D. C., 2001, 'The Gospels for All Christians? A Response to Richard Bauckham', *JSNT* 84: 3–27.

Sim, D. C., 2011. 'Matthew's Use of Mark: Did Matthew Intend to Supplement or to Replace His Primary Source?', *NTS* 57: 176–92.

Simonetti, M. (ed.), 2001. *Matthew 1—13*. Ancient Christian Commentary on Scripture: New Testament 1a; Downers Grove, IL: InterVarsity Press.

Simonetti, M. (ed.), 2002. *Matthew 14—28*. Ancient Christian Commentary on Scripture: New Testament 1b; Downers Grove, IL: InterVarsity Press.

Slingerland, H. D., 1979. 'The Transjordanian Origin of St. Matthew's Gospel', *JSNT* 3: 18–28.

Bibliography

Smit, P.-B., 2010. 'Something about Mary? Remarks about the Five Women in the Matthean Genealogy', *NTS* 56: 191–207.

Stanton, G. N., 1985. 'The Origin and Purpose of Matthew's Gospel: Matthean Scholarship from 1945 to 1980', in H. Temporini and W. Haase (eds), *Aufstieg und Niedergang der römischen Welt*, Teil II (Principat), Band 25 (Religion), Teilband 3. Berlin: de Gruyter: 1889–951.

Stanton, G. N., 1992. *A Gospel for A New People: Studies in Matthew*. Edinburgh: T. & T. Clark.

Stanton, G. N., 1994. 'Revisiting Matthew's Communities', in E. H. Lovering (ed.), *SBL Seminar Papers 1994*. Chico, CA: Scholars Press: 9–23.

Stendahl, K., 1954. *The School of St Matthew and Its Use of the Old Testament*. Acta Seminarii Neotestamentici Upsaliensis XX; Lund: C. W. K. Gleerup.

Stendahl, K., 1968. *The School of St Matthew and Its Use of the Old Testament*. Revised edn; Philadelphia: Fortress Press.

Stendahl, K., 1995. 'Quis et Unde? An Analysis of Matthew 1—2', in G. N. Stanton (ed.), *The Interpretation of Matthew*. 2nd edn; Studies in New Testament Interpretation; Edinburgh: T. & T. Clark: 69–80.

Stewart-Sykes, A., 1995. 'Matthew's "Miracle Chapters": From Composition to Narrative and Back Again', *Scripture Bulletin* 25: 55–65.

Stock, A., 1994. *The Method and Message of Matthew*. Collegeville, MN: Liturgical Press.

Strecker, G., 1963. *Der Weg der Gerechtigkeit*. Göttingen: Vandenhoeck & Ruprecht.

Strecker, G., 1995. 'The Concept of History in Matthew', in G. N. Stanton (ed.), *The Interpretation of Matthew*. 2nd edn; Studies in New Testament Interpretation; Edinburgh: T. & T. Clark: 81–100.

Streeter, B. H., 1927. *The Four Gospels: A Study of Origins*. London: Macmillan and Co.

Suggs, M. J., 1970. *Wisdom, Christology, and Law in Matthew's Gospel*. Cambridge, MA: Harvard University Press.

Thompson, W. G., 1970. *Matthew's Advice to a Divided Community: Mt 17,22—18,35*. Analecta Biblica 44; Rome: Biblical Institute Press.

Thompson, W. G., 1971. 'Reflections on the Composition of Mt 8:1–9:34', *CBQ* 33: 365–88.

Troxel, R. L., 2002. 'Matt 27.51–4 Reconsidered: Its Role in the Passion Narrative, Meaning and Origin', *NTS* 48: 30–47.

Tuckett, C. M., 1983. *The Revival of the Griesbach Hypothesis: An Analysis and Appraisal*. SNTSMS 44; Cambridge: Cambridge University Press.

van Aarde, A., 2000. 'The Carpenter's Son (Mt 13:55): Joseph and Jesus in the Gospel of Matthew and Other Texts', *Neotestamentica* 34: 173–90.

van Aarde, A. and Dreyer, Y., 2010. 'Matthew Studies Today – A Willingness to Suspect and a Willingness to Learn', *HTS* 66(1): Art. #820.

Verseput, D. J., 1987. 'The Role and Meaning of the "Son of God" Title in Matthew's Gospel', *NTS* 33: 532–56.

Viviano, B. T., 1979. 'Where Was the Gospel according to St. Matthew Written?', *CBQ* 41: 533–46.

Viviano, B. T., 2007. *Matthew and His World: The Gospel of the Open Jewish Christians: Studies in Biblical Theology*. NTOA 61; Fribourg: Academic Press/ Göttingen: Vandenhoeck & Ruprecht.

Viviano, B. T., 2009. 'Making Sense of the Matthean Genealogy: Matthew 1:17 and the Theology of History', in J. Corley (ed.), *New Perspectives on the Nativity*. London and New York: T. & T. Clark: 91–109.

Viviano, B. T., 2010. 'God in the Gospel of Matthew', *Interpretation* 64: 341–54.

von Dobschütz, E., 1995. 'Matthew as Rabbi and Catechist', in G. N. Stanton (ed.), *The Interpretation of Matthew*. 2nd edn; Studies in New Testament Interpretation; Edinburgh: T. & T. Clark: 27–38.

Wainwright, E. M., 2009. 'Feminist Criticism and the Gospel of Matthew', in M. A. Powell (ed.), *Methods for Matthew*. Methods for Biblical Interpretation; Cambridge and New York: Cambridge University Press: 84–117.

Wansbrough, H., 2009. 'The Infancy Stories of the Gospels since Raymond E. Brown', in J. Corley (ed.), *New Perspectives on the Nativity*. London and New York: T. & T. Clark: 4–22.

Weren, W. J. C., 2006. 'The Macrostructure of Matthew's Gospel: A New Proposal', *Biblica* 87: 171–200.

Willitts, J., 2007. *Matthew's Messianic Shepherd-King: In Search of 'The Lost Sheep of the House of Israel'*. BZNW 147; Berlin and New York: de Gruyter.

Winkle, R. E., 1986. 'The Jeremiah Model for Jesus in the Temple', *AUSS* 24: 155–72.

Zuffi, S., 2003. *Gospel Figures in Art*. Trans. T. M. Hartmann; Los Angeles: The J. Paul Getty Museum.

Index of Biblical References

Index of Ancient Texts

Early Christian authors of commentaries on Matthew are listed in the main index of names and subjects.

Index of Names and Subjects